# RELATIONSHIPS IN THE ORGANIZATION OF KNOWLEDGE

# Information Science and Knowledge Management

## Volume 2

*Editor-in-Chief:*

J. Mackenzie Owen, *University of Amsterdam, Amsterdam*

*Editorial Board:*

*The titles published in this series are listed at the end of this volume.*

# RELATIONSHIPS
# IN THE ORGANIZATION
# OF
# KNOWLEDGE

*edited by*

## CAROL A. BEAN

*School of Information Sciences,*
*University of Tennessee, Knoxville, TN, U.S.A.*

and

## REBECCA GREEN

*College of Information Studies,*
*University of Maryland,*
*College Park, MD, U.S.A.*

## KLUWER ACADEMIC PUBLISHERS
### DORDRECHT / BOSTON / LONDON

A C.I.P. Catalogue record for this book is available from the Library of Congress.

ISBN  978-90-481-5652-8

Published by Kluwer Academic Publishers,
P.O. Box 17, 3300 AA Dordrecht, The Netherlands.

Sold and distributed in North, Central and South America
by Kluwer Academic Publishers,
101 Philip Drive, Norwell, MA 02061, U.S.A.

In all other countries, sold and distributed
by Kluwer Academic Publishers,
P.O. Box 322, 3300 AH Dordrecht, The Netherlands.

*Printed on acid-free paper*

# Table of Contents

# Introduction

Relationships abound in the library and information science (LIS) world. Those relationships may be social in nature, as, for instance, when we deal with human relationships among library personnel or relationships (i.e., "public relations") between an information center and its clientele. The relationships may be educational, as, for example, when we examine the relationship between the curriculum of an accredited school and the needs of the work force it is preparing students to join. Or the relationships may be economic, as when we investigate the relationship between the cost of journals and the frequency with which they are cited. Many of the relationships of concern to us reflect phenomena entirely internal to the field: the relationship between manuscript collections, archives, and special collections; the relationship between end user search behavior and the effectiveness of searches; the relationship between access to and use of information resources; the relationship between recall and precision; the relationship between various bibliometric laws; etc. The list of such relationships could go on and on.

The relationships addressed in this volume are restricted to those involved in the organization of recorded knowledge, which tend to have a conceptual or semantic basis, although statistical means are sometimes used in their discovery. Despite this limitation to knowledge organization, the range of relationships relevant to our endeavor is extensive, including:

- The many types of bibliographic relationships between units of recorded knowledge;
- Various intratextual and intertextual relationships, including relationships based on text structure, citation relationships, and hypertext links;
- Subject relationships in thesauri and other classificatory structures, including the relationships involved in knowledge discovery; and
- Relevance relationships, including both topical relevance relationships and other user-oriented relevance relationships.

The careful reader will notice that these four categories are not necessarily mutually exclusive.

While knowledge organization has a rich interest in such relationships, the field has no monopoly on semantic associations. Relationships also play an integral role in other fields. For example, discrete mathematics addresses the formal properties of relations, which are defined as sets that express a correspondence between two or more sets; data modeling adopts these mathematical relations, but allows them to have a semantic interpretation (Tsichritzis & Lochovsky, 1982, p. 25). Such relations may express either entity classes (e.g., Companies, Persons, Products) or relationship classes (e.g., Student <enrolls in> Class, Supplier <supplies> Part <for> Project), which are associations between two or more entity classes. (Because "relation" has a technical meaning, we will reserve its use for mathematical and data modeling contexts and for such phrases as "public relations" and "phase relations." Note that all relations are relationships, but not vice versa. We will instead use the term "relationships" exclusively for the notion of semantic association, although the terms "relation" and "relationship" are often used interchangeably outside formal settings.) The ontologies of knowledge representation are also replete with relationships. Furthermore, linguistics has a firm interest in semantic relationships, both when words are considered out of context, where we speak of paradigmatic and lexical relationships, or in specific contexts, where we speak of syntagmatic and thematic relationships. A companion volume, *The Semantics of Relationships: An Interdisciplinary Perspective*, will address relationships in the broader arena.

Because subject relationships are at the very heart of the organization of knowledge, many of the papers in this volume address the topic in one form or another. Papers within the first part of the volume address subject relationships from a general and mostly scheme-independent perspective. Dextre Clarke cogently introduces the three basic thesaural relationships—equivalence, hierarchical, and associative—and briefly discusses the need for greater relational definition in automated contexts. Based on her extensive experience with standards-making, Milstead explains the process by which standards are developed and presents the current standards for thesauri and indexes, focusing on their treatment of relationships. A set of three papers follows, each of which examines subject relationships across contexts: Hudon addresses relationship compatibility in the multilingual thesaurus context, while Bodenreider and Bean explore problems involved in vocabulary integration within the domain of medicine for the *Unified Medical Language System (UMLS);* Beghtol examines the cultural dependence of relational systems (where a culture may be defined by time, place, discipline, school of thought, etc.). Papers from the second part of the volume address the relational structure of several specific thesauri and classification schemes. El-Hoshy thoroughly explores the expression of relationships in the *Library of Congress Subject Headings (LCSH)*, while Molholt and Nelson, Johnston, and Humphreys do the same for the *Art & Architecture Thesaurus (AAT)* and *Medical Subject Headings (MeSH)* respectively. Each of these systems is highly conscious of the importance of relationships and deals with them in somewhat unique ways. Neelameghan introduces a new system, *OMIS*, which cuts across cultures and religious traditions and uses an extensive set of explicit associative ("lateral") associations. Satija explores the role of relationships in the *Colon Classification (CC)*, while Mitchell addresses the relational structure of the *Dewey Decimal Classification (DDC)*.

Several other papers in the first part of the volume address relationships in knowledge organization other than subject relationships. The overview chapter by Green introduces relationships in knowledge organization, based on the four-way classification set out above; along the way, it acts as a guide to the literature of the area and situates the remaining chapters of the volume in a larger context. Tillett reviews her earlier work on bibliographic relationships and ties it together with the IFLA model that has emerged more recently. Bean and Green present a relationally-based view of relevance; in particular, topical relevance is argued to involve relationships beyond topic matching.

We are especially pleased that so many of our colleagues accepted the invitation to contribute to this volume. Their chapters reflect a wealth of experience with the development of knowledge organization systems, grounded in solid understanding of the more theoretical aspects of relationships. We have found their thoughts to be cogent and their writing incisive.

The chapters in this volume present a lively discussion of what we currently know about relationships in the service of knowledge organization, how they are used in current systems, both generally and specifically, and the challenges we face in identifying and making effective use of relationships. Many of the papers further address how a deeper understanding and use of relationships should beneficially affect knowledge organization in the future.

It is impossible for a volume of this nature to express all that needs to be considered and put forth at this time. But it will serve its purpose if it spurs further interest, debate, research, and development.

## References

Tsichritzis, D. C., & Lochovsky, F. H. (1982). *Data Models*. Englewood Cliffs, NJ: Prentice-Hall.

Carol A. Bean
Knoxville, Tennessee

Rebecca Green
College Park, Maryland

# PART I

**Relationships in the Organization of Knowledge: Theoretical Background**

# Chapter 1

# Relationships in the Organization of Knowledge: An Overview

Rebecca Green
*College of Information Studies, University of Maryland, College Park, MD, USA*

**Abstract:**
Relationships are specified by simultaneously identifying a semantic relationship and the set of participants involved in it, pairing each participant with its role in the relationship. Properties pertaining to the participant set and the nature of the relationship are explored. Relationships in the organization of knowledge are surveyed, encompassing relationships between units of recorded knowledge based on descriptions of those units; intratextual and intertextual relationships, including relationships based on text structure, citation relationships, and hypertext links; subject relationships in thesauri and other classificatory structures, including relationships for literature-based knowledge discovery; and relevance relationships.

## 1. BASIC PROPERTIES OF RELATIONSHIPS

Whatever we consider to be the most basic elements of reality, we deem to be things or, more formally, entities. After that, it's all relationships. Relationships are involved as we combine simple entities to form more complex entities, as we compare entities, as we group entities, as one entity performs a process on another entity, and so forth. Indeed, many things that we might initially regard as basic and elemental are revealed upon further examination to involve internal structure, or in other words, internal relationships. So, while entities are primary, they are almost without import without also taking relationships into account. After all, few, if any, of us have ever consciously encountered a pure entity; indeed, it's unclear that our physics has so far identified or will ever identify such.

In the broadest sense, a relationship is an association between two or more entities or between two or more classes of entities. To specify a relationship, we must be able, first, to designate all the parties bound by the relationship and, second, to specify the nature of the relationship.

Designating all the parties bound by the relationship extends beyond simply enumerating the participants. We may distinguish between abstract relationships, on the one hand, which express associations between entity classes (e.g., Person < born in > Place), and concrete relationships, on the other hand, which express associations between specific entities (e.g., Michelangelo < born in > Caprese, Raphael < born in > Urbino). We use abstract relationships, for example, in data modeling, but instantiate those abstract relationships in recording concrete relationships in the actual database. Closer to home, data modeling of

3

C. A. Bean and R. Green (eds.), *Relationships in the Organization of Knowledge*, 3–18.

bibliographic entity classes operates with abstract relationships, but catalogs record concrete relationships.

An important property of the participants bound by a relationship is their number. We refer to this property as a relationship's arity. If there are only two entities or entity classes involved, as is often the case, the relationship is binary. If there are three, we speak of a ternary relationship. We may also speak of any relationship having more than two participants as an n-ary relationship. Kent (1978, pp. 155-160) discusses how any n-ary relationship can be recast as a set of binary relationships by creating a dummy entity (class) to which each of the original participants can be related in turn. If we take the ternary relationship, Supplier < supplies > Part < for > Project, we apply this technique by creating a new dummy entity class, which we will unimaginably call "Dummy," and by relating each of the three participant classes to Dummy: Supplier < supplies > Dummy, Part < supplied for > Dummy, and Dummy < for > Project. Somewhat counterintuitively, the new dummy entity (class) conceptually stands for the entire ternary relationship (although it seems above to stand for only two entity classes at a time, with the identity of those two shifting throughout) and allows the original relationship to be reconstituted. In instantiating this set of relationships, the values given to Dummy will be either arbitrary (e.g., "D00378") and/or (semi-)redundant (e.g., if based on the values of the three participants, as in "Spplr001Pt0027Proj031"). Although the conversion of n-ary relationships into sets of binary relationships can be seen to be conceptually messy, the regularity of binary relationships often makes it an attractive option. The attractiveness is also a danger, since it creates the temptation to restrict relationships to binary relationships without taking the requisite step of creating the intermediating dummy entity (class). When this step is omitted, it is no longer possible to recreate the original relationship. For example, if we wish to model an n-ary relationship among descriptors in a thesaurus (e.g., *buyer*, *seller*, *merchandise*, *money*) and can only use binary *see also* references between the participant types of the relationship to do so, we will not be able to re-capture the full original relationship unless we include references from each term to all three other terms.

Most relationships are asymmetric, meaning that it is not usually the case that if entity A stands in a certain relationship with entity B, then entity B stands in the same relationship with entity A. For example, if A is broader than B, B is not broader than A; if Mary likes John, it is not necessarily the case that John likes Mary. Such relationships are asymmetric. (Examples of symmetric relations include < is a cousin of >, < is a sibling of >, < is a spouse of >.) This asymmetry means that it must be possible to specify of a given entity (class) which participant it is in the relationship. Relationship participants must thus either be ordered or labeled so as to associate with each participant the role it plays in the relationship. This specification marries the ability to designate the participants in the relationship with the ability to indicate the nature of the relationship, since it is the latter that governs what roles participants can play.

Specifying the nature of a relationship is accompanied by its own array of properties to be considered. One of these properties is the cardinality of the relationship. This property is easiest to illustrate with binary relationships. Here the question concerns for some participating member of one entity class how many members of the other entity class it may be associated with through the relationship and vice versa. There are three overall possibilities in the case of binary relationships: one-to-one, one-to-many, and many-to-many relationships. (While a many-to-one relationship is also a logical possibility, it is conventional in such a case to re-order the relationship participants so as to convert the relationship into a one-to-many relationship.) Husband < is currently legally married in a monogamous society to > Wife is a one-to-one relationship: A husband can only be currently legally married to one wife, and vice versa in a monogamous society. Man < is biological father of > Person is a one-to-many relationship: While a person can only have one biological father, a man can be the biological father of many children. Person < is parent of > Person is a many-to-many relationship: A person can be the parent to multiple persons, and a person has more than one parent.

Another property that may be posited of relationships is transitivity. A relationship is said to be transitive if whenever A < is related in a certain way to > B and B < is related in that same way > to C, it is also true that A < is related in that same way > to C. Hierarchical inheritance is a type of transitivity: If a Faceted thesaurus < is a > Thesaurus and a Thesaurus < is a(n) > Index language, then a Faceted thesaurus < is a(n) > Index language.

The single most important aspect of specifying the nature of the relationship that holds between entities or entity classes is identifying the semantics of the relationship. This may be done with various degrees of implicitness/explicitness. (1) One option forgoes any attempt to identify the nature or semantics of the relationship, but counts on the enumeration of participants or participant types to imply an underlying relationship. This option presumably can only work if one relationship type is more likely than any other to occur between two entities or entity classes and this greater likelihood is accessible to the human or machine making use of the relationship. This option underlies the typical use of *see also* or RT (related term) references in thesauri. (2) Closely related to this option is a second one in which a relationship type between entity classes holds by convention. Beghtol (this volume, sect. 2.1) notes, for example that in Ranganathan's PMEST formula, the S(pace) and T(ime) facets are understood to situate the topic of the writing as taking place in the specified Space and Time and not to situate the actual writing of the document, for example, in that Space and Time. (3) A third option simply names the relationship type that holds, which has been the practice of this chapter, e.g., Bibliographic unit < is part of > Bibliographic unit. This option makes the assumption that the user is familiar with the relationship type ("< is part of >") through his or her own personal experience and can access an understanding of the semantics of the experience on the basis of a natural language label. (4) The most explicit option uses a formal language to set forth the semantics of the relationship type. Such an option will commonly be found in knowledge representation systems that incorporate relationship types. Ultimately the symbols of that formal language must be transformed into understanding on the basis of personal experience and probably using the medium of natural language. The third and fourth options are thus closer than they may appear on the surface, and they are certainly more like each other than either is to the first or second option.

Considerable effort has gone into the identification of a comprehensive inventory of relationship types, although this effort has paled beside the effort that has gone into identifying the parallel inventory of entity types. On some small number of relationship types, for example, hierarchical relationships, there is general consensus, but on others, for example, associative relationships, there is only partial consensus. Indeed, it may be appropriate to apply the open (non-enumerable) class vs. closed (enumerable) class distinction to the ideal inventory of relationship types. Examining this same distinction in the context of parts of speech in English will help illuminate the point. We consider nouns, verbs, adjectives, and adverbs to be open classes of words, while pronouns, prepositions, and conjunctions are closed classes. In other words, we would be surprised to hear someone coin a new pronoun, preposition, or conjunction, but new nouns, verbs, adjectives, or adverbs continue to come into the language. Parts of speech correspond roughly to the basic components of the entity-relationship model: Nouns and pronouns tend to name entities; adjectives and adverbs often fulfill the same role as attributes; and verbs, prepositions, and conjunctions generally express relationships. We note that relationships, like entities, have part-of-speech counterparts that constitute open classes and those that constitute closed classes. It is a small leap to hypothesize that there is a set of conceptual relationships that is closed and also a set of such relationships that is open. The closed class corresponds to those relationships expressed linguistically through paradigmatic relationships, for example through hyponymy, meronymy, synonymy, antonymy, and perhaps various series relationships. Specifically, the closed class would include, minimally, hierarchical relationships and equivalence relationships. The open class corresponds to those relationships expressed linguistically through syntagmatic relationships. This class would include those relationships referred to in the LIS world as associative relationships; being open, the membership of the class can never be fully enumerated: Every time a new verb is coined, for example, the potential for the introduction of a new conceptual relationship arises.

To recapitulate: Relationships are specified by simultaneously identifying a semantic relationship and the set of participants involved in it, pairing each participant with its role in the relationship. Properties pertaining to the participant set include the level at which the participants are identified (i.e., as classes of entities or as specific entities) and the number of participants in the relationship. Properties possibly pertaining to the nature of the relationship include cardinality and transitivity. A hypothesis was put forth that the inventory of semantic relationships includes both a closed set of relationships (including mainly hierarchical and equivalence relationships) and an open set of relationships.

## 2. RELATIONSHIPS IN KNOWLEDGE ORGANIZATION

As we examine relationships in the organization or knowledge, we will be concerned both with the types of entities that participate in those relationships and with the semantic types of those relationships. It might seem most natural to go about our investigation by examining relationship types first off, but there are two reasons to start instead with participant types. First, while we can quickly identify major closed class relationship types (and although these hierarchical and equivalence relationships are crucially important in knowledge organization), it is unclear how to identify the presumably far larger set of open class relationships within our context. Second, the relationship types we know up front are ubiquitous and therefore would probably not function well in distinguishing relationships inside the organization of knowledge from those outside. The more effective means of picking out the relationships of concern to us is by looking at the entity types of concern to knowledge organization and then by considering what relationships involve those entity types.

Major entity types in the organization of knowledge include bodies (e.g., authors, translators, editors, publishers), bibliographic units (both intellectual units, e.g., texts, and physical units, e.g., books, serials, Web pages), subjects, concepts, words, knowledge (both public, as conveyed by documents, and private, as held in human minds), and users, with their information needs. Examples of relationships within the organization of knowledge include (the list is not even remotely exhaustive):

- Body < produces > Bibliographic unit,
- Bibliographic unit < is part of > Bibliographic unit,
- Bibliographic unit < describes > Bibliographic unit,
- Bibliographic unit < cites > Bibliographic unit,
- Bibliographic unit < links to > Bibliographic unit,
- Text < has > Subject,
- Concept < in > Text,
- Word < conveys > Concept,
- Knowledge < conveyed by > Text,
- User < has > Knowledge,
- User < has > Information need, and
- Knowledge < addresses > Information need.

Accordingly, we may group relationships in the organization of knowledge into four areas:

- Relationships between units of recorded knowledge that are based on bibliographic descriptions of those units;
- Intratextual and intertextual relationships, including relationships based on text structure, citation relationships, and hypertext links;
- Subject relationships in thesauri and other classificatory structures; and
- Relevance relationships.

## 2.1 Bibliographic Relationships

Bibliographic relationships broadly defined include all relationships involved in the descriptive cataloging of bibliographic units, whether considered as physical or material units, on the one hand, or as intellectual units, on the other hand. The specific set of relationships addressed in this section will be limited to those that involve *only* bibliographic units as participants (as opposed, for instance, to the association between a bibliographic unit and the person(s) who produced it). Such relationships can be considered both abstractly or concretely.

On the abstract level, the two primary questions to be addressed are: (1) What classes of bibliographic entities need to be recognized?, and (2) How are these general classes related to each other? O'Neill and Vizine-Goetz (1989) recognized five classes of bibliographic entities, two of an intellectual nature, namely, Works and Texts, and three of a material nature, namely, Editions, Printings, and Books (although some of their terms sound limited to a single physical format, they are meant to apply broadly). They suggest that these entity types "reflect a hierarchical relationship . . . [that] results from a one-to-many association between the entities at the various levels" (p. 174). However, hierarchical relationships have specific semantic properties (which most of the relationships between these bibliographic entities do not share) and do not result from a pattern of cardinalities. Furthermore, it is not true that all of the relationships in question are one-to-many relationships. Specifically, the relationship that crosses between intellectual and material units—here the Text < is related to > Edition relationship—is a many-to-many relationship, not a one-to-many relationship: A Text may occur in various physical Editions and a physical Edition (for example, an anthology) may contain multiple Texts. The international community (IFLA, 1998) has taken up these same questions in the past decade, agreeing to recognize four types of bibliographic entities: Works, Expressions, Manifestations, and Items. The first two are intellectual units, the last two material. (Specifically, the Printing entity class from O'Neill and Vizine-Goetz lacks a correspondent in the IFLA model.)

On the concrete level, there have been several major scholarly investigations into relationships between specific bibliographic units (for example, Tillett, 1987; Smiraglia, 1992; Vellucci, 1997). Such studies have brought to light, in addition to the relationship types already considered on the abstract level, numerous recursive bibliographic relationships, for example, those centering around the general Work < is related to > Work relationship. The broadest of these (Tillett 1987, summarized in Tillett, 1991a, 1991b, 1992a, 1992b) established seven distinct types of bibliographic relationship, several of which have also been investigated individually (Goossens & Mazur-Rzesos, 1982; McNellis, 1985; Smiraglia, 1992; Leazer & Smiraglia, 1994; Leazer, 1996).

The implementation of bibliographic relationships across bibliographic records is another issue of concern. Tillett (1992a) gives a chronological overview of the various devices used to express bibliographic relationships, and, of course, the various MARC standards provide detailed information on coding such relationships (where there is provision for their explicit expression). Leazer (1993) explicitly proposes using bibliographic relationships to structure bibliographic databases, while Bertha (1993) further suggests that online catalogs make such bibliographic relationships manipulable by end users so they can link between records for related bibliographic entities.

## 2.2 Intra- and Intertextual Relationships

As noted in the previous section, there are numerous recursive bibliographic relationships. Included among these are various equivalence (e.g., Manifestation < is a reprint of > Manifestation, Item < is photocopy of > Item), derivative (e.g., Work < is a translation of > Work, Work < parodies > Work), descriptive (e.g., Work < reviews > Work, Work < provides commentary on > Work), and sequential (e.g., Work < is the sequel to > Work) relationships. Although content is intimately involved in some of these relationships, the relationships still are mostly objective in nature.

Not surprisingly, there are also recursive relationships between bibliographic units that involve content and that are more subjective in nature.[1] Here we will briefly discuss three distinct types of such relationships. The first type relates the various text structural parts of an Expression to each other. The second type concerns Manifestations related through citation, while the third, not unlike the second, involves hypertext links between Items.

An Expression, for example, a particular edition or translation of a Work, has internal structure. Many texts, such as this one, are explicitly divided into sections intended to form a logical overall text structure. Such textual units form coherent semantic units that interrelate to form a whole text and express a complete exposition of some subject in almost the same way that words, properly chosen and ordered, interrelate to form a sentence and express a complete thought. Components of the overall structure yield iteratively to decompositional processes to form smaller and smaller text units.[2] Furthermore, there may be overlapping layers of text structure, where such phenomena as discourse structure and semantic unity are used to define the parts. Text relationships operate on all levels of the breakdown, from macrostructures to microstructures. A vast text structure literature exists, among which Halliday and Hasan (1976) and Crombie (1985) may be singularly mentioned for their coverage of relationship types. Also deserving of attention are recent efforts to define text segments automatically, based on the lexical relationships that interconnect the words within the segment (Hearst, 1997).

Like text structure, citation has also generated a sizeable literature (reviewed, for example, by Liu, 1993). Of relevance to knowledge organization is whether citation relationships between Manifestations are paralleled by semantic relationships between their subject matter. If so, we can use citation relationships either to substitute for or to supplement more conventional means (e.g., subject indexing, keyword searches) in subject searching.[3] Several studies have investigated the correlation between citation and subject similarity. For example, Ali (1993) investigated the overlap between the words in the titles of citing and cited works, while Harter, Nisonger, and Weng (1993) examined semantic relationships between citing and cited documents by looking at the overlap between the subject descriptors assigned to them. Trivison (1987) found that documents bound by a citing relationship had a significantly higher document similarity, as measured by term co-occurrence within the titles and abstracts of the documents, than documents without any citation relationship. Unfortunately, all three studies limited their sense of semantic relationship to the co-occurrence of specific words or phrases, thus ignoring the possible occurrence of such semantic relationships as synonymy and hyponymy. In reality we know very little about the range of semantic relationships between citing and cited documents.

Hypertext links between items are conceptually similar to citation links, in that one physical bibliographic unit (or class of bibliographic units) refers to another; in both cases the link is asymmetric (in other words, the directionality of the link counts). Often both the source location and the destination location of the link are relatively precisely defined, for example, a specific page within a journal article, a particular verse of an epic poem, the beginning of a specific paragraph of text, or even a specific sentence or phrase from the text. Indeed, the primary reason we consider citation relationships and hypertext linkage to be distinct is because of implementational differences. Print-based documents could only make reference to other documents indirectly, through bibliographic citation; electronic documents, however, can make direct reference, via hypertext links, to other electronic documents. This raises two issues beyond those typically associated with citation: Are typed links—that is, links in which the semantic relationship between source and destination is made explicit—beneficial to hypertext users (Baron, Tague-Sutcliffe, & Kinnucan, 1996)?

If so, can link types be generated automatically (Allan, 1997; Agosti, Crestani, & Melucci, 1997; S. J. Green, 1999, Thistlewaite, 1997)? Both questions focus our attention on the inventory of possible link types.

Trigg (1983) has proposed by far the lengthiest list of hypertext link types, eighty in number. However, the majority of those link types (fifty-nine) he categorizes as commentary link types, links between a node and a statement about the node, as contrasted with normal link types, which connect nodes (either internally or externally). Commentary links (e.g., S[tyle]-boring, A[rgument]-strawman, P[roblem]ill-posed) are more like attributes than relationships, but can also be seen as a type of descriptive bibliographic relationship (in which the commentaries in Trigg's system become mini-texts in their own right). Many of his normal link types resemble relationship types we have previously encountered. Some express citation functions; some parallel certain bibliographic relationships (e.g., derivative: links to summarizations, paraphrases, simplifications, updates, corrections; descriptive: links to explanations; sequential: links to continuations); some reflect hierarchical relations (e.g., generalize/specialize, abstraction/example); and some are based on the typical discourse structure of research papers (e.g., methodology, data, argument; in this latter case, Trigg includes several link types that also specify the nature of the argument, i.e., whether it is inductive, deductive, by analogy, or intuitive). Parunak (1991, pp. 313-314) also distinguishes a number of link types, which are grouped under three main link types: association, aggregation, and revision. Association links "are the most common, and reflect various ways in which one node brings another to mind;" in brief, they can be almost any kind of link type at all! Aggregation links reflect part-whole relationships, while revision links are used to mirror the derivative bibliographic link between versions of a text. Other sets of link types are generally small: Frei and Stieger (1995) distinguish only two types of links (referential and semantic), while Thistlewaite (1997) recognizes four (structural, referential, semantic, and contingent). Structural links connect nodes related by the document's structure and thus mirror the discourse structure links previously mentioned; referential links generally function as citation links; semantic links are relatively unbounded and reflect some sort of content relatedness (semantic links and association links are essentially the same thing). Thistlewaite's contingent links, which he argues should not be represented explicitly, reflect relationships that might be important to some person at some time, but that lack general staying power. Such a link prefigures the user-oriented relevance relationships we will take up later. Indeed, while many relationship types pertain in the hypertext context, almost none of them is unique to that context. We find that the same relationship types recur over and over.

## 2.3 Subject Relationships

Overall, the single most important variable in information retrieval is subject. Unfortunately, searching by subject is inherently difficult. For one thing, documents are almost never about just a single subject. For another thing, it is not uncommon for a user statement of need to fail to specify exactly the subject or subjects of materials that can actually help satisfy his or her need. For yet another, there are a seemingly infinite set of subjects. What keeps this situation from being utterly hopeless is the perception that all of these many subjects are related to each other and that this web of subject relationships, if understood, can help users navigate between their needs and the resources that can help meet their needs.

Although we haven't explicitly addressed subject relationships up to this point, we have encountered them already at several turns. For instance, Hearst's (1997) text segmentation technique endeavors to identify subsections of the text that are topically cohesive. Studies that explore semantic relatedness between citing and cited documents were criticized for not taking into account relationships between their subjects. Most hypertext link typologies recognize a broad class of semantic or association relationships, which are essentially subject relationships.

In trying to establish relationships between subjects, we must take into account relationships between concepts. While concepts are often expressed in words, they may also be expressed through a notational system, so it is important to recognize that concepts are the foundational coin of the subject relationship realm. All index languages worthy of the name, whether thesauri, on the one hand, or classification schemes, on the other, address how the concepts within their scope are related to each other.

The task of putting together a comprehensive inventory of relationionship types is not for the faint of heart. Among those in the LIS world who have undertaken such a daunting assignment are Soergel (1967) and Perreault (1994). Myaeng and McHale (1992) review the results of additional efforts along these lines. On the practical side are the various handbooks for constructing thesauri, among which Aitchison, Gilchrist, & Bawden (1997) and Hudon (1994) are some of the more current. Also of a practical nature is Willett's (1975) empirical study of term relationships in ten thesauri.

A great many relational systems recognize a catch-all relationship type, for example, the semantic relationship type of hypertext links or the association relationship of thesauri. At the same time that other relationship types (e.g., equivalence relationships, hierarchical relationships) are closed classes, semantic or associative relationship types seem altogether open. Increasingly greater attention has been placed on such relationships in recent decades. After all, any attempt (as noted above) to identify a comprehensive inventory of relationships must deal extensively with associative relationships. Neelameghan and Maitra (1978) represent a pioneering effort to specify a major set of associative relationships; the continuation of this work can be seen in the system described by Neelameghan (this volume). Coates (1973) offers a basic overview of "syntactic [syntagmatic] relations" in indexing languages, while Spang-Hanssen (1976) compares links and roles—mechanisms used for specifying particular sets of associative relationships—and grammatical relationships in natural languages. Green (1995b) characterizes the nature of such relationships, while Green (1995c) surveys how they have been expressed in various index languages. Vickery (1996) briefly summarizes the history of expressing associative relationships in information retrieval; in doing so, he provides a concentrated set of references to related literature from several fields and over several decades. Empirical work examining specific types of associative relationships or associative relationships in specific domains include Bean (1996) and Khoo (1997). Larger research programs in this arena are outlined in Myaeng & McHale (1992), Khoo (1997), and Green (in press).

The most typical use of subject relationships has been in determining which subject terms are the most appropriate ones to search under. The research agenda centered around associative relationships envisions a second major use in which relationships are used to form more complex (and more precise) subject terms. A third promising use of subject relationships arises in literature-based knowledge discovery. Swanson (1986, 1990, 1993) and Davies (1989) lay out the basic premise that hitherto undiscovered knowledge may be gleaned from bringing together literatures whose subject matter (including, for example, assertions, arguments, evidence) is related in certain ways, although they are not bibliographically related through citation. Because "combinations of potentially related segments of literature can grow at a rate far higher than the capacity of the [scholarly] community to identify and assimilate such relatedness," "the fragmentation of knowledge inevitably will spawn the most important information problems of the future, problems that also are opportunities to create new knowledge by discovering new relationships" (Swanson, 1993, pp. 606, 619). Or, as Davies (1989, p. 275) puts it, "every time a new item of knowledge is created there will be a vast number of potential relationships with existing items and those that prove valid . . . will constitute more knowledge awaiting discovery." Lindsay and Gordon (1999, p. 575) summarize the published work of Swanson and more recently Swanson and Smalheiser, in which this phenomenon is exemplified in the medical literature. Davies points out that Swanson's work has almost exclusively focused on knowledge discovery based on inferences from transitive (causal) relationships of the form "$A$ causes $B$" and "$B$ causes $C$," while other relationship types (for example, finding apparent conflict between theories and reported data) would apply to other categories of literature relatedness, potentially leading to new knowledge. Swanson (1991, pp. 282-283) specifically lays out the logical structure of relatedness leading to one of his literature-based knowledge discoveries. More recently, work has focused on the development of algorithmic approaches to identifying related articles in support of literature-based knowledge discovery (Gordon & Lindsay, 1996; Swanson & Smalheiser, 1997; Smalheiser & Swanson, 1998; Gordon & Dumais, 1998; Lindsay & Gordon, 1999).

## 2.4 Relevance Relationships

The relationality of relevance has long been recognized. For example, Saracevic characterizes "relevance as a measure of effectiveness between a source and a destination in a communication process. A measure is a relation. Relevance is also a relation" (1976, p. 91; emphasis in original omitted). In similar fashion, Lancaster and Warner (1993, p. 47) characterize relevance and utility in terms of relationships between a document and a user, a request, and/or a need. More specifically we may say that relevance relationships refer to the relationships between a user and his or her need, on the one hand, and those sources relevant to the need (that is, those sources of potential usefulness in the resolution of the need), on the other.

Establishing relevance as a relationship at this level is simply a matter of definition. Of far greater import would be the specification of which aspects of the user and the user's need, on the one hand, and which aspects of sources, on the other hand, participate in establishing relevance relationships and what the exact nature of these relationships may be.

There is general consensus that the single most important aspect of the user's need and of the document within the relevance relationship is topicality, although this is by no means a sufficient condition to generate relevance. But topicality relationships do not begin to exhaust the relationality involved in relevance. A host of other criteria also contribute to (the perception of) relevance. Studies by, for example, Halpern and Nilan (1988), Nilan, Peek, and Snyder (1988), Schamber (1991), and Barry (1994) have isolated numerous factors beyond topicality that affect users' judgments of document relevance; a related group of studies by, for example, Kwašnik (1991) and Barreau (1995) have specifically investigated how individuals organize their personal document space, whether physical or electronic—documents assumed to be relevant to the user, because they have been retained—and have similarly identified sets of factors affecting their decisions. Barry, for instance, identified twenty-three extra-topical criteria, which she grouped into seven broad classes of criteria, namely, those pertaining to the information content of documents (e.g., scope, validity, clarity, recency), the user's previous experience and background (e.g., ability to understand, content novelty), the user's beliefs and preferences (e.g., subjective validity, affectiveness), other information and sources within the information environment (e.g., consensus, external verification), the sources of document (e.g., source quality, source reputation), the document as a physical entity (e.g., obtainability, cost), and the user's situation (e.g., time constraints, relationship with author). Each of these factors may be involved in unique types of associations relating relevant material to the user need. However, the relational aspects of these associations have not been addressed in depth.

While it has generally been agreed that a topical relationship exists between a need and the material that can (help) resolve it, discussions of topicality have often wrongly made the simplifying assumption that relatedness means sameness (R. Green, 1995a). Harter points out the oddity of equating topical relevance with simply being on the same topic. After noting that the equation of relevance with "on the [same] topic" diverges from the everyday meaning of *relevance*, he gives two quite apt examples that hammer home the point: "That there was a drought in South Dakota in 1985 was relevant to my vacation plans there that year. Developments in computer technology are relevant to the future careers of students enrolled in schools of library and information science" (1992, pp. 602-603). Clearly the topics of the two parts of each of those examples are conceptually related, but not the same. Indeed, the relationships involved in topical relevance may be quite complex and may range across the full array of semantic relationship types (R. Green & Bean, 1995; Bean & Green, this volume).

## 3. PURPOSES OF RELATIONSHIPS IN KNOWLEDGE ORGANIZATION

On the one hand, the relationships involved in knowledge organization are both numerous and often complex. On the other hand, their very magnitude and complexity militate against their consistent use by information professionals, much less by end users. Even when subject relationships have been kept to the bare minimum—equivalence, hierarchical, associative—there is sometimes lack of consensus on how to treat a specific relationship, and end users often don't understand what is being communicated by the standard relationship notations. At the same time, end users typically understand the relationships of concern to their information situations intuitively. Naturally, some raise the question whether a deeper and/or broader emphasis on relationships would be at all beneficial to knowledge organization or would only get in the way.

While it may be true that the usefulness of explicit relationships is minimal for many end users, they may also be useful to others. But the real rationale for focusing on relationships comes from the dual combination of the continuing explosion of information and its recording in myriad forms with the increasing management of an ever increasing supply of information sources by automated means. The intuitive understanding that humans bring to relationships is not shared by computational devices. At the same time, the expression and manipulation of relationships is perhaps our best hope for infusing higher quality into our retrieval systems. This higher quality may come in the form of greater precision, achieved by specifying relevant topical relationships, as well as by specifying relationships involving other user-centered relevance criteria, thus being able to filter out those materials that are likely to be found less useful. Conversely, if we learn how to reason on these relationships, the higher quality may also come in the identification of relevant sources that would otherwise not have been retrieved at all, for example, if we can retrieve sources that are relevant by analogy.

## Endnotes

1. Tillett's inventory of bibliographic relationships includes a shared characteristic relationship, for which subject is a possible characteristic. This refers to a relationship where Work < has the same subject heading assigned to it as > Work or Work < is assigned to the same class as > Work. Thus this relationship is derived objectively from previously made subject cataloging decisions.

2. Of course, in reality, the smaller text units appeared first and by accretion formed the whole. It is only in turning from generation to analysis that the notion of decomposition makes sense.

3. Scholars often prefer literature searches based on following bibliographic references over straight subject-oriented searches in indexing and abstracting services. A study by R. Green (2000) demonstrates the complementarity of the two approaches. By implication, citation-based searching can also be used to find literature relevant to a user need.

## References

Agosti, M., Crestani, F., & Melucci, M. (1997). On the use of information retrieval techniques for the automatic construction of hypertext. *Information Processing & Management, 33,* 133-144.

Aitchison, J., Gilchrist, A., & Bawden, D. (1997). Structure and relationships. Sect. F in *Thesaurus Construction and Use: A Practical Manual* (3rd ed.). London: Aslib.

Ali, S. N. (1993). Subject relationship between articles determined by co-occurrence of keywords in citing and cited titles. *Journal of Information Science,* 19, 225-232.

Allan, J. (1997). Building hypertext using information retrieval. *Information Processing & Management,* 33, 145-159.

Baron, L., Tague-Sutcliffe, J., & Kinnucan, M. (1996). Labeled, typed links as cues when reading hypertext documents. *Journal of the American Society for Information Science,* 47, 896-908.

Barreau, D. K. (1995). Context as a factor in personal information management systems. *Journal of the American Society for Information Science,* 46, 327-339.

Barry, C. L. (1994). User-defined relevance criteria: An exploratory study. *Journal of the American Society for Information Science,* 45, 149-159.

Bean, C. A. (1996). Analysis of non-hierarchical associative relationships among Medical subject headings (MeSH): Anatomical and related terminology. In R. Green (Ed.), *Knowledge Organization and Change: Proceedings of the Fourth International ISKO Conference,* 80-86. Frankfurt am Main: INDEKS Verlag.

Bertha, E. (1993). Inter- and intrabibliographical relationships: A concept for a hypercatalog. In A. H. Helal & J. W. Weiss (Eds.), *Opportunity 2000: Understanding and Serving Users in an Electronic Library,* 211-223. Essen: Essen University Library.

Coates, E. J. (1973). Progress in documentation: Some properties of relationships in the structure of indexing language. *Journal of Documentation,* 29, 390-404.

Crombie, W. (1985). Semantic relations between propositions: An outline. Chap. 2 in *Process and Relation in Discourse and Language Learning.* London: Oxford University Press.

Davies, R. (1989). The creation of new knowledge by information retrieval and classification. *Journal of Documentation,* 45, 273-301.

Frei, H. P. & Stieger, D. (1995). The use of semantic links in hypertext information retrieval. *Information Processing & Management,* 31, 1-13.

Goossens, P. & Mazur-Rzesos, E. (1982). Hierarchical relationships in bibliographic descriptions: Problem analysis. In A. H. Helal & J. W. Weiss (Eds.), *Hierarchical Relationships in Bibliographic Descriptions: INTERMARC Software-subgroup Seminar 4,* 13-128. Essen: Essen University Library.

Gordon, M. D. & Dumais, S. (1998). Using latent semantic indexing for literature based discovery. *Journal for the American Society for Information Science,* 49, 674-685.

Gordon, M. D. & Lindsay, R. K. (1996). Toward discovery support systems: A replication, re-examination, and extension of Swanson's work on literature-based discovery of a connection between Raynaud's and fish oil. *Journal for the American Society for Information Science,* 47, 116-128.

Green, R. (1995a). Topical relevance relationships: Why topic matching fails. *Journal of the American Society for Information Science,* 46, 646-653.

Green, R. (1995b). Syntagmatic relationships in index languages: A reassessment. *Library Quarterly,* 65, 365-385.

Green, R. (1995c). The expression of conceptual syntagmatic relationships: A comparative survey. *Journal of Documentation,* 51, 315-338.

Green, R. (2000). Locating sources in humanities scholarship: The efficacy of following bibliographic references. *Library Quarterly,* 71, 201-229.

Green, R. (In press). Developing an inventory of thesaural relationships. In W. Schmitz-Esser (Ed.), *Lines of Thought in Knowledge Organization: 10 Years Anniversary*

*Festschrift: ISKO—International Society for Knowledge Organization, 1989-1999.*
Würzburg: ERGON-Verlag.

Green, R. & Bean, C. A. (1995). Topical relevance relationships: An exploratory study and preliminary typology. *Journal of the American Society for Information Science,* 46, 654-662.

Green S. J. (1999). Lexical semantics and automatic hypertext construction. *ACM Computing Surveys* [Online], 31(4), 22 paragraphs. Available: <http://www.cs.brown.edu/memex/ACM_HypertextTestbed/papers/48.html> [2000, 14 August].

Halliday, M. A. K. & Hasan, R. (1976). *Cohesion in English.* London: Longman.

Halpern, D. & Nilan, M. (1988). A step toward shifting the research emphasis in information science from the system to the user: An empirical investigation of source-evaluation behavior information seeking and use. In *ASIS '88, Proceedings of the 51st ASIS Annual Meeting,* 169-176.

Harter, S. P. (1992). Psychological relevance and information science. *Journal of the American Society for Information Science,* 43, 602-615.

Harter, S. P., Nisonger, T. E., & Weng, A. (1993). Semantic relationships between cited and citing articles in library and information science journals. *Journal of the American Society for Information Science,* 44, 543-552.

Hearst, M. A. (1997). TextTiling: Segmenting text into multi-paragraph subtopic passages. *Computational Linguistics,* 23, 33-64.

Hudon, M. (1994). La structure sémantique du thésaurus. Chap. 2 in *Le Thésaurus: Conception, Élaboration, Gestion.* Montréal: Éditions ASTED.

IFLA Study Group on the Functional Requirements for Bibliographic Records. (1998). *Functional Requirements for Bibliographic Records: Final Report.* München: K.G. Saur.

Kent, W. (1978). *Data and Reality: Basic Assumptions in Data Processing Reconsidered.* Amsterdam: North-Holland.

Khoo, C. S.-G. (1997). The use of relation matching in information retrieval. *LIBRES* [Online], 7(2), 70 paragraphs. Available: <http://aztec.lib.utk.edu/libres/libre7n2/khoo.html> [2000, February 9].

Kwašnik, B. H. (1991). The importance of factors that are not document attributes in the organisation of personal documents. *Journal of Documentation,* 47, 389-398.

Lancaster, F. W. & Warner, A. (1993). *Information Retrieval Today.* Arlington, VA: Information Resources Press.

Leazer, G. H. (1993). *A Conceptual Plan for the Description and Control of Bibliographic Works.* D.L.S. dissertation, Columbia University.

Leazer, G. H. (1996). Recent research on the sequential bibliographic relationship and its implications for standards and the library catalog: An examination of serials. *Cataloging & Classification Quarterly,* 21(3/4), 205-220.

Leazer, G. H. & Smiraglia, R. P. (1994). Toward the bibliographic control of works: Derivative bibliographic relationships in the online union catalogue. *Annual Review of OCLC Research 1994,* 19 paragraphs. [Online]. Available: <http://www.oclc.org/oclc/research/publications/review94/part3/smiragla.htm> [2000, February 9].

Lindsay R. K., & Gordon M. D. (1999). Literature-based discovery by lexical statistics. *Journal of the American Society for Information Science*, 50, 574-587.

Liu, M. (1993). Progress in documentation: The complexities of citation practice: A review of citation studies. *Journal of Documentation*, 49, 370-408.

McNellis, C. H. (1985). Describing reproductions: Multiple physical manifestations in the bibliographical universe. *Cataloging & Classification Quarterly*, 5(3), 35-48.

Myaeng, S. H. & McHale, M. L. (1992). Toward a relation hierarchy for information retrieval. In B. H. Kwašnik & R. Fidel (Eds.), *Advances in Classification Research, Proceedings of the 2nd ASIS SIG/CR Classification Research Workshop*, 101-113. Medford, NJ: Learned Information.

Neelameghan, A. & Maitra, R. (1978). *Non-hierarchical Associative Relationships among Concepts: Identification and Typology* (part A of FID/CR report no. 18). Bangalore: FID/CR Secretariat.

Nilan, M. S., Peek, R. P., & Snyder, H. W. (1988). A methodology for tapping user evaluation behaviors: An exploration of users' strategy, source and information evaluating. In *ASIS '88, Proceedings of the 51st ASIS Annual Meeting*, 152-159.

O'Neill, E. T. & Vizine-Goetz, D. (1989). Bibliographic relationships: Implications for the function of the catalog. In E. Svenonius (Ed.), *The Conceptual Foundations of Descriptive Cataloging*, 167-179. San Diego: Academic Press.

Parunak, H. V. D. (1991). Ordering the information graph. In E. Berk & J. Devlin (Eds.), *Hypertext / Hypermedia Handbook*, 299-325. New York: Intertext Publications.

Perreault, J. M. (1994). Categories and relators: A new schema. *Knowledge Organization*, 21, 189-198.

Saracevic, T. (1976). Relevance: A review of the literature and a framework for thinking on the notion in information science. *Advances in Librarianship*, 6, 79-138.

Schamber, L. (1991). *Users' Criteria for Evaluation in Multimedia Information Seeking and Use Situations*. Ph.D. dissertation, Syracuse University.

Smalheiser, N. R., & Swanson, D. R. (1998). Using ARROWSMITH: A computer-assisted approach to formulating and assessing scientific hypotheses. *Computer Methods and Programs in Biomedicine*, 57, 149-153.

Smiraglia, R. P. (1992). *Authority Control and the Extent of Derivative Bibliographic Relationships*. Ph.D. dissertation, University of Chicago.

Soergel, D. (1967). Some remarks on information languages, their analysis and comparison. *Information Storage and Retrieval*, 3, 219-291.

Spang-Hanssen, H. (1976). *Roles and Links Compared with Grammatical Relations in Natural Languages*. Lyngby: Dansk Teknisk Literaturselskab.

Swanson, D. R. (1986). Undiscovered public knowledge. *Library Quarterly*, 56, 103-118.

Swanson, D. R. (1990). The absence of co-citation as a clue to undiscovered causal connections. In C. L. Borgman, (Ed.), *Scholarly Communication and Bibliometrics*, 129-137. Newbury Park, CA: Sage Publications.

Swanson, D. R. (1991). Complementary structures in disjoint scientific literatures. In *SIGIR '91: Proceedings of the Fourteenth Annual International ACM SIGIR Conference on Research and Development,*, 280-289. New York: ACM Press.

Swanson, D. R. (1993). Intervening in the life cycles of scientific knowledge. *Library Trends*, 41, 606-631.

Swanson D. R., & Smalheiser N. R. (1997). An interactive system for finding complementary literatures: A stimulus to scientific discovery. *Artificial Intelligence*, 91, 183-203.

Thistlewaite, P. (1997). Automatic construction and management of large open webs. *Information Processing & Management*, 33, 161-173.

Tillett, B. B. (1987). *Bibliographic Relationships: Toward a Conceptual Structure of Bibliographic Information Used in Cataloging*. Ph.D. dissertation, University of California, Los Angeles.

Tillett, B. B. (1991a). A taxonomy of bibliographic relationships. *Library Resources & Technical Services*, 35, 150-158.

Tillett, B. B. (1991b). A summary of the treatment of bibliographic relationships in cataloging rules. *Library Resources & Technical Services*, 35, 393-405.

Tillett, B. B. (1992a). The history of linking devices. *Library Resources & Technical Services*, 36, 23-36.

Tillett, B. B. (1992b). Bibliographic relationships: An empirical study of the LC machine-readable records. *Library Resources & Technical Services*, 36, 162-188.

Trigg, R. H. (1983). *A Network-based Approach to Text Handling for the Online Scientific Community*. Ph.D. dissertation, University of Maryland.

Trivison, D. (1987). Term co-occurrence in cited/citing journal articles as a measure of document similarity. *Information Processing & Management*, 23, 183-194.

Vellucci, S. L. (1997). *Bibliographic Relationships in Music Catalogs*. Lanham, MD: Scarecrow Press.

Vickery, B. (1996). Conceptual relations in information systems [letter to the editor]. *Journal of Documentation*, 52, 198-200.

Willetts, M. (1975). An investigation of the nature of the relation between terms in thesauri. *Journal of Documentation*, 31, 158-184.

# Chapter 2

# Bibliographic Relationships

Barbara B. Tillett
*Library of Congress, Washington, DC, USA*

**Abstract:**
    The realm of conceptual modeling of the bibliographic universe presents another view of the theoretical foundations of bibliographic relationships as reflected in cataloging rules and practices. Linking devices used to indicate bibliographic relationships in past and present catalogs will continue to evolve with changes in technologies that are used to create catalogs.

## 1. BACKGROUND

    For centuries, librarians have created catalogs with the intention of enabling persons to find what they are looking for by author, title, or subject. This includes bringing all the works of an author together and all editions of a work together, as well as bringing together all the materials on a given subject (Cutter, 1904; Lubetzky, 1969; O'Neill & Vizine-Goetz, 1989). Library catalogs are even intended to help a person choose material by edition or literary or topical character as documented by Cutter (1904, p. 12). Cutter's objectives of the catalog are accomplished using the cataloging convention of author/title entries with uniform headings to collocate all the works of an author.

    Catalogs have also provided a surrogate method of navigating among the materials in a library's collections or the entire bibliographic universe, through bibliographic and authority records that indicate relationships among the various materials. Some of these relationships are implicit while others are explicit and have been conveyed through various linking devices. Linking devices continue to evolve with the changes in technologies used to create catalogs (Tillett, 1992a). Before looking at linking devices, we shall consider the basic bibliographic relationships.

    Tillett's (1987) analysis of cataloging rules led to the identification of categories of relationships that have been provided in the Anglo-American tradition. Her taxonomy identified seven types of bibliographic relationships derived from this analysis of cataloging rules as follows:

- **Equivalence relationships**, which hold between exact copies of the same manifestation of a work or between an original item and reproductions of it, so long as the intellectual content and authorship are preserved. Included here are copies, issues, facsimiles and reprints, photocopies, microforms, and other similar

19

*C. A. Bean and R. Green (eds.), Relationships in the Organization of Knowledge,* 19–35.

reproductions.

- **Derivative relationships** (called horizontal relationships in UNIMARC, 1994), which hold between a bibliographic work and a modification based on the work. These include:
  - Variations or versions of the work, such as editions, revisions, translations, summaries, abstracts, and digests;
  - Adaptations or modifications that become new works but are based on the earlier work;
  - Changes of genre, as with dramatizations and novelizations; and
  - New works based on the style or thematic content of the work, as with free translations, paraphrases, imitations, and parodies.
- **Descriptive relationships**, which hold between a bibliographic entity and a description, criticism, evaluation, or review of that entity, such as that between a work and a book review describing it; also included are annotated editions, casebooks, commentaries, critiques, etc.
- **Whole-part** (or part-whole) **relationships** (called vertical relationships in UNIMARC or hierarchical relationships in Goossens & Mazur-Rzesos, 1982), which hold between a bibliographic entity and a component part of the entity, as is the case between an anthology and an individual selection taken from it or between a series and one of its volumes.
- **Accompanying relationships**, which hold between bibliographic entities and their accompanying materials. In some cases one entity is predominant and the other subordinate to it, as is the case between a text and its supplements or between one bibliographic entity and another which provides access to it (e.g., concordances, indexes, catalogs of libraries). In other cases the entities are of equal status but have no specific chronological arrangement, as is the case with parts of a kit.
- **Sequential relationships** (called chronological relationships in UNIMARC), which hold between bibliographic entities that continue or precede one another, as between the successive titles of a serial, sequels of a monograph, or among the various parts of a numbered series.
- **Shared characteristic relationships**, which hold between bibliographic entities that are not otherwise related but coincidentally have a common author, title, subject, or other characteristic used as an access point in a catalog, such as a shared language, date of publication, or country of publication (Tillett, 1987, pp. 24-25; Tillett, 1991; Goossens & Mazur-Rzesos, 1982; UNIMARC, 1994).

This taxonomy indicates requirements for relationships that can be used when designing and building bibliographic systems.[1]

## 2. IFLA MODEL

Since Tillett's 1987 analysis there have been several modeling exercises described in the literature, most significantly those that led to the IFLA *Functional Requirements for Bibliographic Records* (IFLA, 1998; ELAG, 1999). These exercises suggested a new approach to that taxonomy of bibliographic relationships, as viewed against the hierarchy of four bibliographic entities: *work, expression, manifestation,* and *item* (IFLA, 1998). These are entities that are the result of intellectual or artistic activity that has led to objects named or described in bibliographic records. There are of course other entities in the bibliographic universe, also noted in the IFLA study, such as *persons* and *corporate bodies* that have "**responsibility relationships**" to *works, expressions, manifestations,* and *items* (IFLA, 1998, p. 14). There are also entities that are in a "**subject relationship**" with *works,* including *persons* and *corporate bodies* and even other bibliographic entities, but also *concepts, objects, events,* and *places.*

## 3. PRIMARY RELATIONSHIPS

The entities of *work, expression, manifestation,* and *item* have implicit relationships among themselves, which the IFLA study called "**primary relationships**" (fig. 1):

A *work* may be realized through one or more than one *expression* (hence the double arrow on the line that links *work* to *expression*). An *expression,* on the other hand, is the realization of one and only one *work* (hence the single arrow on the reverse direction of that line linking *expression* to *work*). An *expression* may be embodied in one or more than one *manifestation;* likewise a *manifestation* may embody one or more than one *expression.* A *manifestation,* in turn, may be exemplified by one or more than one *item;* but an *item* may exemplify one and only one *manifestation.* (IFLA, 1998, p.13)

Figure 1 is a variation of the IFLA figure. Notice the double line between *work/expression* and *manifestation/item* to show the partition between the entities in the physical world that have been recorded and those that are unrecorded intellectual or artistic content. *Works* and *expressions* are intellectual or artistic content. Those may be the thoughts of a creative person or performances of *works,* but once they are recorded or captured in some physical form, the result is a *manifestation.* One exemplar—one instance—of the *manifestation* is called an *item.* Catalogers typically deal with *item*s and place *items* in their existing collections, giving them characteristics of call numbers, locations, piece identifiers, or notes that uniquely locate or describe those *items;* these are *item*-level data elements in a bibliographic or holdings record. Catalogers also use the *item* to describe the general characteristics that apply to all copies, that is, the *manifestation.* Manifestation-level data elements include the place of publication, publisher, date of publication, physical characteristics, title and statement(s) of responsibility found on the chief source of information, edition statement, series statement, and notes that apply to all copies. And in describing the *manifestation,* they mention the embodied *expression* or *work,* such as through uniform titles or subject headings. So all four of the entity classes may be represented in a single bibliographic record. In the electronic environment, a cataloger may also describe and actually provide a direct link to an *item* that will be remotely accessed. This combines description and access with actually obtaining an exemplar of the desired work, and the process of creating the bibliographic record and identifying relationships with other bibliographic entities continues.

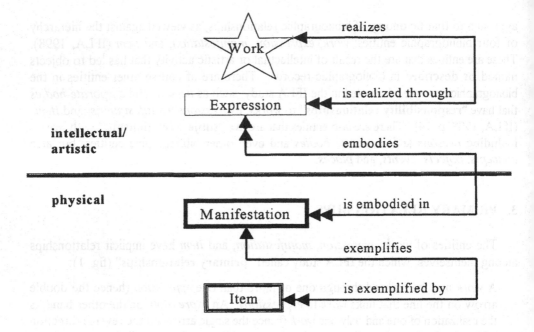

Figure 1. Entity-relationship model—Primary relationships

Within these primary relationships there are other implicit relationships, such as an implicit "**sibling relationship**" between the various *expressions* of a *work*, between the various *manifestations* of an *expression*, and between the various copies (i.e., *items*) of a *manifestation* (IFLA, 1998, p. 59).

## 4. CONTENT RELATIONSHIPS

As noted in the model above, works and expressions are the intellectual or artistic content. Equivalence, derivative, and descriptive relationships can be viewed with this model as applying to works, and hence also hold among the expressions of that work, the manifestations of that work, and the items containing that work in a transitive or inheritance relationship. Content relationships apply across the different levels of entities and exist simultaneously with primary relationships. Content relationships can even be seen as part of a continuum of intellectual or artistic content and the farther one moves along the continuum from the original *work*, the more distant the relationship, as shown in figure 2.

These close **content relationships** have been the primary focus of most relationships described in catalogs (Tillett, 1987; Tillett, 1992b; Smiraglia, 1992; Vellucci, 1994, 1997; Leazer, 1993; Smiraglia & Leazer, 1999). As shown by the dotted vertical line in figure 2, *Anglo-American Cataloguing Rules* have declared a cut-off point for determining when the intellectual or artistic content has changed so much that it constitutes a new work for purposes of entering a record for it in a library catalog. Up to that point the works are considered the same, and the expression has varied; in the case of equivalence relationships

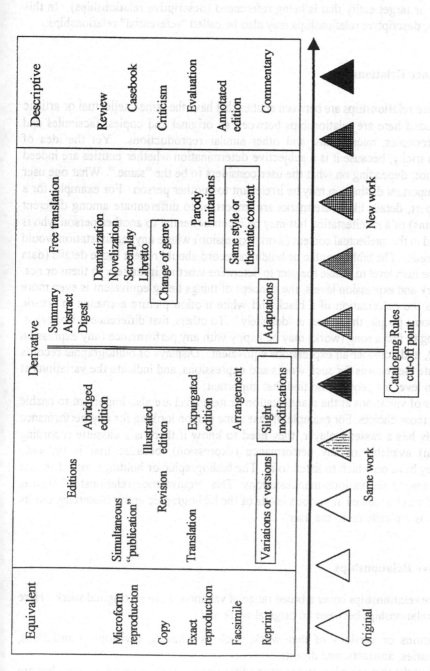

Figure 2. Content relationships—Categories and examples

the manifestation has varied, but the work and/or the expression are the same. We identify these content relationships by linking devices in the bibliographic record for the new manifestation, pointing backwards to some original entity (equivalence and derivative relationships) or target entity that is being referenced (descriptive relationships). In this latter situation, descriptive relationships may also be called "referential" relationships.

## 4.1 Equivalence Relationships

**Equivalence relationships** are between entities that have the same intellectual or artistic content. Included here are relationships between an original and copies, facsimiles and reprints, photocopies, microforms, and other similar reproductions. Yet the idea of equivalence is tricky, because it is a subjective determination whether entities are indeed equivalent or not, depending on what the user considers to be the "same." What one user considers an important distinction may be irrelevant to another person. For example, for a rare book expert, details like watermarks are important to differentiate among different exemplars (items) of a manifestation but may be inconsequential to another person who is more interested in the intellectual content (work/expression) where any manifestation would meet his/her needs. The bibliographic or holdings record should reflect those details (data elements) at the item level to enable the user to determine whether it matters to them or not.

At the work and expression levels, the concept of things being equivalent is even more subjective. Is the colorization of a black and white motion picture a change in artistic content? To some people, the answer is "definitely." To others, that difference is irrelevant. Someone trying to find a song (work) may be happy with any performance (any expression of that work), and consider all expressions equivalent. Displays of bibliographic records should collocate the records for such works and expressions, and indicate the variations at the expression level for people who find that important.

Indications of variations at the manifestation or item level are also important to enable users to make those choices. For example, if that same person looking for any performance of a song only has a cassette player, they need to know if there is a cassette recording (manifestation) available of any performance (expression), because that is the only equipment they have on which to listen to it. The bibliographic or holdings record should differentiate among the various manifestations. This "equivalence relationship" then is subjective and can be viewed at various levels of the bibliographic entity hierarchy, but its determination is typically up to the user.

## 4.2 Derivative Relationships

**Derivative relationships** cover a broad range of variations from an original work. Here are included relationships between an original work and

- Variations or versions of that work, such as editions, revisions, translations, summaries, abstracts, and digests;
- New works that are adaptations or modifications that become new works but are

based on the earlier work;
- New works that are changes of genre, as with dramatizations and novelizations; and
- New works based on the style or thematic content of other works, as with free translations, paraphrases, imitations, and parodies.

For some electronic materials, the content changes over time, either by augmenting the content with additional material or by revising the content. Specifically, "integrating entities" (Hirons, 1999) are works and expressions that have their content evolving over time within the same manifestation, such as some loose-leaf publications or some electronic texts or objects that continuously augment the corpus of intellectual or artistic content. For these works, there may be no earlier recorded work to relate to. However, a derivative relationship may exist with earlier versions if they continue to exist.

## 4.3 Descriptive Relationships

**Descriptive relationships**, sometimes called referential relationships during the deliberations on the IFLA study, include relationships between a target work or expression or manifestation and a new work that refers to the target. Examples are the relationships between a work and a review or casebook describing that work, a criticism and the work being criticized, an evaluation of an original work and the work being evaluated, and a commentary and the work being commented upon.

Some authors have included descriptive or referential relationships and even accompanying relationships as derivative relationships (Smiraglia, 1992; Leazer, 1993; Smiraglia & Leazer, 1999). There may be a subtle line of demarcation between a variation of a work and when a work describes or refers to an earlier work, such as a criticism or commentary (descriptive or referential relationship), or is intended to be a companion or tool to facilitate use of another work, such as a concordance (accompanying or companion relationship). Then again, such subtleties may not be important for these content relationships, and it may be more useful to categorize derivative and descriptive together.

## 5. WHOLE-PART AND PART-TO-PART RELATIONSHIPS

There are other types of relationships that deal with the components or aggregates of *works*, namely **whole-part relationships**. These types of relationships are particularly interesting with electronic materials where images and text and/or sound become components of the whole and need to be addressed and brought together (aggregated) for displays, yet often are stored as separate components (fig. 3, A). Another whole-part example is an anthology or a finite set (whole) with its distinctive, separate works (parts) (fig. 3, B). Others still may continually add to the corpus of content, as print serials and electronic serials may do, and we consider those just to be the growing or evolving components (parts) of a single work (fig. 3, C).

Yet the part-to-part relationship between the individual components of a serial or between a prequel and sequel is considered a **sequential relationship** (fig. 4). Among other

WHOLE-PART RELATIONSHIPS

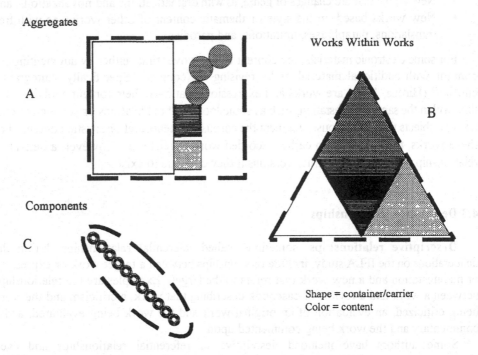

Figure 3. Whole-part relationships or aggregates/components

things, sequential relationships are important for ordering and assisting a user in determining the sequence of the parts for finding information.

**Accompanying relationships** (fig. 4), called companion relationships in discussions during the IFLA study, hold between an entity intended to be used with or to augment another entity. Examples are supplementary maps intended as a companion to a video, a computer disk that accompanies a textbook, and accompanying plates intended to illustrate a main text. The pieces can be viewed either as dependent parts of a whole or as separate entities in their own right that can exist independently of each other, but are packaged together. In this latter situation, the accompanying or companion relationship can also be viewed as existing beyond the end of the continuum of close **content relationships** (beyond the right end on fig. 2), because the entities are (or contain) different works that complement the content of another work that is another component of the whole. So the entities in an accompanying relationship are each considered a component part of a whole, while entities in close content relationships are separate, independent entities. The relationship is "x accompanies y" or "x is a companion to y" or the reverse ("y is accompanied by x"), or we may choose to make this a one-directional relationship for "companion" works that are viewed as independent. In any case, we have a work that accompanies the intellectual or artistic content of another.

## PART-TO-PART RELATIONSHIPS

### (Component-to-Component)

Accompanying Relationships                    Sequential Relationships

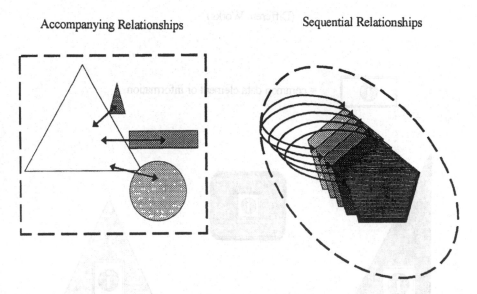

Figure 4. Part-to-part relationships

## 6. SHARED CHARACTERISTIC RELATIONSHIPS

There is yet another type of relationship that can be described that holds between different *works* that share any element in common (other than an element described by one of the other types of relationships). We could establish a **shared characteristic relationship** for whatever element we found useful. Some people might like us to use the color or size of the binding as significant characteristics for locating items, and indeed some storage facilities and early libraries in monasteries used size as an element for identifying, organizing, storing, and shelving. We might also use the date of publication, country of publication, language, or "format/media/carrier" as useful elements for relating manifestations that share that characteristic of interest. Some of these data elements, like language and country of publication have appeared in machine-readable cataloging records since the late 1960s, but we still lack an exhaustive and mutually exclusive listing of format/media/carrier elements. Shared characteristic elements are used for retrieval either directly or as limits or filters to a search.

The relationship then is entity A has the characteristic X in common with entities B, C, . . . N. This is a very useful relationship to make and will be easier to make in future catalogs, where data elements can be more easily manipulated to collocate bibliographic records. This is shown in figure 5 as a data element for some bit of information ( ▣ ) that is shared among several entities, and potentially can be used as a retrieval element.

## SHARED CHARACTERISTIC RELATIONSHIPS

### (Different Works)

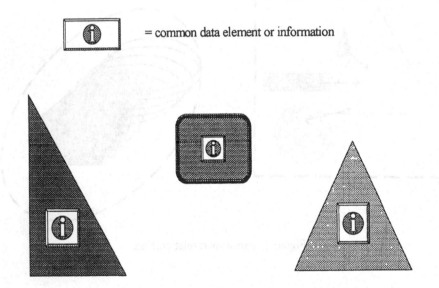

Figure 5. Shared characteristic relationships

So which relationships are worth noting in our catalogs for the users? We have traditionally been concerned about the economics of providing information in cataloging records and typically have concentrated on those relationships that are economical to provide. User studies are difficult to perform, and as a consequence we do not have good information on what users really need. And who are the users of bibliographic information? The useful relationships may vary depending on whether the user is a publisher providing an inventory of goods, a researcher trying to track down scholarly works, an Internet user following paths to information, or someone wanting to find a movie at a local library. These categories of useful relationships are still being debated in the metadata world. The importance of bibliographic relationships is well recognized by such groups as the inventors and future users of Digital Object Identifiers and the participants in the Dublin Core Metadata Initiative. The Dublin Core Relations Working Group[2] has started identifying what they believe are the useful relationships to include in metadata, but much more needs to be done to provide for bibliographic relationships for materials on the Internet. In addition, our cataloging rules should be more explicit about relationships.

## 7. LINKING DEVICES

Cataloging rules have provided ways to indicate bibliographic relationships and to bring together related entities in catalog displays, but this interconnection of rules and catalogs is weakening. The types of linking devices used in the Anglo-American cataloging tradition (table 1) have changed over time reflecting the technological capabilities available in the catalog (Tillett, 1992a).

---

**Linking Devices**

- Main entry
- Uniform title
- Added entry
- Dash entry
- Analytical entry
- Multilevel description
- Edition statement
- Series statement
- Physical description addition
- Note
- Reference
- Hypertext link
- Integrated record displays from shared data in databases

---

Table 1. Linking devices

During the time of book and handwritten card catalogs, linking devices to relate bibliographic entities included shared main entries, analytical entries, dash entries, references, notes, edition statements, series statements, additions to physical description (namely the "+" sign to indicate accompanying materials; see fig. 6), and holdings annotations.

---

387 p. : ill. ; 27 cm. + teacher's notes

---

Figure 6. Example of additions to physical description

When printed card catalogs were introduced around 1900, the new device of an added entry was used to express relationships and that device made its way into cataloging rules of that era. Many of the old devices were continued in online catalogs, but some, like dash entries, were prematurely abandoned. Dash entries, also called dashed on entries, were a useful space saving device in book and card catalogs to record added copies or other editions or accompanying materials within the same entry/record as the main manifestation (fig. 7). The dash or multiple dashes served as ditto symbols to indicate the above main entry and description applied to the additional manifestation being described in the dash entry. An electronic dashed on entry might save space for online displays.

---

**Cole, Ralph Dayton, 1873-1932.**
       Custer, the man of action: address by Colonel Ralph
D. Cole.
       (*In* Ohio archæological and historical quarterly. Columbus,
O., 1932. 23ᶜᵐ Vol. XLL, p. 631-654. illus. (ports.))

— Copy 2. Detached.

---

Figure 7. Example of a dash entry, "copy 2"
(from the 1941 *A.L.A. Rules*, p. 226)

More recent online catalogs have introduced a new device of hypertext links to relate bibliographic entities and to connect the surrogate bibliographic records with the actual items. We can now link bibliographic records to the digital objects and electronic texts they describe. In the MARC 21 format this is done through the 856 field or a subfield where the address of the digital object is recorded. We can also use the online catalog to connect to intermediary tools like electronic finding aids that in turn can retrieve desired items for the user.

For several years the concept of "executable" relationships has been discussed. Daniel and Lagoze called these "distributed active relationships" or "DARs" for the digital environment (Daniel & Lagoze, 1997). Future systems development offers many more opportunities for users to navigate through the bibliographic universe and has the potential to show the user the available pathways that may be of interest and actually take them to those resources electronically.

We also now have the ability to limit or filter, as well as to search for shared characteristics (data elements) in our online catalogs. These capabilities and new devices will continue to expand with the imagination for future system designers.

## 8. SUMMARY OF RELATIONSHIPS

To summarize the relationship types operating among bibliographic entities, there are:

- **Primary relationships** that are implicit among the bibliographic entities of work,

expression, manifestation, and item;
- Close **content relationships** that can be viewed as a continuum starting from an original work, including equivalence, derivative, and descriptive (or referential) relationships;
- **Whole-part and part-to-part relationships**, the latter including accompanying relationships and sequential relationships; and
- **Shared characteristic relationships.**

As noted in the IFLA model, there are also two other very important types of relationships in the bibliographic universe. These are:

- **Responsibility relationships** between the four bibliographic entities (*work, expression, manifestation, item*) and entities for *persons* and *corporate bodies*; and
- **Subject relationships** between *works* and entities that can be subjects: another *work, expression, manifestation, item, person, corporate body, concept, object, event,* and *place* (IFLA 1998, pp. 14-15).

## 9. RECOMMENDATIONS AND FUTURE AGENDA

We are seeing catalogs move farther away from the control of cataloging rules. Commercial and "home-grown" systems have each taken their own paths, resulting in a great variety of online catalogs and displays (Carlyle, 1999). A user in one library cannot predict how bibliographic information will be presented from one library or information system to another, even with the Z39.50 standard. Some vendors see standardization efforts for OPAC displays, such as those recommended by IFLA, as stifling their competitive edge (Yee, 1999; Yee & Layne, 1998). Where is the win-win solution?

Perhaps it will be found in future catalogs. The opportunity exists to move beyond the current "record" structure and beyond relational and even the current object-oriented databases. For economic reasons we will continue MARC formats (MARC 21, UNIMARC, etc.) for communicating records, but we now have other options for displays and structures in local and shared systems. Future computer architectures will bring increased flexibility in manipulating data elements and relating entities and digital objects. Cataloging rules and catalogs themselves should build on the new opportunities that technology offers us at this time, yet it may be too soon to take that leap, given the economic impact of such a jump.

Now more than ever, bibliographic relationships need to be more explicit, so users understand the paths they are offered in an online catalog or on the Internet. Users are no longer limited to the catalog of a single institution. Collections are now accessible worldwide. We must assure normalization or consistency in the displays and in the presentation of data to users, particularly for relationships, so the pathways are clear. How can we take best advantage of computer capabilities for expressing bibliographic relationships and provide for them in cataloging rules and catalogs of the future?

We should take positive steps toward the goal of improved devices for expressing important bibliographic relationships. Our cataloging rules should be changed to ensure consistency in the formulation and display of relationships, yet in a manner that allows for expansion to accommodate future relationships we have not yet dreamed of (Wainwright,

1991). New devices should be used within our computer-based records (bibliographic, authority, holdings, etc.) to facilitate user-viewed displays that present relationships graphically through pictures or text, or even directly, as we can do now through hypertext links or "executable" relationships. Who knows what devices might be invented in the future?

Rule changes are needed. Cataloging rules should be more explicit about the types of relationships worth including and should provide appropriate consistency in the methods used to express relationships. For example, reproductions can be considered to be in equivalence relationships to the originals, yet we continue to catalog facsimiles differently from other reproductions. Consistency in treatment would benefit users' understanding of relationships.

A thorough analysis of the structure of the *Anglo-American Cataloguing Rules*, commissioned by the Joint Steering Committee for Revision of the Anglo-American Cataloguing Rules (Delsey, 1999a, 1999b) will lead to many improvements. We need to be sure those improvements include explicit provisions for relationships, both in what the cataloger creates and in what the user sees in displays. In order to deal efficiently with online cataloging, our rules need a fresh review that focuses on computer-based cataloging.

Bibliographic records created by catalogers are no longer the finished product that the user sees or even should see. The cataloger creates a MARC record and the computer system manipulates the data in that record for various displays. Displays should indicate content relationships and pertinent characteristics to enable users to choose the entity that meets their needs. Links and relationship types could be coded to enable the display of pertinent notes or other navigational information in the user's language. Cataloging rules should save the catalogers' time while enabling better displays for users.

We need more than the linking of the bibliographic, holdings, item, and authority records, because we now have a user expectation of linking directly to the bibliographic object. The specific relationship to the linked object must be clear to the user navigating the bibliographic universe.

A multi-tiered root/branch structure for "multiple versions" was suggested for primary relationships in 1989 (Tillett, 1989; Multiple, 1990). The proposal was to handle the cataloging and display problems of various manifestations (particularly same content in different carriers) by linking the descriptions and access elements of various manifestations and physical items to the descriptions and access points of the work they contained. This was important to alleviate redundant information in record creation (to reduce cataloging costs) by utilizing the hierarchical "inheritance" among linked records and to improve collocation of online displays for easier understanding by users. Heaney (1995) proposed a similar model in looking at object-oriented cataloging. Many online library systems now can accommodate such a multi-tiered approach, and the display of primary bibliographic relationships among bibliographic entities can be realized. All systems should enable users to easily find what they need and offer pathways to related materials.

The IFLA model optimizes bibliographic control and minimizes bibliographic input, increasing data integrity. It can be used for objects other than publications, such as materials in museums or archives. It also maximizes retrieval possibilities, but it has not yet been tested. We need new systems that build on this model.

Libraries created systems that behaved in known ways. Computer systems and the

Internet challenge that stability. The Internet has a broader spectrum of users than an individual library has. Items are more varied than in the past and increasingly come in mixed media. Users can now do new things with the items, including copying them directly and manipulating them to formulate new works. Continuous updating can occur online, making citation and even location or retrieval of a particular version more difficult, if not impossible. The Internet is for the most part uncontrolled, and could greatly benefit by library experience with controlled vocabularies and bibliographic access and retrieval methods. However, both Internet search engine providers and libraries could improve their services to users by providing quality links that clearly indicate specific bibliographic relationships.

The opportunity is here. Let's take it.

## Endnotes

1. For a complete historical background on research in bibliographic relationships see Vellucci (1998).

2. See the report from the Dublin Core Metadata Initiative, Relations Working Group (1997).

## Acknowledgments

I would like to thank the following people (in alphabetical order) who served as readers and provided excellent comments to assist in the preparation of this chapter: Allyson Carlyle, Paula Goossens, Olivia Madison, Ron Murray, Elaine Svenonius, Arlene Taylor, Sherry Vellucci, and the editors, Carol Bean and Rebecca Green.

## References

Carlyle, A. (1999). User categorisation of works: Toward improved organisation of online catalogue displays. *Journal of Documentation*, 55, 184-208.
Cutter, C. A. (1904). *Rules for a Dictionary Catalog* (4th ed. rewritten). Washington, DC: U.S. Government Printing Office.
Daniel, R. & Lagoze, C. (1997). Extending the Warwick framework: From metadata containers to active digital objects. *D-Lib Magazine* [Online], 44 paragraphs. Available: http://www.dlib.org/dlib/november97/daniel/11daniel.html [2000, February 9].
Delsey, T. (1999a). *The Logical Structure of the Anglo-American Cataloguing Rules—Part I* [Online]. Available: <http://www.nlc-bnc.ca/jsc/aacrdel.htm> [2000, February 9].
Delsey, T. (1999b). *The Logical Structure of the Anglo-American Cataloguing Rules—Part II* [Online]. Available: <http://www.nlc-bnc.ca/jsc/aacrdel2.htm> [2000, February 9].

Dublin Core Metadata Initiative. Relations Working Group (1997). *Relation Element Working Draft 1997-12-19* [Online]. Available: <http://purl.org/dc/documents/working_drafts/wd-relation-current.htm> [2000, February 10].

ELAG (1999). European Library Automation Group (ELAG) Workshop 4. User benefits from a new bibliographic model: Follow-up of the IFLA Functional Requirements Study. *International Cataloguing and Bibliographic Control*, 28, 80-81. (Also available online: <http://ifla.inist.fr/IV/ifla64/084-126e.htm> [2000, February 9].)

IFLA Study Group on the Functional Requirements for Bibliographic Records. (1998). *Functional Requirements for Bibliographic Records: Final Report.* München: K. G. Saur.

Goossens, P. & Mazur-Rzesos, E. (1982). Hierarchical relationships in bibliographic descriptions: Problem analysis. In A. H. Helal & J. W. Weiss (Eds.), *Hierarchical Relationships in Bibliographic Descriptions: INTERMARC Software-subgroup Seminar 4*, 13-128. Essen: Essen University Library.

Heaney, M. (1995). Object-oriented cataloging. *Information Technology and Libraries*, 14, 135-153.

Hirons, J. (1999). *Revising AACR2 to Accommodate Seriality: Report to the Joint Steering Committee for Revision of AACR* [Online]. Available: <http://www.nlc-bnc.ca/jsc/ser-rep0.html> [2000, February 9].

Leazer, G. H. (1993). *A Conceptual Plan for the Description and Control of Bibliographic Works.* D.L.S. dissertation, Columbia University.

Lubetzky, S. (1969). *Principles of Cataloging.* Los Angeles, CA: Institute of Library Research, University of California.

*Multiple Versions Forum Report: Report from a Meeting Held December 6-8, 1989, Airlie, Virginia.* (1990). Washington, DC: Network Development and MARC Standards Office, Library of Congress, 1990.

O'Neill, E. T. & Vizine-Goetz, D. (1989). Bibliographic relationships: Implications for the function of the catalog. In E. Svenonius (Ed.), *the Conceptual Foundations of Descriptive Cataloging*, 167-179. San Diego: Academic Press.

Smiraglia, R. P. (1992). *Authority Control and the Extent of Derivative Bibliographic Relationships.* Ph.D. dissertation, University of Chicago.

Smiraglia, R. P. & Leazer, G. H. (1999). Derivative bibliographic relationships: The work relationship in a global bibliographic database. *Journal of the American Society for Information Science*, 50, 493-504.

Tillett, B. A. B. (1987). *Bibliographic Relationships: Toward a Conceptual Structure of Bibliographic Information Used in Cataloging.* Ph.D. dissertation, University of California, Los Angeles.

Tillett, B. B. (1989). Hierarchical approach to materials in multiple formats: General description. Paper delivered and distributed at the LC/CLR Forum on "Multiple Versions."

Tillett, B. B. (1991). A taxonomy of bibliographic relationships. *Library Resources & Technical Services*, 35, 150-158.

Tillett, B. B. (1992a). The history of linking devices. *Library Resources & Technical Services*, 36, 23-36.

Tillett, B. B. (1992b). Bibliographic relationships: An empirical study of the LC machine-readable records. *Library Resources & Technical Services*, 36, 162-188.

UNIMARC (1994). *UNIMARC Manual Bibliographic Format* (2nd ed.). München: K. G. Saur. Update 1, 1996 and Update 2, 1998.

Vellucci, S. L. (1994). *Bibliographic Relationships among Musical Bibliographic Entities: A Conceptual Analysis of Music Represented in a Library Catalog with a Taxonomy of the Relationships Discovered.* D.L.S. dissertation, Columbia University.

Vellucci, S. L. (1997). *Bibliographic Relationships in Music Catalogs.* Lanham, MD: Scarecrow Press.

Vellucci, S. L. (1998). Bibliographic relationships. In *The Principles and Future of AACR: Proceedings of the International Conference on the Principles and Future Development of AACR, Toronto, Ontario, Canada, October 23-25, 1997*, 105-147. Ottawa: Canadian Library Association; Chicago: American Library Association.

Wainwright, E. (1991). Implications of the dynamic record for the future of cataloguing. *Cataloguing Australia*, 17 (3/4), 7-20.

Yee, M. M. (1999). *Guidelines for OPAC Displays. Prepared for the IFLA Task Force on Guidelines for OPAC Displays* (draft) [Online]. Available: <http://www.ifla.org/VII/s13/guide/opac.htm> [2000, February 9].

Yee, M. M. & Layne, S. S. (1998). *Improving Online Public Access Catalogs.* Chicago: American Library Association.

# Chapter 3

# Thesaural Relationships

Stella G. Dextre Clarke
*Information Consultant, Luke House, West Hendred, Oxon, UK*

**Abstract:**
   A thesaurus in the controlled vocabulary environment is a tool designed to support effective information retrieval (IR) by guiding indexers and searchers consistently to choose the same terms for expressing a given concept or combination of concepts. Terms in the thesaurus are linked by relationships of three well-known types: equivalence, hierarchical, and associative. The functions and properties of these three basic types and some subcategories are described, as well as some additional relationship types commonly found in thesauri. Progressive automation of IR processes and the capability for simultaneous searching of vast networked resources are creating some pressures for change in the categorization and consistency of relationships.

## 1. INTRODUCTION

   Pick up any of the thesauri widely used for information retrieval (IR) and at first glance you will see a highly developed knowledge structure, comprising terms and relationships between them. The relationships are of several distinct and mutually exclusive types. If the terms are viewed as nodes in a semantic network, then the relationships serve as a complex pathway or navigation guide through the network. It is evident that the thesaurus is the product of intense intellectual analysis, with potential uses in artificial intelligence, machine translation, and other automated applications.

   Closer scrutiny, however, reveals problems. The categorization of relationship types in the typical thesaurus often looks inconsistent and/or incomplete. What rules did the editor follow when deciding whether a given term pair should be linked hierarchically, associatively, or by equivalence? If precise rules have not been followed, then the usefulness of the relationships in automated applications will be severely limited. Some inconsistencies arise from sloppiness, but others appear to be deliberate. Why do thesaural relationships so often appear idiosyncratic?

   This chapter explores the relationship types in typical thesauri along with some reasons for the observed variations and inconsistencies. The description will be limited to thesauri intended as controlled vocabularies for use by human indexers and searchers in IR. This is the type of thesaurus for which standards have been developed, especially the international standard ISO 2788 (International Organization for Standardization, 1986) and the U.S. national standard ANSI/NISO Z39.19 (National Information Standards Organization, 1994).

37

C. A. Bean and R. Green (eds.), *Relationships in the Organization of Knowledge*, 37–52.

The main relationship types recommended in these standards will be taken as the "rules" from which departures may often be observed. (Thesaural standards are discussed in detail in Milstead, this volume.) Some additional relationships not in the standards but observed in many good thesauri will also be described. New applications are creating a demand for thesauri that extend or depart from the standard relationship requirements. But first we shall consider the functions that a thesaurus and its relationships are expected to serve. Understanding the functions is the key to understanding the practices followed.

## 2. PURPOSES AND USES OF THESAURAL RELATIONSHIPS

A simple assumption underlies the design of a controlled vocabulary: To identify relevant items among a large set of documents, it is only necessary that the person searching uses exactly the same term or combination of terms as did the person indexing. A thesaurus, which is one type of controlled vocabulary, is the guide to the terms available for indexing and searching. Everything in it is designed to assist both searchers and indexers to express a given concept in exactly the same way. At first sight a thesaurus may look like a list of terms, but more fundamentally it is a list of concepts, with terms present as identifiers for the underlying concepts.

The inclusion of relationships is intended primarily to guide users to the selection of the index term(s) most appropriate for expressing a given concept/query. Typically, a user starts with a term, which may or may not adequately express the desired concept. The relationships present can help in three possible ways:

- By giving for the term found by the user a context that clarifies its scope and indicates whether it is appropriate,
- By leading to other terms to supplement or replace the first term, and
- By making it easy to replace terms or apply additional ones, especially in the electronic search environment.

Most thesauri are not stand-alone reference works, but are tools designed to support IR in one or more particular databases. And so they have features taking into account:

- The likely background of users—both searchers and indexers,
- The development history of the database, and
- Anticipated capabilities of search software and search interface(s).

Unfortunately, conflicts can arise between the recommendations of the standards and the style of relationships deemed most acceptable to existing users. The rules may then be quietly ignored.

Despite such lapses, some basic rules are always applied. To be worthy of the name "thesaurus," a controlled vocabulary must incorporate a minimum of three types of relationship, namely equivalence, hierarchical, and associative. The three basic types have been widely recognized for at least three decades. Willetts (1975) describes their use in ten important thesauri of the time, including the 1967 editions of two very influential works: the *Thesaurus of Engineering and Scientific Terms* (1967) and the *NASA Thesaurus* (National Aeronautics and Space Administration, 1967). See also Vickery (1971), Lancaster (1986), and Aitchison, Gilchrist, & Bawden (1997).

## 3. THE EQUIVALENCE RELATIONSHIP

In the context of a monolingual thesaurus, equivalence is the relationship between a pair of synonyms or quasi-synonyms. (The equivalence that obtains between corresponding terms in the different languages of a multilingual thesaurus is discussed by Hudon, this volume.) The relationship is directional, linking terms of unequal status. One of them is designated the "preferred term" or "descriptor," while the other is known as a "non-preferred term," "lead-in term," or "non-descriptor." Here are two typical thesaurus entries showing the reciprocal equivalence relationship:

```
guarantee                          warranty
    UF    warranty                     USE    guarantee
```

The function of the relationship is to guide the user to the term that is preferred for both indexing and searching. In the above case, the instruction "USE" tells the indexer and the searcher to prefer the term "guarantee" for the concept of "warranty"; the reciprocal abbreviation "UF" means "use for."

Note that the equivalence relationship is often used between terms that are not true synonyms. More accurately, they are terms whose meaning is sufficiently close to the desired concept that it is convenient to treat them as equivalent, for the purposes of the database(s) to be indexed/searched. Terms such as "porcelain," "bone china," and "crockery," which might be individual descriptors in a thesaurus for the ceramics industry, could well be treated as equivalents in a thesaurus for more general use. Which relationship to apply between these terms is a subjective decision, depending on the likely scope and depth of the document collection to be indexed, as well as the background and likely interests of the users who will be searching it.

In practice, many different types of equivalence are observed in well-developed thesauri, as shown in table 1; this list is by no means exhaustive.

Some examples in table 1 show equivalence sets rather than simple pairs. Where there are more than two terms in the set, one will be shown as the preferred term, and an equivalence relationship will link it to each other member of the set. The first eleven types in the table are straightforward enough, but the last two merit discussion.

The "perfume" example among the quasi-synonyms is drawn from the *BSI ROOT Thesaurus* (1985), a tool designed for indexing standards and regulations. Plainly eau de cologne is not the same thing as perfume. But since both products are likely to be covered in the same few relevant standards and regulations, indexing and searching efficiency are improved by using just one term to cover both concepts. For similar pragmatic reasons, equivalence may be established between terms like "smoothness" and "roughness," which at first sight seem direct opposites. Behind each of these terms lies the concept of describing the degree to which a surface evidences physical irregularities, raised portions, and hollows. This concept is the one wanted in the indexing vocabulary, and it could be phrased in terms either of smoothness or of roughness. Arbitrarily, one of these may be chosen as the preferred term and the other as the lead-in. The aim of

| Equivalence type | Examples |
|---|---|
| Common/scientific names | mad cow disease/bovine spongiform encephalopathy |
| Non-proprietary/trade names | adhesive plaster/band-aid/elastoplast |
| Standard names/slang | supplementary earnings/perks |
| Abbreviations, acronyms | AIDS/auto-immune deficiency syndrome |
| Lexical variants | color/colour; edema/oedema; databases/data-bases/data bases |
| Inverted entries | electric cables/cables, electric |
| Terms from different cultures sharing a common language | elevators/lifts; splinter/sliver/skelf |
| Terms of different linguistic origin | buying/purchasing; thermal resistance/heat resistance |
| Competing terms for emerging concepts or technologies | phasmid/phagemid; lap-top computers/notebook computers |
| Current/outdated terms | capacitors/(electric) condensers |
| Irregular plurals | mouse/mice |
| Quasi-synonyms | perfume/eau de cologne; smoothness/roughness |
| Specific concepts subsumed in a broader concept | flavour/bitterness/sweetness; handling machinery/cranes/extractors |

Table 1. Types of equivalence commonly noted in thesauri

a controlled vocabulary and its relationships is not to teach people the correct meaning of terminology, but to assist them in the practical business of IR.

The two examples for the last type of equivalence relationship in table 1 come from *AGROVOC* (1997) (used for indexing the *AGRIS* database) and illustrate how equivalence may be established between terms of differing levels of specificity. A user interested in the concept of "sweetness" needs to be told, firstly, that this term is not valid for searching *AGRIS*, and secondly, that the most appropriate search term is "flavour." Thus an equivalence relationship is established between two terms that could hardly be considered synonymous. This practice of subsuming a narrower concept under a broader heading is sometimes known as "upward posting."

## 3.1 Partial Equivalence

The vast majority of thesaural relationships link pairs of terms, but complex three-way relationships do sometimes occur when a compound term is to be factored. Thus *AGROVOC* recommends:

mechanical harvesting
    USE    harvesting
    AND   mechanical methods

Reciprocal entries are also required to ensure that users of the constituent terms know what is going on. In the above case these are:

harvesting
    UF+   mechanical harvesting

mechanical methods
    UF+   mechanical harvesting

Note that there is no intrinsic property of the term "mechanical harvesting" that dictates that it should be factored. The *CAB Thesaurus* (1995), which has a scope similar to that of *AGROVOC* but a much greater level of specificity throughout, admits the pre-coordinated term "mechanical harvesting" as a descriptor and shows a hierarchical relationship between this and "harvesting." The differences in choice of relationship shown by these two thesauri are no doubt based on judgments concerning the characteristics of the content and users of their respective databases, rather than on semantic properties of the indexing vocabularies.

Some thesauri include another type of partial equivalence:

beans, faba                                        *from CAB Thesaurus*
    USE    faba beans
    OR     Vicia faba

The USE . . . OR relationship occurs rarely because it can usually be avoided by providing two lead-in entries with different qualifiers.

## 3.2 Dialectal Forms

Substantial differences in terminology can occur when two or more peoples share a common language, such as the differences in American and European usages in English, Spanish, and Portuguese. Although most thesauri treat this as a normal case of equivalence, consistently preferring the spelling and usage of one culture over the other, difficulties for users can arise.

For example, the *CAB Thesaurus* serves two different databases, namely *CAB ABSTRACTS* and *AGRICOLA*. The former has a track record of decades of British house style; the latter has an equally established tradition of American usage. Neither of the database producers was prepared to risk alienating its users by switching to transatlantic usage, so they agreed to introduce a new form of relationship: AF/BF standing for the reciprocals American Form/British Form. Users are expected to interpret AF/BF as a sort of equivalence relationship in which the directionality is reversed depending on which database is to be searched.

The *Art & Architecture Thesaurus* (1994) (*AAT*) adopts a similar approach, in distinguishing dialectal variants from any other type of synonym. American usage is consistently preferred in the printed thesaurus, and British forms (called UK Alternate Descriptors) appear as lead-ins, introduced with the symbol UK or UKALT (reciprocal SEE).

## 4. THE HIERARCHICAL RELATIONSHIP

This relationship is assigned to a pair of terms when the scope of one of the terms totally includes (is broader than) the scope of the other. The Broader Term is designated BT and the Narrower Term NT. Here are examples showing how such relationships are typically displayed in thesaurus entries:

| citrus fruits | lemons | limes |
|---|---|---|
| NT lemons | BT citrus fruits | BT citrus fruits |
| limes | | |

The primary function of the hierarchical relationship is to alert the user to alternative terms that might be used to convey the same concept, but at a different level of specificity. A search at one level could fail to retrieve relevant items indexed either at the broader level or at a narrower level. Careful manipulation of hierarchically related terms allows the user to broaden or narrow a search at will.

An additional function of the hierarchical relationship is to clarify scope. Knowing that "limes" is narrower than the concept of "citrus fruits," the user will not confuse the term with the mineral lime spread on farm fields or even the ornamental trees of the same name.

Three types of hierarchical relationship are accepted in the international standard: generic, whole-part, and instantial. In some thesauri the three types are distinguished formally by using these abbreviations:

- BTG/NTG    Broader Term (Generic)/ Narrower Term (Generic)
- BTP/NTP    Broader Term (Partitive)/ Narrower Term (Partitive)
- BTI/NTI    Broader Term (Instantial)/ Narrower Term (Instantial)

However, most thesauri do not find it necessary to make the distinction explicit. Each of the types will now be described.

### 4.1 The Generic Hierarchical Relationship

This is the case of the citrus fruits (above) and others where the broader term names a class or category, and each of the narrower terms names a subset of that class, but not an individual instance of it. Some examples are:

| mammals | chemical properties |
|---|---|
| NT carnivores | NT acidity |
| primates | alkalinity |
| rodents | flammability |

engines
  NT       internal combustion engines
           jet engines

## 4.2  The Whole-Part Hierarchical Relationship

The four types of whole-part relationship usually accepted as hierarchical are those occurring among geographic entities, parts of the body, disciplines of study, and social structures.  Here are examples of each:

Mexico                                    *from Macrothesaurus*
  BT       Latin America
           North America

heart                                     *from AGROVOC*
  BT1      cardiovascular system
    BT2    body parts

anthropology                              *from Macrothesaurus*
  BT       social sciences

UNESCO                                    *from CAB Thesaurus*
  BT1      UN

Notice that the above examples do not include any parts of machines, or buildings, or networks, or indeed some of the most typical cases of the whole-part relationship.  In practice, certain thesauri list some components of vehicles and other engineering structures as Narrower Terms, but generally machine parts are treated as associatively related (see below), if they are linked at all.

## 4.3  The Instantial Hierarchical Relationship

In this case the narrower terms are not types or parts of the broader, but rather individual instances of them.  Each instance forms a class of just one member; often the narrower terms are proper names.  For example:

Classical languages                       *from Thesaurus of ERIC Descriptors*
  NT       Latin
           Sanskrit

Deserts                                   *from CAB Thesaurus*
  NT1      Gobi Desert
  NT1      Kalahari Desert
  NT1      Mojave Desert
  NT1      Sahara Desert

## 4.4  Policy Differences in Different Thesauri

Although the standards advise applying the hierarchical relationship only to the three types described, some well-respected thesauri extend its use to a wider type of subject hierarchy comparable to that in library classification schemes. The medical/pharmaceutical vocabularies *Medical Subject Headings* (1998) (*MeSH*) and *EMTREE* (1997), both very popular with their users, present their descriptors in fully developed polyhierarchical "tree structures," extending to eight levels or more. Among the parent-child relationships (indicated implicitly by hierarchical indentation) are many that do not conform to the three types admitted by the standards (Bean, 1998). In *MeSH* for example, "Absorption," "Crystallography," and "Solubility" are sibling terms, all children of "Physical Chemistry." Of the three, only "Crystallography" would be admitted by ISO 2788 as a true NT.

The *BSI ROOT Thesaurus* (*ROOT*) superficially resembles *MeSH*, in that its Subject Display presents all descriptors within fully developed hierarchies similar to the tree structures. Unlike *MeSH*, however, the *ROOT* Alphabetical Index spells out which parent-child relationships are BT/NT and which are RT/RT. Thus *ROOT* avoids transgressing the standard, but one wonders to what extent getting it correct has helped users.

The *INSPEC Thesaurus* (1997) is more explicitly liberal in its interpretation of hierarchical relationships. For example, "Aircraft control" is considered to be a Narrower Term of "Aircraft," even though it is neither a type, nor a part, nor an instance of aircraft. It would not be easy to show whether such departures from the standard's recommendations affect retrieval of information from the *INSPEC* database for the better or for the worse.

Other differences of approach can arise when relationships are not invariably valid. Svenonius (1997) suggests that a distinction should be made between "logical hierarchies" and "perspective hierarchies." She considers the genus-species and membership-instance relationships to be logical in that independently of context, any member of the narrower class can be deduced to be a member of the broader. In contrast, "perspective hierarchies" depend on point of view. She asserts that the logical hierarchies are useful for broadening, narrowing, and exploding searches; the perspective hierarchies are said not to be useful for any of these purposes but rather for disambiguating the search terms.

A similar situation occurs with materials, substances, agents, crops, etc., in the context of their application. Consider the following pairs:

- Analgesics/aspirin
- Insecticides/DDT
- Medicinal plants/foxgloves
- Fur-bearing animals/minks

Some thesauri treat these as BT/NT pairs; others consider the relationship to be associative because in each case the particular agent or organism can have an existence unconnected with the use(s) to which it might be put.

## 4.5 Relationships in Complex Hierarchies

Many levels of hierarchy are possible. Depending on the interests of its users, a thesaurus may not enumerate all the theoretically possible levels intermediate between the top and the bottom of the hierarchy. The hierarchical superstructure of the term "cattle" in *EMTREE*, a thesaurus for the pharmaceutical industry, gives the following progression:

<pre>
cattle                                from EMTREE
    bovids
        artiodactyla
        ungulate
            placental mammals
            mammal
                vertebrate
</pre>

Shown below is the subtly different entry for "cattle" in the *CAB Thesaurus*. These examples illustrate that the concept of hierarchical level in thesauri is not absolute but relative, and that the choice of levels is driven by perceived user needs rather than theoretical principles. In other words, the presence of BT/NT relationships, even if the convention BT1, BT2, etc., is used to distinguish between levels, does not indicate what semantic distances separate the pairs of linked terms. In different thesauri, a case could be made for giving the immediate BT of cattle as ruminants, or as mammals, or as animals.

The *CAB Thesaurus* entry also illustrates polyhierarchical relationships. Thus two different terms ("livestock" and "skin producing animals" in the example) that share a common Narrower Term ("cattle") are not necessarily related to each other: Not all livestock are considered skin producing animals and vice versa.

<pre>
cattle                                from CAB Thesaurus
    BT1    Bos
        BT2    Bovidae
            BT3    ruminants
                BT4    artiodactyla
                    BT5    mammals
    BT1    livestock
        BT2    animals
    BT1    skin producing animals
        BT2    animals
</pre>

Both the *CAB Thesaurus* (through the 1995 edition) and *EMTREE* routinely display all the hierarchical levels admitted. Some other thesauri show broader and narrower term relationships to only a single level up or down respectively. A typical entry in the *INSPEC Thesaurus*, Alphabetical Display section, shows hierarchical relationships as follows:

<pre>
aircraft control                      from INSPEC Thesaurus
    NT     aircraft landing guidance
    BT     aerospace control
           aircraft
    TT     automation
           computer applications
           vehicles
</pre>

"Aerospace control" and "aircraft" are Broader Terms of "aircraft control," both just one level up from the latter. "TT" stands for "Top Term," another form of hierarchical relationship showing the top node or level of each hierarchy to which the entry term belongs. In between the Top Terms and the immediate BTs, there may be any number of broader terms at intermediate levels. Regardless of the length and complexity of the intervening hierarchical pathway(s), "TT" is not semantically different from "BT."

## 5. THE ASSOCIATIVE RELATIONSHIP

Any paradigmatic inter-term relationship that is not hierarchical, nor of equivalence, is nowadays usually described as "associative." (Willetts [1975] called it "affinitive.") The function of associative links is to alert the user to terms that he might wish to apply *instead of or as well as* the term he first thought of. Associative relationships are usually shown with the abbreviation "RT," standing for "Related Term." Reciprocal entries must always be provided, and the reciprocal of RT is RT. Here are some examples:

<table>
<tr><td>magnets</td><td></td><td></td><td>from INSPEC Thesaurus</td></tr>
<tr><td></td><td>RT</td><td>ferromagnetism</td><td></td></tr>
<tr><td></td><td></td><td>magnetic circuits</td><td></td></tr>
<tr><td></td><td></td><td>magnetic cores</td><td></td></tr>
<tr><td></td><td></td><td>magnetic fields</td><td></td></tr>
<tr><td></td><td></td><td>magnetisation</td><td></td></tr>
<tr><td>planned communities</td><td></td><td></td><td>from Thesaurus of ERIC descriptors</td></tr>
<tr><td></td><td>RT</td><td>housing</td><td></td></tr>
<tr><td></td><td></td><td>planning</td><td></td></tr>
<tr><td></td><td></td><td>urban renewal</td><td></td></tr>
<tr><td>trains</td><td></td><td></td><td>from Macrothesaurus</td></tr>
<tr><td></td><td>RT</td><td>railway transport</td><td></td></tr>
<tr><td></td><td></td><td>railways</td><td></td></tr>
</table>

Neither ISO 2788 nor ANSI/NISO Z39.19 gives a really clear definition of the associative relationship, but both suggest that there ought to be a strong mental association between the terms. ISO 2788 indicates that the relationships in a thesaurus should be *a priori* rather than syntactical. In contrast, Lancaster (1986, pp. 45-47) maintains that the associative relationship is not paradigmatic but syntagmatic; however, his examples are quite similar to those in the standard. To add to the complications, a gray area lies between the definitions of hierarchical and associative links. As corroborated by Milstead (1995), "Any thesaurus developer knows that it is possible—though highly undesirable—to spend an inordinate amount of time debating whether a given relationship should be hierarchical (BT/NT) or associative (RT/RT)."

Despite the difficulties with definitions, all the authorities make it clear that the main function of the RT links is to suggest additional or alternative terms for indexing or retrieval. The presence of an RT link therefore depends more on the thesaurus editor's feel for what will serve the users than on a precise semantic analysis. For example, the *INSPEC* editor appointed "Ferromagnetism" as an RT of "Magnets," but not the more obvious term "Magnetism" (although the thesaurus does contain this descriptor), presumably to help users find the right level of specificity. Most editors give high priority to providing RT links between terms with overlapping meanings, unless an equivalence relationship is more appropriate.

## 5.1 Subcategorization of Associative Relationships

Perhaps in search of that elusive definition, many researchers have attempted to subcategorize the associative relationships found in thesauri. Table 2 provides the fourteen categories noted by Aitchison, Gilchrist, and Bawden (1997). In similar analyses, both Lancaster (1986) and Raitt (1980) enumerate ten categories, only some of which coincide with each other or with Aitchison et al. In a study of explicit parent-child relationships in *MeSH*, after instantial and generic relationships are excluded, Bean (1998) reports finding 67 other distinct relationship types, most of which would be considered associative. Aitchison et al. also cite a 1965 study by Perreault, in which 120 different types of relationship were enumerated! In eight thesauri studied by Willetts (1975), a total of 4252 pairs of terms linked by RT were analyzed. She categorized the terms according to the five fundamental facets of Entity, Activity, Abstract concept, Property, and Heterogeneous term. A total of fifteen facet pair combinations is possible, and Willetts found examples of all fifteen in each of the thesauri. When she further categorized the pairs according to the nine distinct relations derived by Farradane, Datta, and Poulton (1966) from experimental psychology, the result included 53 different combinations of relation/facet pair. Confused by such a variety of usages, she concluded, "There is no consistent pattern of relations in use." The same may be said of most thesauri today.

## 5.2 Rules for Identifying Associative Relationships

Rigorous consistency is rarely observed among published thesauri. In the entry for "Railways," for example, *Macrothesaurus* gives RT "Trains," but in the entry for "Roads" it makes no mention of "Automobiles" or any other of the vehicle descriptors in the thesaurus. In the *BSI ROOT Thesaurus*, the entry for "Wheels" shows RTs "Wheel centres," "Wheel rims," and "Spokes"—an obvious case of whole-part relationships. But the entries for "Cycles" or "Motor vehicles" make no mention of "Wheels," although wheels are just as fundamental to these vehicles as spokes or rims are to wheels. It is easy to see one practical reason for this: The list of parts of any complex machine is simply too lengthy to include. Conversely, if "Wheels" were to have an RT for every device, machine, or structure of which these can be a component, where would the list stop? Attempts to be consistent and comprehensive in applying semantic rules can lead to lists of RTs so long that they actually can impede users in finding the related terms they really need help with. If the user is a computer, however, the situation is different. Because a computer can manipulate long lists of terms there is much to gain from rigorously applied rules for relationships. But the human user has human failings as well as intelligence. Thesaurus editors typically try to respect both.

| Type of associative relationship | Examples |
|---|---|
| Terms with overlapping meanings | Ships RT Boats |
| Whole-part associative | Nuclear reactors RT Pressure vessels |
| Discipline or field of study, and phenomena studied | Seismology RT Earthquakes<br>Ethnography RT Primitive societies |
| Operation or process and its agent or instrument | Velocity measurement RT Speedometers<br>Turning RT Lathes |
| Occupation and person in that occupation | Accountancy RT Accountants |
| Action and product of the action | Roadmaking RT Roads |
| Action and its patient | Teaching RT Students |
| Concept and its properties | Surfaces RT Surface properties<br>Women RT Femininity |
| Concept and its origins | Water RT Water wells<br>Information RT Information sources |
| Causal dependence | Erosion RT Wear<br>Injury RT Accidents |
| A thing or action and its counter-agent | Pests RT Pesticides<br>Crime RT Crime prevention devices |
| Raw material and its product | Aggregates RT Concrete<br>Hides RT Leather |
| Action and property associated with it | Precision measurement RT Accuracy<br>Communication skills RT Communication |
| Concept and its opposite | Single people RT Married people<br>Tolerance RT Prejudice |

Table 2. Types of associative relationship with examples, listed by Aitchison et al.

Molholt (1996) reports some success in applying consistent rules for RTs, given a thesaurus with rigorous hierarchical structure. But how to formulate rules that really help the user is not yet clear. Users typically need help when, for example, the wanted concept is hard to put into words, or could be expressed in a multiplicity of ways, or could rather easily be confused with another concept having a similar descriptor.

Maniez (1988) echoes the philosophy of ISO 2788 in saying, "Logico-semantic categories [of relationships] are useful, but only as means subordinate to the aims of information indexing and retrieval." He stresses the importance of associative links between the following:

• Terms with overlapping meanings,

- Terms with high co-occurrence rates among titles and/or indexing fields, and
- Terms related by "extrasemantic" factors, such as causation-effect (e.g., between Braking and Side-slipping) or structural similarity (e.g., between Eskimo and Turkish languages).

Unfortunately, none of the above may be translated into a simple semantic rule for consistent application, although the usefulness of co-occurrence data in identifying associatively linked term pairs is supported by Svenonius (1988).

# 6. OTHER THESAURAL RELATIONSHIPS

It is not unusual for a published thesaurus to include unique relationship types in addition to the equivalence, hierarchical, and associative categories already considered. This section will briefly describe just two additional types that are in fairly general use.

## 6.1 Relationships at the Macro Level

In those thesauri that present descriptors in a faceted or otherwise classified display, some means is needed to guide users from the alphabetical index to the correct position in the classified display. The chosen mechanism is often a class code or notation, which can be viewed as relating the descriptor to the overall structure of the subject field. (See Aitchison, Gilchrist, & Bawden 1997, pp. 47, 91-134.) Examples may be seen in *Macrothesaurus*, the *BSI ROOT Thesaurus*, the *AAT*, *MeSH*, and *EMTREE*.

The *Thesaurus of Engineering and Scientific Terms* (*TEST*) and the *Thesaurus of ERIC Descriptors* use a different style of display, but again they provide each descriptor with a code or number, relating that descriptor to a broad subject group.

A comparable device is the Top Term relationship described in Section 4.5 above. TT relates a term not only to the individual term at the top of its hierarchy but to the whole of the hierarchy of which it forms a part.

## 6.2 Links to Other Coding Schemes

Increasingly, searchers expect to be able to cross boundaries, either to search databases in clusters or to use the results from one in the search statement for another. One way to aid the process is to provide linkages from the terms in one thesaurus to the names or codes found in another nomenclature or coding scheme, preferably a more universal one. This type of relationship is not described in ISO 2788, but neither is it proscribed, and instances of it will become much more common in the future. Some examples found in today's thesauri include Chemical Abstracts Registry Numbers, assigned to names of chemicals; notations from the International Union of Biochemistry Enzyme Commission, applied to names of enzymes; and codes from ISO 3166, *Codes for the representation of names of countries*, applied to names of countries. Bodenreider and Bean (this volume) discuss

relationships across controlled vocabularies in more detail, and Beghtol (this volume) and
Neelameghan (this volume) deal with intercultural and interdisciplinary links.

## 7. IMPLICATIONS FOR THE FUTURE

We have now taken stock of the main types of relationship to be found in the thesauri
widely used today for IR in databases that employ vocabulary control. Most of these
databases and corresponding thesauri have their roots in assumptions, techniques, and
conventions that were developed in the 1960s and led to publication of national and
international standards in the 1970s. At that time computerized IR was in its infancy. The
selection of terms for indexing and/or searching was a process performed intellectually by
humans, specifically for one database with a single controlled vocabulary. In very many
applications, the original assumptions are still valid, the rules for determining thesaural
relationships are still appropriate, and the scope for subjective interpretation can be
beneficial. But the assumptions begin to break down where processes are automated and/or
multiple databases are to be searched simultaneously.

So long as the main function of the relationships is to guide the human user to select the
most appropriate term(s), precise subcategorization of relationships is often unnecessary.
Consider a searcher looking up "Ships." Among the NTs he finds "Fishing vessels," "Cruise
boats," and "Queen Elizabeth." His decision on which of the terms to include in his search
will depend more on his prior knowledge than on guidance as to which relationships are
instantial, generic, partitive, etc. But a computer using the NTs for query expansion may
well need relational guidance. Artificial intelligence applications may make inferences from
a knowledge base or ontology that could look rather similar to a thesaurus, but would
necessarily distinguish between instantial and partitive relations. Automation is creating a
demand for thesauri with relationships that are subcategorized and more consistently
assigned.

A different pressure comes from the trend towards searching multiple databases (indexed
with different thesauri) at one pass, as well as full-text databases and heterogeneous
resources on intranets or the Internet. In such cases the human searcher needs a "search
thesaurus" rather than a controlled vocabulary. In the search thesaurus there is no such
thing as a preferred term. A directional equivalence relationship is irrelevant: What is
wanted are equivalence sets, including as many as possible of the different terms and
expressions that may have been used by different authors for the same concept. Terms that
are hierarchically or associatively related may also be useful but are less easy to specify, for
when we lose the controlled vocabulary convention of limiting one term to one meaning, the
relationship between one term and another varies with context. When relationships in search
thesauri are subcategorized, the useful subcategories typically group terms applicable to
particular databases rather than terms with a common semantic relationship.

While enumerating the various sorts of thesaural relationship observed in controlled
vocabularies, we noted a plethora of subjectivities and inconsistencies, occurring both
among and within thesauri. Such inconsistencies are abhorrent to any tidy mind, and
especially to the developers of ontologies and artificial intelligence applications. But most
of the inconsistencies in good thesauri are not due to sloppiness or accident; rather, they

represent the best efforts of editors to design thesauri that serve their intended application. Until the use of controlled vocabularies for human indexing and searching has become economically unsustainable, such inconsistencies are likely to persist.

## 8. CONCLUSIONS

- The practice of including three main relationship types (equivalence, hierarchical, and associative) in thesauri for controlled vocabulary applications is well established and stable, although the definition of each type varies slightly from one thesaurus to another.
- Subcategories of these types, as well as special new relationships, are distinguished in some thesauri but such distinctions are unlikely to be adopted as standard practice.
- Inconsistencies between thesauri may arise from the need to serve particular user groups with established traditions and subject-specific needs.
- Inconsistencies in term relationships within thesauri are often based on pragmatic and subjective decisions about what will serve human users best.
- Relationships pointing to corresponding terms/codes in other vocabularies are likely to become more prevalent in the Internet era, and should cause no conflict with standard recommendations.
- Conflicts do arise when a traditional thesaurus is adapted to automated applications and/or to situations without vocabulary control:
  - Automated applications may require new categories of relationship as well as greater rigor in assigning the standard categories.
  - Applications for human searching without vocabulary control may require equivalence sets instead of preferred/non-preferred equivalence relationships.
  - Relationship categories in search thesauri may be based on source database rather than semantic significance.
- Rules optimized for one application cannot reasonably be expected to apply equally to others. Hence the thesaurus genus can be expected to evolve towards several different species with different styles of relationship as information science and technology advance.

## References

*AGROVOC Multilingual Agricultural Thesaurus.* (1997). Rome: Food and Agriculture Organization of the United Nations.

Aitchison, J., Gilchrist, A., & Bawden, D. (1997). *Thesaurus Construction and Use: A Practical Manual* (3rd ed.). London: Aslib.

*Art & Architecture Thesaurus.* (1994). (2nd ed.; T. Petersen, Dir.). New York: Oxford University Press.

Bean, C. A. (1998). The semantics of hierarchy: Explicit parent-child relationships in MeSH tree structures. In W. Mustafa el Hadi, J. Maniez, & S.A. Pollitt (Eds.), *Structures and*

*Relations in Knowledge Organization: Proceedings of the Fifth International ISKO Conference*, 133-138. Würzburg: Ergon Verlag.

*BSI ROOT Thesaurus* (2nd ed.). (1985). Milton Keynes, England: British Standards Institution.

*CAB Thesaurus* (3rd ed.). (1995). Wallingford, Oxon: CAB International.

*EMTREE Thesaurus 1997*. (1997). Amsterdam: Elsevier Science.

Farradane, J., Datta, S., & Poulton, R. K. (1966). *Report on Information Retrieval by Relational Indexing*. London: City University.

*INSPEC Thesaurus*. (1997). London: Institution of Electrical Engineers.

International Organization for Standardization. (1986). *Documentation—Guidelines for the Establishment and Development of Monolingual Thesauri* (2nd ed.). [Geneva:] ISO. (ISO 2788-1986(E))

Lancaster, F. W. (1986). *Vocabulary Control for Information Retrieval*. Arlington, VA: Information Resources Press.

*Macrothesaurus for Information Processing in the Field of Economic and Social Development* (5th ed.). (1998). Paris: OECD Development Centre.

Maniez, J. (1988). Relationships in thesauri: Some critical remarks. *International Classification*, 15, 133-138.

*Medical Subject Headings* (MeSH). (1998). Bethesda, MD: National Library of Medicine.

Milstead, J. L. (1995). Invisible thesauri: The year 2000. *Online & CDROM Review*, 19, 93-94.

Molholt, P. (1996). Standardization of inter-concept links and their usage. In R. Green (Ed.), *Knowledge Organization and Change: Proceedings of the Fourth International ISKO Conference*, 65-71. Frankfurt am Main: INDEKS Verlag.

National Aeronautics and Space Administration. (1967- ). *NASA Thesaurus*. Washington, DC: National Aeronautics and Space Administration.

National Information Standards Organization. (1994). *Guidelines for the Construction, Format, and Management of Monolingual Thesauri*. Bethesda, MD: NISO Press. (ANSI/NISO Z39.19-1993).

Raitt, D. I. (1980). Recall and precision devices in interactive bibliographic search and retrieval systems. *Aslib Proceedings*, 37, 281-301.

Svenonius, E. (1988). Design of controlled vocabularies in the context of emerging technologies. *Library Science with a Slant to Documentation*, 25, 215-227.

Svenonius, E. (1997). Definitional approaches in the design of classification and thesauri and their implications for retrieval and for automatic classification. In *Knowledge Organization for Information Retrieval: Proceedings of the Sixth International Study Conference on Classification Research*, 12-16. The Hague: FID.

*Thesaurus of Engineering and Scientific Terms*. (1967). New York: Engineers Joint Council and U.S. Department of Defense.

*Thesaurus of ERIC Descriptors* (13th ed.; J. E. Houston, Ed.). (1995). Phoenix, AZ: Oryx Press.

Vickery, B. C. (1971). Structure and function in retrieval languages. *Journal of Documentation*, 27, 69-82.

Willetts, M. (1975). An investigation of the nature of the relation between terms in thesauri. *Journal of Documentation*, 31, 158-184.

# Chapter 4

# Standards for Relationships between Subject Indexing Terms

Jessica L. Milstead
*The JELEM Company, Indian Head, MD, USA*

**Abstract:**
Relationships between the terms in thesauri and indexes are the subject of national and international standards. The standards for thesauri enumerate and provide criteria for three basic types of relationship: equivalence, hierarchical, and associative. Standards and guidelines for indexes draw on the thesaurus standards to provide less detailed guidance for showing relationships between the terms used in an index. The international standard for multilingual thesauri adds recommendations for assuring equal treatment of the languages of a thesaurus. The present standards were developed when lookup and search were essentially manual, and the value of the kinds of relationships has never been determined. It is not clear whether users understand or can use the distinctions between kinds of relationships. On the other hand, sophisticated text analysis systems may be able both to assist with development of more powerful term relationship schemes and to use the relationships to improve retrieval.

## 1. INTRODUCTION

Relationships among terms used for subject indexing may be divided into two very general types: semantic and statistical ("co-occurrence"). A semantic relationship is inherent—it always applies to a given pair of terms, regardless of whether they happen to be used together in a document or not. A co-occurrence relationship, on the other hand, is document-dependent, and does not imply a semantic relationship. Two terms with no relationship in meaning may co-occur within the same document, or even within the same sentence.

### 1.1 Available Standards

Only semantic relationships are the subject of formal standards and guidelines, and this chapter is limited to such relationships. The discussion is limited to:

- The American national standard for thesauri (National Information Standards Organization, 1994) (referred to as the American or ANSI/NISO thesaurus standard),
- The International Organization for Standardization (1986) standard for thesauri

*C. A. Bean and R. Green (eds.), Relationships in the Organization of Knowledge, 53–66.*

(referred to as the international or ISO thesaurus standard),
- The NISO technical report which provides guidelines for indexes (Anderson, 1997) (referred to as the NISO indexes guideline), and
- The International Organization for Standardization (1996) standard for indexes (referred to as the international or ISO standard for indexes).

The two thesaurus standards are similar in many respects, but there are some significant differences. The provisions of the ISO standard for indexes are in the same spirit as those of the international thesaurus standard, with specific application to the needs of indexes. The NISO technical report draws on the ANSI/NISO thesaurus standard, applying its provisions to the specific requirements of indexes. While this technical report does not have the force of a standard, it serves as an authoritative guideline for the field; since standards for vocabularies are more like guidelines than prescriptive standards in any case—they use "should" far more than they use "shall"—it is not going too far afield to include the guideline. Most thesauri are designed specifically to serve the needs of indexing for one or more databases, making it worthwhile to consider the thesaurus and index standards together.

This chapter is limited to English-language standards, both for reasons of accessibility and because the different structures of other languages could impose different requirements on the relationship structure. The British Standards Institution standards for thesauri (1987) and indexes (1996) match the ISO standard, so they are not considered here. No Canadian or Australian standards in this area were found, and the New Zealand standard for indexes is adopted from the ISO standard.

Meanwhile, devices such as semantic networks are so new that no standards exist for them. The standards for thesauri and, to a lesser extent, those for indexes, form the body of material that can be drawn on in a discussion of standards for subject relationships.

## 1.2  The Standard Development Process

These standards are developed and maintained by a formal process. The American National Standards Institute (ANSI) is a private nonprofit organization which coordinates development of standards in the United States. ANSI does not itself develop standards; instead, it accredits standard-setting bodies in specific areas. NISO is the body accredited by ANSI to develop standards for information services. ISO is an international standards organization that works through a number of technical committees. These technical committees are the international equivalent of the ANSI-accredited standards organizations in the U.S. ISO's Technical Committee 46 is the international counterpart of NISO.

All of these groups work in a similar fashion. Consensus and openness are watchwords. Standards are not imposed from above; instead, they are developed in an open environment. Typically, a committee of experts is formed representing the major stakeholders and constituencies with an interest in the projected standard. The committee deliberates over a period ranging from months to years (in cases that are complex or where consensus is difficult to achieve). It may consult with other experts, and is likely to issue one or more drafts of the proposed standard for review by interested parties. When the draft is considered ready, it is submitted for a vote. In the U.S. it goes to the voting members of the particular standards organization, such as NISO. In ISO, the country members of a particular technical committee vote on the draft.

It is in the balloting process that the requirement for consensus becomes most evident. While a large majority is required for adoption of a standard, in practice the committee that develops the standard is expected to make a serious attempt to resolve every negative vote. In the U.S., ANSI monitors the process very closely. NISO submits ballot results with supporting data when recommending approval of an ANSI/NISO standard, and unresolved negative votes must be explained in detail. The process of developing a standard is difficult—and can be very painful—but the goal is to assure that the standard is one that will be accepted in the field and widely adopted.

On occasion it is impossible to reach a consensus. The reasons vary. Interests may be so diverse that the various stakeholders are unable to reach a compromise. Sometimes change in an area is rapid, or major issues are unresolved, so that a standard is perceived not to be useful. In other cases, developments in the field outrun the standards development process, so that by the time a draft is ready it is already out of date. In some of these cases, particularly where a full draft standard was developed by a committee, NISO may choose to issue the document as part of its technical report series. These documents do not have the force of a standard, but they record the work of experts, and can serve as a basis for later standards work in the area.

In the U.S., the adoption of standards is voluntary, while in other countries there is likely to be more government involvement, and standards are more likely to become law. The national and international standards bodies work closely together, and it is quite common for a national body to adopt or adapt an international standard for approval as its national standard. Conversely, a national standard may become the basis for an international standard, though modification is more likely because of the more complex requirements of the international environment.

The standards development process does not end when a standard is adopted. In the U.S. standards are required to be reviewed every five years. At that time they can be reaffirmed, revised, or withdrawn; a ballot of the voting members of the standard-setting organization is required. By ANSI's rules, if a standard has not been reaffirmed or revised after ten years, it is automatically withdrawn. Thus, standards are required to be kept current.

The NISO web page provides especially useful descriptions of the national standards process (National Information Standards Organization, 1998) as well as of international standards (National Information Standards Organization, 2000).

## 2. KINDS OF RELATIONSHIPS

The standards for thesauri define three basic kinds of relationship, each with a typical notation:

- Equivalence (Use/Used for—USE/UF),
- Hierarchical (Broader Term/Narrower Term—BT/NT), and

- Associative (Related Term/Related Term—RT/RT).

There is a fundamental difference between the equivalence relationship and the hierarchical and associative relationships. The latter are defined between pairs of preferred terms, i.e., terms that are authorized for use in indexing. In equivalence relationships, one term of a pair is authorized for indexing and the other is forbidden from use, referring to the preferred term instead.

The relationships are always reciprocal; that is, if there is a relationship between Term A and Term B, the complementary relationship between Term B and Term A applies. Furthermore, relationships are conceived as being between pairs of terms. A given term may have the same kind of relationship (e.g., RT) to several terms, but the fact that several terms have the same relationship to another term does not automatically imply that those terms are themselves related to each other in any way.

The thesaurus standards also permit variants of each of the three kinds of relationship. For instance, a specialized type of hierarchical relationship may be used for parent and subsidiary companies. Alternatively, abbreviations and acronyms may have a specialized type of equivalence relationship to the full form of a term. Nevertheless, any specialized relationship belongs to one of the three categories of equivalent, hierarchical, and associative. The standards for indexes use this same tripartite distinction, but in a less formal way.

The International Organization for Standardization standard for multilingual thesauri (1985) follows the general pattern of the standard for monolingual thesauri, with addition of some provisions that are specifically applicable to the situation of multiple languages. These aspects are treated separately here.

In this chapter, equivalence relationships are discussed first, followed by relationships between preferred terms (hierarchical and associative) and issues of multilingual thesauri. The chapter finishes with a consideration of the future of relationships between terms in subject vocabularies.

## 3. EQUIVALENCE RELATIONSHIPS

In standard thesauri, one of two or more closely related terms is selected as the "preferred" term for indexing and retrieving a concept; the other terms are nonpreferred, and become cross-references leading to the preferred term. The equivalent terms may be:

- True synonyms, such as popular/scientific names, or current/outdated terms,
- Lexical variants, such as irregular plurals or full names/abbreviations, or
- Quasi-synonyms, representing closely related concepts which are treated as synonymous for purposes of the scheme, such as wetness/dryness.

The typical thesaurus notation for equivalence relationships is Use/Used For (USE/UF), but the notation is not an inherent part of the standards. The standards allow for specific types of equivalents, such as acronyms and abbreviations, to be distinguished by a different notation.

A special case of a "quasi-synonym" is the relationship between a compound term and its components where the compound term is split into two simple terms for indexing and searching (e.g., coal mining / coal + mining). In these cases the equivalent of the compound term is the intersection (logical AND) of the pair of simple terms. A common notation for this relationship is USE AND (or USE+ / UF+).

This type of relationship must be distinguished from the case where one term leads to multiple equivalents (e.g., appraisal / assessment, evaluation), where the equivalent is the union (logical OR) of the equivalent terms.

The standards for indexes call for making references from nonpreferred to preferred equivalents, using criteria that are similar to those of the thesaurus standards. The ISO indexes standard prefers "see" as the notation in the index, while the NISO indexes guideline allows for use of different notations to distinguish synonymous terms from other equivalents. Neither of the documents calls for showing the reciprocal reference (the equivalent of a UF reference), for good reason—the standards for indexes are dealing solely with user-oriented products, not with the editorial tools used to produce and manage them. The NISO guideline recognizes that display in "non-displayed" (i.e., electronic) indexes requires somewhat different methods, pointing out that such methods are not yet well established.

Equivalence relationships demonstrate clearly the basic retrieval system design for which subject vocabularies have traditionally been intended, that of print on paper, where it is generally impracticable to repeat exactly the same information at multiple access points. When electronic systems were developed, the same paradigm of preferring one term of a group of equivalents continued to be followed. Computing resources and memory were scarce and precious, and a design was in place that had worked reasonably well for many years.

Today, however, it is perfectly possible to design a system in which equivalent terms are treated as a "cluster," with no one term in a cluster considered preferable to any other. Any term in a cluster may be used in indexing, and a search on any term retrieves documents indexed with all of the terms in the cluster.

However, the old paradigm still has some value, and it should not be mindlessly discarded. Take a seemingly trivial example:

> Cars
> USE Automobiles

A user who is directed in this fashion is shown just what will happen to her query, so that if she desires something other than automobiles, a bad translation of the query can be avoided. However, if a searcher for "cars" is automatically redirected to "automobiles" in an index file, the individual who was actually searching for railroad cars or mine cars will not be favorably impressed by the capabilities of the system.

It is practical, however, to treat term equivalents as clusters if the interface dialogue is designed in a way that prevents false associations, and the NISO guideline for indexes recommends this option. In the obvious case, where the query term matches two or more thesaurus terms, the system can show all of the hits to the user and query him as to which one is wanted. More complex is the circumstance where the query term is unambiguous in terms of the thesaurus, but it matches a nonpreferred term. Can it be assumed that the lead to a preferred term is correct? Not always. The context of the searcher's query may be quite different from the context of the thesaurus, leading to a unique match that is incorrect. Information system designers need to pursue the equivalence cluster option with caution, but they should not avoid it. When it is possible to be quite certain that an equivalence is correct in the larger world rather than just the limited world of a given thesaurus, the automatic switching option can be adopted. When it is not possible to be so certain, then a dialogue with the user must take place.

This implies a need for distinguishing kinds of equivalence relationships, at least for internal purposes. For instance, abbreviations that are made unambiguous by qualification can be treated as interchangeable with the full form to which they are equivalent, as can lexical variants. However, quasi-synonyms represent a different kind of "equivalence," and should probably be tagged differently in the system.

This is not to suggest that when users are interacting directly with the thesaurus they should be forced to deal with additional kinds of notations. When they are looking at the thesaurus display itself, the assumptions behind equivalents are reasonably obvious, so that an incorrect equivalent can be avoided. It is when the thesaurus sits behind the interface as a tool to be applied by the system that more precise specification of equivalence relationships is required, in order to assure that searchers are not given wrong results without explanation.

## 4. HIERARCHICAL RELATIONSHIPS

The ANSI/NISO and ISO thesaurus standards recognize three kinds of hierarchical relationship: genus-species, instance, and part-whole.

The genus-species ("is-a"—a dog is a mammal) relationship is the traditional one; it was treated as hierarchical in the first edition of the American thesaurus standard (American National Standards Institute, 1980). The instance relationship ("is an example of"—the Alps are an example of a mountain region) is new, but can easily be conceived as a variant of the genus-species relationship. The boundary between a species and an instance can become fuzzy; the distinction in the standard examples seems to be that named entities, such as a specific mountain range, are considered "instances." It seems very likely that "instances" were treated as hierarchical even before the specific type of relationship was distinguished.

The actual language of the present standards is illuminating. Both thesaurus standards use almost exactly the same language to introduce their discussion of the generic relationship: "This relationship identifies the link between a class [or category—in the ISO thesaurus standard] and its members or species." The ANSI/NISO thesaurus standard goes on to state that "[narrower term] *is a* [broader term]." Allowing for purely grammatical differences in number, any individual instance *is a* case of its broader group; for example, the Alps *is a* mountain region. When justifying the instance relationship, the standards point out that the Alps "are neither kinds nor parts of mountain regions," even though the "kind of" language is not used in the discussion of the generic relationship. There the language is simply "is a". Even the "all and some" test used for generic relationships applies to instances if grammatical number is ignored: all "Alps" (even though there is only one) are "mountain regions"; some (one) "mountain regions" are (is) "Alps."

Both standards treat whole-part relationships ("is a part of"—the skull is part of the head) as hierarchical, but these are still not universally accepted. The first edition of the American thesaurus standard treated whole-part relationships as associative, and there is still some preference in the field for limiting hierarchical relationships to class inclusion (Lancaster, 1995). The whole-part relationship is limited to four main classes of terms: systems and organs of the body, geographic locations, disciplines or fields of discourse, and hierarchical organizational structures.

One critical difference between the American and international thesaurus standards is in the rigor of the requirements for a hierarchical relationship. The ISO standard allows use of a hierarchical relationship that is not universally valid if a thesaurus is limited to a narrow subject area in which the relationship applies. An example is:

  Turbines
    Compressors
      Blades

in a thesaurus limited to turbine engineering. While the standard cautions that this kind of subordination must be restricted to limited fields where the implicit limitation will be universally assumed, this provision is still dangerous. It cannot be assumed that users—or thesaurus editors or indexers—will always and forever check the hierarchy to verify the context of a term. It is also worth noting that the example is a whole-part relationship that does not fall into one of the four types specifically permitted in the standards.

In most other respects, the provisions of the American and international thesaurus standards are essentially identical. They both recommend that hierarchical relationships be made only between terms that refer to the "same basic kind of concept," e.g., thing, property, etc. They both permit the use of notation to distinguish the different kinds of hierarchical relationship, e.g., BTG/NTG to indicate Broader Term Generic/Narrower Term Generic. Such notations may be attractive from a logical and editorial point of view, but it seems unlikely that they are of great assistance to human users. Any user who cares about the distinction between a genus-species and a part-whole relationship will probably be able to determine which is true in a given case without the assistance of notation. However, the notational distinctions are only permitted; they are not required. They need not be used unless they add value in a particular situation.

Provisions for hierarchical relationships have grown more complex over the years. For instance, the first edition of the American thesaurus standard states (p. 13): "The BROADER TERM (BT) reference is employed to refer from a term representing a member of a class of concepts to the term naming that class . . ." It goes on to prohibit whole-part relationships from being treated hierarchically, except for geographic names and "other limited cases." Present-day standards first list the three different types of hierarchical relationship (generic, instance, and whole-part) and then go into detail about each.

The first point that becomes obvious by comparing the earlier and later standards is that the language of the earlier standard ("a member of a class of concepts") covers both the generic and the instance types of hierarchical relationships. The "Alps" is a member of the class "mountain regions" just as much as "cocker spaniels" are a member of the class "dogs." These two types may be "logically different," as the present-day standards state, but the difference appears to have little import either for design of vocabularies or for tagging and retrieval of information.

For part-whole relationships, the standards have moved from almost complete rejection of hierarchy to acceptance in a limited set of circumstances (body parts, geographic locations, disciplines, and organizational structures). The ISO thesaurus standard appears to be ambivalent about the limitation, since it allows for machinery parts (Turbines / Compressors), as discussed above, in special situations, even though the example given is logically incorrect. The ANSI/NISO thesaurus standard excludes from the hierarchical relationship cases where a part can belong to multiple wholes.

There seems to be no particular logical reason why the part-whole relationship should not be generally applicable. It only has to meet the test of being always true, just as with the other hierarchical relationships. Just as a cat is not necessarily a pet, a compressor is not necessarily a part of a turbine, and the same logical test can be applied in both cases. It is possible that, as the standards for thesauri evolve, acceptance of the part-whole relationship as hierarchical will grow.

Elsewhere in this volume (in the chapter by Dextre Clarke) examples are given which demonstrate clearly that application of the hierarchical relationship in actual thesauri is frequently not nearly as rigorous as the standards recommend. An operation may be subordinated to a physical entity, or a subordination that does not always apply may be treated as hierarchical. It is very tempting to do this, and it is easy to make the argument that a user who wants everything on the broader subject would expect information on the narrower subject to be included. However, actual development experience has repeatedly demonstrated that extending the criteria for hierarchical relationships is fraught with dangers. Any attempt to define broader criteria (rather than just deciding on the relationships *ad hoc*) runs into problems. Subordinations may seem intuitively correct in one case and intuitively incorrect in another. Or, it may be possible to make an argument in either direction for the subordination. For instance, should an object be subordinated to an operation that is uniquely carried out upon it, or vice versa? Unless a better, rigorously definable substitute can be found, it is preferable to stick with the provisions of the standard. The developer must keep in mind that others will come after her; their mental maps of the world may differ from hers in ways that make it impossible for them to conform readily to a particular set of non-standard criteria.

The notion of polyhierarchy is fully accepted in the standards. Terms may belong to more than one hierarchy or sub-hierarchy, and the hierarchical relationships may be of the same type (e.g., organs—the musical variety—are both keyboard instruments and wind instruments, all of which are kinds of musical instruments), or different (e.g., the skull is a kind of bone and is a part of the head). This represents a change from the first edition of the American thesaurus standard. The older edition accepts polyhierarchy in theory, but partly justifies its avoidance of hierarchical whole-part relationships by the fact that making such relationships "would result in multiple hierarchies for a significant proportion of terms, thereby significantly increasing the complexity of the thesaurus" (p. 14). One can conjecture that the reluctance to include polyhierarchical relationships in the thesaurus was at least partly due to the fact that software for thesaurus management was limited to non-existent at the time—but this is just a conjecture. Another possible influence is the view of some researchers that in classification, any entity belongs to one, and only one, class (Jacob, 1992). If the developer of a thesaurus intends it to be used for classification in this sense, then polyhierarchy cannot be permitted. However, while this view may have some use in theory, it does not reflect the way in which entities are really associated—unless the classes are so finely divided that many will have only one member.

## 5. ASSOCIATIVE RELATIONSHIPS

The thesaurus standards define associative relationships negatively, as any non-hierarchical relationship between a pair of preferred terms (i.e., any non-hierarchical, non-equivalence relationship). Both standards provide extensive lists of kinds of relationships that are associative, dividing them into two types: descriptors belonging to the same hierarchy or category, and those belonging to different hierarchies or categories. The standards emphasize, however, that the grounds for associating descriptors belonging to different hierarchies are representative, not exhaustive. Table 1 shows the kinds of associations listed in the thesaurus standards as warranting an RT relationship. Except as noted, the associations appear in both standards. The first two items in the table are associations between terms in the same hierarchy; the remainder are associations between different hierarchies.

| Kind of association | Example |
|---|---|
| Siblings with overlapping meanings | boats RT ships |
| Familial/derivational | children RT parents |
| Discipline and object of study | zoology RT animals |
| Operation/process and its agent/instrument | heating RT furnaces |
| Thing and its counter agent | plants RT herbicides |
| Action and its product | weaving RT cloth |
| Action and its target | harvesting RT crops |
| Concepts and their unique properties | perception RT acuity |
| Concepts related to their origins (ISO only) | Dutch RT Netherlands |
| Concepts linked by causal dependence | bereavement RT death |
| Concept and its unit of measurement | length RT meter (measure) |
| Phrases in which the noun is not a true broader term | heart RT artificial hearts |

Table 1. Grounds for associating terms via the RT relationship

In a way, these relationships are simultaneously the easiest and the most problematic of the standard thesaurus relationship types to understand and evaluate. An associative relationship by definition is any semantic relationship that is neither equivalent nor hierarchical. This makes them easy—once it has been determined that the relationship between the terms is not one of equivalence or hierarchy, then it must be associative. On the other hand, a negatively defined subset is too amorphous to be of much assistance if relationships are to be used for any purpose more sophisticated than direct suggestion to users of additional or alternative query terms. For instance, automatic query expansion based on Related Term relationships could be of value in either user dialogue or automatic search procedures, if distinctions could be made among the kinds of related terms that would minimize irrelevant retrievals. Dextre Clarke (this volume) references a variety of categorizations of associative relationships. The variations in number and kind make it clear that such categories are largely "in the eye of the beholder."

Tests of retrieval might show that certain kinds of categorization of associative relationships could be useful, but it is highly likely that application of these categorizations would have to be automatic to be practical. Simply deciding between associative and hierarchical, or between equivalent and non-equivalent, can be time-consuming and complex; trying to make finer distinctions manually is likely to be counterproductive. However, linguistic analyses, such as are carried out by the DR-LINK system (Liddy, 1998), detect types of associative relationships at a much more granular level, and finer distinctions in relationships will probably surface in text analysis and retrieval systems rather than in standard thesauri.

## 6. PROVISIONS FOR MULTILINGUAL THESAURI

The ISO standard for multilingual thesauri (International Organization for Standardization, 1985) first refers to the monolingual thesaurus standard for general provisions about relationships. It then considers the extent to which relationships between pairs of specific terms should correspond in the different languages of a thesaurus. The standard tends to prefer exact equivalence across languages, even when terms or hierarchical/associative relationships must be devised that are not justified by usage in one of the languages. Relationships in multilingual thesauri are discussed in more detail in Hudon (this volume); the treatment here is limited to the provisions of the standard.

Equivalence relationships need not correspond across languages, however. The standard recognizes that synonyms and quasi-synonyms will be language-specific, and that even when it is required that all preferred terms be matched by corresponding terms in each language, there need not be cross-language equivalents for all nonpreferred terms.

In the case of hierarchical relationships, this standard recognizes that cultural differences may result in equivalent terms appearing to be part of different hierarchies in different languages. The recommendation is that such terms be treated as polyhierarchical, including them in both hierarchies in all languages.

The standard is ambiguous in its provisions for associative relationships. It states in section 12.4.2: "Before an associative relationship which has been recognized in one language is transferred to another, it should be examined to determine the extent of its validity. If it appears to apply to only one group of language users, it should generally be excluded." The standard goes on to state that in such a case the terms themselves should be re-examined to verify that they actually refer to the same concept, but that there will be a richer variety of relationships in a multilingual thesaurus because of the viewpoints of the different language groups. What is not made explicit is whether an associative relationship that applies in only one language is to be excluded from the thesaurus completely, or only from the language(s) to which it is not applicable. However, given the general preference of the standard for making the different language versions exactly equivalent in both preferred terms and relationships, it seems reasonable to infer that the intention is to exclude any associative relationship which cannot reasonably be applied across all of the languages of the thesaurus.

While the standard's recommendation that: "All the languages should be regarded as having equal status from the viewpoint of thesaurus construction" (p. 6) is admirable, it seems to have been carried to an extreme. The standard recognizes that one language may contain terms that have no counterpart in another, and that culture affects the perceived relationships between terms. "Equal status" should not have to mean inventing terms in one language just because an equivalent term exists in another language. The purpose of a thesaurus is to serve indexing and retrieval; users of a thesaurus and of the system it supports are going to be looking for the concepts they know. A middle ground, perhaps supporting the borrowing of terms from the other language when required for indexing, would have been of more service to users. This is the way that languages frequently operate in any case, borrowing from another language that already has a needed concept.

## 7. VALUE OF THE RELATIONSHIP TYPES

How much detail is worthwhile in relationship types? That is, how many different kinds of relationships should be specified? The present thesaurus standards allow for up to six pairs (USE/UF, USE+/UF+, BTG/NTG, BTI/NTI, BTP/NTP, and RT/RT). Soergel (1974) calls for distinguishing as many as four or five types of equivalence relationships, six types of hierarchical relationships, and 10 types of associative relationships, though he does not advocate including this level of complexity in the user version of the thesaurus. Aitchison, Gilchrist, & Bawden (1997) basically follows the ISO standard. Most thesauri in use today apply only three or four of the standard relationships (USE/UF, BT/NT, RT/RT and sometimes USE+/UF+).

Yet no one appears to have asked the basic question: Why do we distinguish different kinds of relationships rather than simply indicating that a relationship of some kind exists? Rather, the need to make a distinction is taken for granted, the only issues seeming to be the fineness of the distinctions and the criteria for them. As humans, and particularly as organizers of information or knowledge, we find the building of schemes interesting for its own sake, but this is not a valid reason for expending the resources in staff and money to build them. The traditional purpose of distinguishing relationship types should be to facilitate user navigation of the vocabulary, generally for the purpose of improving indexing and retrieval results. This purpose still dominates present-day standards, not least because when they were developed human search still dominated retrieval. Although the number of kinds of relationships is quite limited in present-day standards, even this specification of types may be of limited direct value to many users. Users do not necessarily recognize that "BT" and "NT" mean a relationship is hierarchical and "Use" and "UF" mean the terms are equivalent, while "RT" means the relationship is something else—that something being unspecified.

For a thesaurus developer, even deciding when a relationship is hierarchical or part/whole can be difficult. The decision is fairly easy when concrete objects (e.g., truck/motor vehicle) are the issue. However, in a world where the same entity may be a "particle" (i.e., concrete) or a "wave" (not concrete), depending on how the observer happens to be looking at the entity at the moment, deciding whether something is a "thing" or a "process" may not only be difficult, but is likely to be futile.

The effort is worth it if we are making distinctions that actually assist users in locating desired information more easily, but it is not worth it solely from the point of view of "logical" organization of the vocabulary. Research to determine the value to humans of term relationships in an indexing vocabulary would be useful, even in today's environment where more automatic text analysis is available. Results are still improved if humans can state their information needs more clearly, and assistance in navigating a vocabulary can contribute to such clarification.

## 8. FUTURE OF THE RELATIONSHIPS

These standards were all developed in an environment where indexing and retrieval were manual and Boolean logic was the primary tool for searching. Furthermore, the basic assumption was that searchers were experts in a subject field and/or in the techniques of searching. The environment today is different. A variety of techniques are used for searching, including Boolean logic, proximity searching, statistical tools, and natural language processing. Frequently full text of documents or of surrogates such as abstracts is available for searching, making it possible to use assigned index terms and the text of the document in tandem to enhance retrieval. At the same time, a far greater variety of users are searching directly, and it is not possible to assume either the same level of sophistication in searching or the ability and willingness to use information retrieval tools such as thesauri.

The standards also reflect the fact that until recently print on paper was the dominant—or only—means of providing access to a thesaurus. The ANSI/NISO thesaurus standard (approved 1993) gives less than half as much space to its section on screen display as to the section on print display. Furthermore, the print display section is able to go into detail, e.g., specifying the need for running heads on pages, while the screen display section is much more general. The ISO thesaurus standard (approved 1986, recently reaffirmed) only discusses print displays. Basic assumptions about means of display probably constrained the design of these standards even more than the developers realized. When the ISO standard was being developed in the early and mid 1980s, online services had been available for several decades, but graphic displays were uncommon—and HTML was unheard of. There would have been a clear break between the thesaurus "display" intended for users, and means of accessing the thesaurus database for editorial purposes; the latter was not a "display," so the only concern of the standard was with paper.

By the time the ANSI/NISO thesaurus standard was under development in the early 1990s, it was clear that the situation was changing, but there still were not a variety of sophisticated displays to serve as models. These standards can only reflect the situation of their time, and the time has changed dramatically. It is time to take another look at the use of relationships between terms, to investigate whether the current types still serve a useful purpose or new ones must or should be developed. We can separate the display from the database in our thinking far better than was formerly the case; editors can view the thesaurus in one way, searchers in another, and some future, as yet undesigned, system can view it in yet another. Therefore, we should be thinking both about what kinds of relationships can be useful at all, and to whom or to what they will be useful.

Text analysis software can make use of richer semantic analysis of both kinds of terms and relationships between them.    While manual analysis of terms is extremely labor-intensive, systems that can perform these functions automatically exist today.  As the thesaurus standards come up for review, the different ways in which it is possible to use the relationships between terms in analysis and searching of text should be considered, as well as the tools that are available to facilitate development of richer kinds of relationships for use in automatic retrieval systems.

When the ANSI/NISO thesaurus standard was reviewed in 1998, it was reaffirmed with the recommendation that the need for a standard for electronic thesauri be investigated. NISO convened a workshop of experts on November 4-5, 1999, to address this issue. Some of the most important recommendations of the workshop bore on the issue of term relationships.  There was general recognition that thesauri use a great many variants of relationships (also demonstrated in a report produced by the American Library Association Subject Analysis Committee [1997]).  In addition, the participants in the workshop recommended that the new standard embrace a wide range of vocabulary control and management tools, not just the Z39.19 standard thesaurus.  This automatically implies even more diversity in relationships.

The participants recommended that a much richer, hierarchically organized, set of relationships be developed.  Interfaces should support easy movement from more specific to more general types of relationships where necessary (e.g., from "Abbreviation" to "Variant" for a thesaurus that does not support an "Abbreviation" relationship type).  There was also support for development of a registry of relationship types.

There is reason to expect that provisions for semantic relationships in controlled vocabularies will become much more extensive in a future standard, though this does not automatically mean that users will need to be aware of all of the kinds of relationships in order to use a particular vocabulary.

# References

Aitchison, J., Gilchrist, A., & Bawden, D. (1997). *Thesaurus Construction and Use: A Practical Manual* (3rd ed.). London: Aslib.

American Library Association, Subject Analysis Committee, Subcommittee on Subject Relationships/Reference Structures. (1997). *Final Report to the ALCTS/CCS Subject Analysis Committee* [Online].    Available: <http://www.ala.org/alcts/organization/ccs/sac/rpt97rev.html> [2000, February 15].

American National Standards Institute. (1980). *American National Standard Guidelines for Thesaurus Structure, Construction, and Use.* New York: ANSI. (Z39.19-1980)

Anderson, J. D. (1997). *Guidelines for Indexes and Related Information Retrieval Devices.* Bethesda, MD: NISO Press. (NISO-TR-02-1997).

British Standards Institution. (1987). *Guide to Establishment and Development of Monolingual Thesauri* (2nd ed.). London: BSI. (BS 5723:1987)

British Standards Institution. (1996). *Information and Documentation. Guidelines for the Content, Organization and Presentation of Indexes.* London, BSI. (BS ISO 999:1996)

International Organization for Standardization. (1985). *Documentation—Guidelines for the Establishment and Development of Multilingual Thesauri.* [Geneva:] ISO. (ISO 5964-

1985(E))

International Organization for Standardization. (1986). *Documentation—Guidelines for the Establishment and Development of Monolingual Thesauri* (2nd ed.). [Geneva:] ISO. (ISO 2788-1986(E))

International Organization for Standardization. (1996). *Information and Documentation—Guidelines for the Content, Organization and Presentation of Indexes.* [Geneva:] ISO. (ISO 999:1996(E))

Jacob, E. K. (1992). Classification and categorization: Drawing the line. In B. H. Kwašnik & R. Fidel (Eds.), *Advances in Classification Research, Proceedings of the 2nd ASIS SIG/CR Classification Research Workshop,* 67-83. Medford, NJ: Learned Information.

Lancaster, F. W. (1995). [Review of the book *ASIS Thesaurus of Information Science and Librarianship*]. *Library & Information Science Research,* 17, 189-194.

Liddy, E. D. (1998). Natural language processing for information retrieval and knowledge discovery. In P.A. Cochrane & E. H. Johnson (Eds.), *Visualizing Subject Access for 21ˢᵗ Century Information Resources,* 137-147. Champaign, IL: Graduate School of Library and Information Science, University of Illinois. (Clinic on Library Applications of Data Processing, 1997).

National Information Standards Organization. (1994). *Guidelines for the Construction, Format, and Management of Monolingual Thesauri.* Bethesda, MD: NISO Press. (ANSI/NISO Z39.19-1993).

National Information Standards Organization. (1998). *Frequently Asked Questions* [Online]. Available: <http://www.niso.org/faq.html> [2000, February 29].

National Information Standards Organization. (2000). *International Standards* [Online]. Available: <http://www.niso.org/internat.html> [2000, February 29].

Soergel, D. (1974). *Indexing Languages and Thesauri: Construction and Maintenance.* Los Angeles: Melville Publishing.

# Chapter 5

# Relationships in Multilingual Thesauri

Michèle Hudon
*École de Bibliothéconomie et des Sciences de l'Information, Université de Montréal, Montréal, QC Canada*

**Abstract:**
Because the multilingual thesaurus has a critical role to play in the global networked information world, its relational structure must come under close scrutiny. Traditionally, identity of relational structures has been sought for the different language versions of a multilingual thesaurus, often leading to the artificialization of all target languages. The various types of cross-lingual and intralingual relations found in thesauri are examined in the context of two questions: Are all types of thesaural relations transferable from one language to another? and Are the two members of a valid relation in a source language always the same in the target language(s)? Two options for resolving semantic conflicts in multilingual thesauri are presented.

## 1. MULTILINGUALITY IN TODAY'S INFORMATION WORLD

The amazing technology now at our disposal makes it possible to imagine that "what the greatest minds of the last two thousand years have dreamt of: to make the sources of information accessible to anybody, anywhere, at any time, and most important of all: in any language" (Wellisch, 1973, p. 162) will some day be achieved. But while the extensive network infrastructure capable of moving data, information, and knowledge across national boundaries is already available, "much remains to be done before linguistic barriers can be surmounted as effectively as geographic ones" (Oard, 1997).

It is now possible for users throughout the world to access massive amounts of information in any language, and for information producers to make the results of their work available in their mother tongue, confident that this will not in itself preclude or limit access to them (Peters & Pichi, 1997). This new situation has given rise to a flurry of research projects focusing on cross-language information retrieval (CLIR), a rejuvenated concept defined as: "the retrieval of any type of object composed or indexed in one language with a query formulated in another language" (Soergel, 1997). Multilingual text retrieval is useful where a collection contains documents in such a large number of languages that it would be impractical to form a query in each one of them, where document contents are in more than one language, and where the user is not sufficiently fluent in a collection's language to express a query in that language, but can make use of the documents themselves (Oard & Dorr, 1996). The World Wide Web is one environment where users may need help in the form of language tools if they are to gain access to resources most appropriate to their needs.

67

C. A. Bean and R. Green (eds.), *Relationships in the Organization of Knowledge*, 67–80.

Three techniques for cross-language retrieval are currently studied: machine translation (MT) and knowledge-based and natural language corpus-based methods. Machine translation does not yet perform at an optimal level because of its inability to cope with semantics, even in restricted domains: It is no secret that "ambiguity resolution has been one of the principal problems in natural language computing, especially with reference to MT and associated efforts" (Sedelow & Sedelow, 1994, p. 246). For the moment at least, it appears that the most promising CLIR results may come from the integration of multilingual lexical instruments (e.g., multilingual thesauri) and corpus-based methods (Oard & Dorr, 1996). Research has demonstrated that explicit thesaural relational structures could be helpful to sort out specific unambiguous conceptual content from a potentially ambiguous text (Sedelow & Sedelow, 1994).

The multilingual thesaurus is as popular today as it was when first proposed in the 1970s to support the work of indexers and searchers in the European Community. In the global information world, the multilingual thesaurus performs three well-defined functions:

- Allowing individuals to use the language that they feel most at ease with so they can formulate queries as simply and intuitively as possible,
- Providing interpretation support to access information within documents written in a foreign language, and
- Facilitating the integration of information provided in various languages.

For the multilingual thesaurus to be most useful and efficient in these tasks, its relational structure should reflect the multiple ways of "seeing" the world that its multilingual and multicultural users bring with them when querying an information system.

## 2. THE MULTILINGUAL THESAURUS

The thesaurus has been described as a "series of semantic networks, each of which is built-up by a collection of junctions (key words or principal headings) connected by various relationships" (Bianucci et al., 1992, p. 59). The genuine multilingual thesaurus is one in which not only the junctions but also the relationships are represented in more than one language.

The first multilingual thesauri were developed rapidly, preserving the standardized structure of the monolingual thesaurus, and using the same design principles. Much emphasis was initially put on compatibility of structures across languages: Strong compatibility resulted from full correspondence of concepts and relations, while weak compatibility resulted from correspondence between concepts but not necessarily between conceptual relations. Multilingual thesauri were often built by translating an existing monolingual thesaurus, most likely one in the English language. Equal status of languages did not appear to be a major concern, and little feedback from the target language—which could potentially lead to a modification of the source language—was allowed. A most unfortunate consequence of this approach was that cross-language equivalences were forced where they did not exist (e.g., one source term, no target term), or were ignored or eliminated where they did exist (e.g., one source term, two or more target terms), and questionable relational structures were established. Although many individuals advocated more flexibility in relational structures and true cultural representativeness, the social, cultural, and political considerations related to any manipulation of natural language were brushed aside, and existing practices were little affected. Although thesaurus designers and users who were not native English speakers believed that the linguistic problems had to be more important than the organizational ones in the construction of a multilingual thesaurus, no official proposal for an alternate model was ever made. The particularities of the multilingual thesaurus with regard to issues of conceptual overlap and differences in relational structures have not been studied in depth, as though multilingual thesauri were language-neutral and culture-neutral objects.

Information users, however, are aware of the very real problems traditionally associated with multilingual indexing and retrieval languages (IRLs):

- "Stretching" a language to fit a foreign conceptual structure until it becomes barely recognizable to its own speakers,
- Transferring a whole relational structure from one cultural context to another whether appropriate or not, and
- Translating terms literally from the source language into meaningless expressions in the target language.

To avoid such problems, it has been recommended that multilingual tools be built from the ground up, starting with distinct banks of terms (one for each language represented) and developing distinct structures through semantic relationships, with immediate help from native speakers of each one of the thesaurus languages.

A critical function of the thesaurus is that of helping users in making sense. The defining function of thesaurus relationships is well established: Relationships "define," admittedly not always very clearly, by providing a context of sorts that determines the place of a concept in its semantic environment, and by supplying more or less explicit information on the intension and extension of this concept. Relationships also serve as navigational aids to arrive at the intended destination or at the most interesting destination on a semantic map. In a multilingual context, both the defining and navigational functions of thesaural relations acquire even more importance.

This essay looks at both types of relationships found in thesauri: the interpreting relationship, which links concepts and words to explain meaning, and the conceptual relationship, which links concepts. For convenience, all examples are selected in the language pair English-French. English and French have been in close contact for centuries and their native speakers, in large part, live in similar environments and share popular culture, occupations, lifestyles, etc.; yet the conceptual and lexical structures of French and English exhibit significant differences. Comparable examples could be found in any language pair appearing in a multilingual thesaurus.

## 3. CROSS-LANGUAGE RELATIONSHIPS IN MULTILINGUAL THESAURI

Languages are conceptual and lexical structures that reflect the way in which their speakers see and interact with the realities of the external world (e.g., objects, events, etc.) and of their own internal world (e.g., emotions). One need not subscribe entirely to the precepts of the Sapir-Whorf hypothesis to recognize that in the best of cases, there still does not exist an exact concordance between two languages in their way of defining concepts and terms, of categorizing and relating concepts, of representing time and space, of characterizing abstract entities, etc. (Maniez, 1997). In every language, a particular term covers a certain area of a semantic field, which can and will vary slightly from one language to another. Differences in the way various natural languages express realities are connected to differences in the political, economic, philosophical, religious, and cultural conditions of the life of the people who speak them.

This makes it difficult (some have said theoretically impossible) to translate one natural language into another. Herein lies a problem with which translators, terminologists, and also multilingual thesaurus designers are all too familiar. Such evidence has led at least one terminologist to question the feasibility of establishing multilingual terminological banks (Otman, 1996); the same comment could apply also to multilingual thesauri.

The first critical step in the design of a multilingual thesaurus is the creation of parallel lexicons to allow for basic cross-lingual communication. Those parallel lexicons are composed of cross-lingual term equivalents, ideally true synonyms across languages. Descriptor equivalence is thus described as a "correspondence on the semantic level with or without correspondence on the formal level" (Merilaïnen, 1997, p. 110). The differences in the conceptual structuring of various languages increase the number of cross-lingual quasi-synonyms in a multilingual thesaurus: Across languages, what appears as a relation of equivalence is often closer to a relation of similarity.

The interpreting relationship between a concept and its verbal representation is evidently not always transferable from one language to another. Concepts verbalized by a single term in one language can be expressed by more than one term in another because of differences in the specificity of natural languages (e.g., the French MOUTON is equivalent to both SHEEP and MUTTON in English). Ambiguity is created when a term in one language has more than one cross-lingual equivalent, representing very distinct concepts (e.g., the French BEAU-PÈRE is equivalent to both STEPFATHER and FATHER-IN-LAW in English). One term may exist in one language for which no equivalent is found in another, presumably because the concept represented in the source language does not exist in the target culture. Finding appropriate equivalents may be especially difficult if concepts do not have a stable lexical support, that is, if the interpreting relationships are weak; this is often the case in the special languages of the social sciences.

The question of conceptual and lexical equivalence across languages has been covered extensively in the international guidelines for thesaurus design and in many textbooks (e.g., see Aitchison, Gilchrist, & Bawden, 1997, and ISO 5964-1985). The identification of cross-lingual equivalents is considered relatively unproblematic, and pragmatic procedures appear sufficient to cope with differences in interpreting relationships in various languages. Cross-language equivalents are seen as perfect examples of dynamic equivalence, i.e., "dependent on factors—inside or outside the linguistic domain—connected to the situation where the equivalence is established" (Merilaïnen, 1997, p. 110). Although this leads to the inclusion in multilingual thesauri of cross-lingual equivalents that would not necessarily be tolerated in natural language, an effort is made to maintain the essential symmetrical quality of the equivalence relation: If A = B is acceptable to native speakers of A, then B = A should also be acceptable to native speakers of B.

Five degrees of cross-lingual equivalence are described in the guidelines:

- Exact equivalence (true cross-lingual synonymy; e.g., SUN = SOLEIL),
- Inexact equivalence (cross-lingual quasi-synonymy with a difference in viewpoint, e.g.; ALCOHOL EDUCATION = ÉDUCATION ANTIALCOOLISME),
- Partial equivalence (cross-lingual quasi-synonymy with a difference in specificity; e.g., NUTS = NOIX),
- Single-to-multiple equivalence (different number of verbal representations for a concept in the source and target languages; e.g., READABILITY and LEGIBILITY = LISIBILITÉ), and
- Non-equivalence (e.g., LATCHKEY CHILDREN = ?).

Much emphasis has been put on potential solutions to the last two problems caused by cases of single-to-multiple equivalence and by non-equivalence. Only a brief survey of those solutions is provided here; detailed descriptions can be found in the latest versions of various guidelines for multilingual thesaurus design.

There are two distinct cases of single-to-multiple equivalence. The first exists where the target language contains more than one equivalent of the source term (i.e., too many target terms), a problem encountered frequently in the language pair English-French. A single-to-multiple equivalence is created de facto every time a source term in English must be translated by French terms that exhibit gender specific forms (e.g., TEACHERS = ENSEIGNANT and ENSEIGNANTE). Thesaurus designers have dealt with this relatively simple case by subsuming the feminine form of a term under its masculine form, an approach supported by grammarians in their decision to simplify the language.

Three solutions have been proposed for the problem of too many target terms:

- The creation of pre-combined descriptors in the target language, for example (EP = employé pour, "used for"):

| Source | Target |
|---|---|
| FUELS | CARBURANT + COMBUSTIBLE |
| | EP  Carburant |
| | EP  Combustible |

- A modification/specification of the source term, e.g., by addition of a qualifier, for example:

| Source | Target |
|---|---|
| FUELS (MOTORS) | CARBURANT |
| FUELS (HEATING) | COMBUSTIBLE |

- The downgrading of one or more of the target terms to the status of non-descriptor, with a link to the preferred term, for example:

| Source | Target |
|---|---|
| FUELS | CARBURANT |
| | EP  Combustible |

The second case of single-to-multiple equivalence is encountered when the target language can only represent the source concept through a combination of terms (i.e., not enough target terms).  Three solutions have again been proposed:

- A formal recommendation in the target version to use many descriptors, providing the information system allows for this, for example:

| Source | Target |
|--------|--------|
| HEATING | CHAUFFAGE |
| SOLAR ENERGY | ÉNERGIE SOLAIRE |
| SOLAR HEATING | CHAUFFAGE + ÉNERGIE SOLAIRE |

- The creation of an equivalent in the form of a coined term (or neologism), for example:

| Source | Target |
|--------|--------|
| HEATING | CHAUFFAGE |
| SOLAR ENERGY | ÉNERGIE SOLAIRE |
| SOLAR HEATING | CHAUFFAGE SOLAIRE |

- The establishment of one or more non-descriptors in the source language, with a link to the preferred term(s), for example:

| Source | Target |
|--------|--------|
| HEATING | CHAUFFAGE |
| SOLAR ENERGY | ÉNERGIE SOLAIRE |
| Solar heating | |
| USE HEATING and | |
| SOLAR ENERGY | |

Orphans (i.e., descriptors appearing in one language version but without equivalent in at least one of the other versions) naturally have not been tolerated in multilingual thesauri where identity of structures was required.  The simplest solution to the non-equivalence problem has always been to remove the orphan from the source language lexicon, but cases of non-equivalence can not always be solved so easily.  Three solutions to the problem of non-equivalence have been offered:

- A change of status for the orphan, which is transformed into an intralingual synonym and linked to a descriptor with which it shares essential characteristics; for example, as there is no exact French equivalent for the term "Teenagers":

| Source | Target |
|--------|--------|
| ADOLESCENTS | ADOLESCENT |
| UF Teenagers | |

- The import of the source term into the target language; for example since the concept Régime pédagogique exists only in Québec and has no exact equivalent in the English language:

| Source (French) | Target (English) |
|-----------------|-------------------|
| RÉGIME PÉDAGOGIQUE | RÉGIME PÉDAGOGIQUE |

- The creation of an equivalent (neologism) in the target language, for example:

| Source | Target |
|--------|--------|
| LATCHKEY CHILDREN | ENFANT À CLÉ |

Any concept existing in a particular culture can likely be described with a number of words in any other language, but the thesaurus must express concepts with terms composed of a restricted number of verbal forms. The previous examples show quite clearly that even with such a restriction, it is still possible to achieve lexical coincidence in a pair of languages by "artificializing" one or both of the languages to some degree. Most of the solutions proposed to the above cases of single-to-multiple equivalence and non-equivalence involve the creation of artificial lexical nodes. Relations linking these nodes to other artificial or legitimate nodes in the network will also be artificial. Such artificialization, realized in part through the manipulation of interpreting relationships within a natural language, is deemed acceptable in the context of designing a tool to access an information system: Equivalence relations, whether applied within or across languages, are relations between terms considered to have equal value for information retrieval and for information retrieval only.

The solutions proposed to the most common cases of inexact cross-lingual equivalence may lead to a belief that these problems arise from some gap in the lexicon rather than differences in the deep semantic structure of languages. We can simplify the surface structure of the multilingual thesaurus, but underlying conceptual overlap and conflicts remain. Cross-lingual equivalents that look the same and are good translations of one another, but that do not in fact represent the same concept, are a frequent occurrence in thesauri.

The following examples reveal the complexity of relationships between concepts and verbal representations presented as equivalent in the language pair English-French. In the first example, the source term has seemingly but a single equivalent in the target language. A closer analysis of the French equivalent, however, shows that two concepts of a very different nature are in fact subsumed under a single verbal representation, and that only one of them can be considered equivalent to the English concept.

| Source | Target |
|--------|--------|
| LITERACY | ALPHABÉTISATION |

*Definitions:*

English LITERACY:
> Ability of an individual to read and write at the level required to fulfil his or her own self-determined objectives as family and community member, citizen, and worker.

French ALPHABÉTISATION:
> (1) The process of acquiring the basic reading, writing, and number skills required to fulfil an individuals's own self-determined objectives as family and community member, citizen, and worker.
> (2) The result of this process.

In the second example, source and target concepts and verbal representations are interrelated in such a way that it becomes difficult to perceive their intension and differentiating characteristics. One might expect the concept behind the term EDUCATION to cover the same ground in Western societies, even where different languages are spoken.

But in fact, French ÉDUCATION has a more restricted meaning than the English EDUCATION, and is better distinguished from the concept of ENSEIGNEMENT than EDUCATION is from TEACHING. The following example shows the complexity of the network of relations linking widely used terms in this field:

| Source | Target |
|--------|--------|
| EDUCATION | ÉDUCATION |
| | ENSEIGNEMENT |
| | FORMATION |
| TEACHING | ENSEIGNEMENT |
| INSTRUCTION | ENSEIGNEMENT |
| | INSTRUCTION |

Experience has shown that ten to fifteen percent of descriptors in a source language will lack an exact conceptual equivalent in another. Because cross-lingual equivalents do not necessarily cover the same area of a semantic field and because they often represent concepts that are not equivalent to one another, it stands to reason that the relational structures in each language version of a multilingual thesaurus should exhibit at least minor variations. Otman (1996) insists that it should never be assumed that the network of relationships for a concept can be automatically transferred from one language structure to another, even if it appears possible to assign a label to this concept in *n* languages.

## 4. INTRALINGUAL RELATIONSHIPS OF EQUIVALENCE, INCLUSION, AND OTHER ASSOCIATIONS

When one puts side by side several monolingual and independently developed thesauri describing the same domain of knowledge or activity in different natural languages, it quickly becomes clear that the relational structures of these thesauri do not fully coincide, even if they are built around the same lexical nodes. Thesaurus developers with different linguistic backgrounds and from different cultural environments do not organize the world according to the same pattern and do not link concepts in the same way.

Since relations in a thesaurus are used to navigate a semantic field and to reach a destination on a semantic map, the tradition of replicating relational structures from one linguistic version to others in a multilingual thesaurus is equivalent to assuming that all individuals can find their way on the same map, and that nobody will mind being forced to travel on the same path as everybody else.

A discussion of intralingual relationships in a multilingual thesaurus raises two distinct questions: Are all types of thesaural relations transferable from one language version to the others? Are the two members of a valid relation in a source language always transferable to the target language(s)?

### 4.1 Universality of Thesaural Relationships

Iyer (1995) suggests that the quest for universal structures in the human mind is no longer merely an area of philosophical interest to us. The use of universals would allow us to link different classification schemes and indexing tools by way of switching languages and generic umbrella systems.

In the 1970s and early 1980s, one of the phenomena carefully investigated for universality or relativity was that of semantic relations. This was considered an important issue because semantic relations constitute one of the building blocks of thought and expression. It has long been recognized that "identification of cultural relativity for some or all relations would also have practical implications for translation and cross-cultural communication generally" (Raybeck & Herrmann, 1990, p. 453). The current proliferation of electronic networks facilitating the sharing of resources among peoples of widely divergent educational, cultural, and linguistic backgrounds, will likely herald a resurgence of interest in this important issue.

In the fields of anthropology and cross-cultural psychology, applied research has led to the conclusion that there is considerable cross-cultural agreement on the meaning and use of semantic relations (Herrmann & Raybeck, 1981; Chaffin & Herrmann, 1984; Romney, Moore & Rusch, 1997). In experiments using concrete (e.g., animals) as well as more abstract (e.g., emotions) concepts, evidence points to specific types of relationships that are recognized equally easily and used with equal frequency and accuracy by diverse groups of people; the relation between opposites, the part-whole relation, and the relation between cause and effect are cited as the relationships most strongly agreed upon (Raybeck & Herrmann, 1990). Evidence also suggests several cross-cultural differences in the perception of relations. Even if the philosophical discussion is not of immediate interest to him, the thesaurus specialist finds here reassurance that the basic relational structure used in thesauri is one most users will recognize and be able to navigate. The findings of these studies also support the assertion in ISO 5964 that "the fundamental relationships described in ISO 2788 (*Guidelines for the Establishment and Development of Monolingual Thesauri*) are regarded as language-independent and also culture-independent" (International Organization for Standardization, 1985, p. 25). Those relations are that of equivalence, of inclusion (or hierarchical relation), and of association (or associative relation).

## 4.2 Relation of Equivalence

Identity of relational structures across languages has never been considered essential where internal relations of equivalence were concerned; the wide variety of these has been described by Iyer (1995, pp. 62-64). It has been taken for granted that non-descriptors would not necessarily match in every language, since the number of synonyms, antonyms, and quasi-synonyms for each term in a language depends on the lexical richness of this language.

Since at some point in time many multilingual thesauri resulted from the translation of a thesaurus in the English language to French, Spanish, German, etc., and since the non-descriptors were not systematically translated, it has often seemed as though English had a much larger stock of words than the target languages. The same phenomenon may still occur where a bilingual or multilingual thesaurus is developed by an individual who can speak several languages: The sets of equivalents in this person's first language will tend to be more populated than sets of equivalents in the other languages.

## 4.3 Relation of Inclusion (Hierarchical Relation)

The guidelines for the development of multilingual thesauri state that "as a general rule, any hierarchy which the users of one language regard as logically acceptable should appear to be equally valid when its terms have been translated into another language" (International Organization for Standardization, 1985, p. 26). This is most likely accurate when exact cross-lingual equivalents are used to construct the hierarchy. But what happens in the ten to fifteen percent of cases where we start with inexact equivalents, with concepts that have different intension and extension?

The main problem related to the hierarchical relation in multilingual thesauri has long been seen as one relating to the absence of a hierarchical level in one of the conceptual structures. The example of the generic NUTS, which has no exact French equivalent, has been frequently chosen to illustrate what is not only a lexical gap but also a structural one. In this case, however, a relatively easy solution has been applied, with the specific NOIX acquiring a larger extension to become a class term and an acceptable equivalent for the English NUTS. But what happens when it comes to listing the specific objects, where NOIX, as the exact equivalent of WALNUT, cannot reappear as its own narrower term?

The guidelines also suggest that where it is not possible to achieve exact equivalence at the level of the individual terms, it may not be possible to translate the source hierarchy into the target language (International Organization for Standardization, 1985, p. 26). Given that in many cases we do indeed start with terms that refer to slightly different concepts, we should expect to see discrepancies in the hierarchies. The main question is whether these discrepancies will become obstacles for the efficient use of a multilingual thesaurus by any of the native speakers of languages represented. In the term record shown below, all narrower terms (English NT; French TS = terme spécifique) refer to relatively well-defined objects, and although one term at least (REGISTRE SOCIAL) is not much used in French, the arrangement presented appears perfectly acceptable to a French speaker.

| *Source* | *Target* |
|---|---|
| REFERENCE MATERIALS | OUVRAGES DE RÉFÉRENCE |
| NT Atlases | TS Atlas |
|     Bibliographies |     Bibliographie |
|     Dictionaries |     Dictionnaire |
|     Directories |     Répertoire |
|     Social registers |     Registre social |
|     Thesauri |     Thésaurus |

The logic of the hierarchical structure, however, breaks down when what must be represented is more abstract and less clearly defined. The example already discussed at the end of section 3 provides an interesting case in point: The cross-lingual equivalence established between EDUCATION and ÉDUCATION may lead to the following:

| Source | Target |
|---|---|
| EDUCATION | ÉDUCATION |
| NT Adult education | TS Éducation des adultes |
| Agricultural education | Enseignement agricole |
| Career education | Préparation à une carrière |
| Civic education | Instruction civique |
| Compulsory education | Scolarité obligatoire |
| Cooperative education | Formation en alternance |
| Free education | Enseignement gratuit |
| Higher education | Enseignement supérieur |
| Private education | Enseignement privé |
| Progressive education | Pédagogie progressiste |
| Vocational education | Enseignement professionne |

The differences in the inventories of narrower terms are not just lexical in nature: They are truly conceptual. When a French speaker looks at the French part of the thesaurus, even after the alphabetical order has been restored, the listing of narrower terms still does not look quite right and may not be that useful for both defining and navigational purposes. Not surprisingly, the initial inexact equivalence has transferred itself to the next level of specificity. It is important to realize that the unusual aspect of the list of French narrower terms is not a factor of the inclusion relation itself: All the specific concepts represented by narrower terms in French are indeed in a genus-species relationship with another concept, but in all but one case the correct broader term is not the one appearing here (i.e., ÉDUCATION). The example in no way invalidates the inclusion relationship in general; it only calls into question the identity of the members of that relationship in this case.

The cross-lingual equivalence established above between LITERACY and ALPHABÉTISATION would also generate irregularities in the hierarchical structures of the English and French versions of a thesaurus. Because the French ALPHABÉTISATION represents two concepts of different nature, its list of narrower terms will include terms that represent entities (identified as [e] below), and terms that represent processes (identified as [p]); this will not be the case in the English version of the same tool. At best, the ambiguity created at the top level will remain through the hierarchical structure. But it will be impossible to transfer the hierarchy where the source and target terms do not belong to the same class of concepts. RURAL LITERACY INSTRUCTION and ALPHABÉTISATION EN MILIEU RURAL are exact cross-lingual equivalents; while the French term clearly belongs to the hierarchy of ALPHABÉTISATION, the English term will appear as a narrower term under LITERACY INSTRUCTION, not under LITERACY.

| Source | Target |
|---|---|
| LITERACY [e] | ALPHABÉTISATION [e, p] |
| NT Basic literacy [e] | TS Alphabétisation de base [e, p] |
| Bilingual literacy [e] | Alphabétisation bilingue [e, p] |
| French language literacy [e] | Alphabétisation en français [p] |
| Functional literacy [e] | Alphabétisation fonctionnelle[ e] |
| Immigrant literacy [e] | Alphabétisation des immigrants [p] |
| [Rural literacy instruction][p] | Alphabétisation en milieu rural [p] |
| Universal literacy [e] | Alphabétisation universelle [e] |
| Women's literacy [e] | Alphabétisation des femmes [p |

## 4.4  Other Associative Relations

If the linguistic versions of a multilingual thesaurus are developed independently, it is likely to be in the sets of associative relationships that the most important discrepancies will appear. These discrepancies are more likely a direct consequence of the fuzzy character of the associative relationship as it appears in thesauri than the result of potentially divergent views of the world that individual thesaurus designers may have. The part-whole relation, the cause-effect relation, and the sign-significance relation are among the most constantly and correctly identified by individuals from various cultures. Differences in case relations (agent-action, action-object, etc.) would likely occur where a conceptual gap exists in a particular culture: A tool that is not in use in a society and has no designation in its language, for example, could not be related to a process or a product existing in the culture.

If the types of associative relationships that should be retained in the thesaural structure were clearly identified and better defined, sets of related terms in the different linguistic versions of a multilingual thesaurus would be very similar if not identical, providing that the concepts and terms thus related had exact equivalents in the other languages. Pairs of related terms appearing in one version only, owing to differences in perceptions and connotations, could be considered for their validity in the other languages and transferred if appropriate. Accordingly, the guidelines suggest that "a multilingual thesaurus should usually contain a richer variety of associative relationships than a monolingual thesaurus in the same field, since it [benefits] from the viewpoints of different language users" (International Organization for Standardization, 1985, p. 27).

## 5.  RELATIONAL STRUCTURES IN COMPUTERIZED MULTILINGUAL THESAURI: INTEGRATION OR PRESERVATION?

As long as thesauri were mainly used by human indexers and searchers, issues related to conceptual and structural differences across languages could be seen as relatively unimportant as far as consequences on retrieval were concerned. But as thesauri come to be used more and more in a fully computerized mode, with minimal or no input from a human mind able to resolve semantic conflicts, the relational structure of a multilingual thesaurus must come under close scrutiny: If conflicts are not resolved, the system cannot perform optimally.

Two options are currently under consideration as a way to resolve conflicts in multilingual thesauri. The first option proposes the integration of the various possible relational structures into one and the generation of a "common" structure (Soergel, 1997). Where identity of structures in all languages is still required, this option is certainly superior to the traditional adaptation of the target language relational network to fit that of the source language. It does re-establish linguistic and cultural equality in a somewhat unfortunate manner by artificializing all languages involved and assumes that more will be better than less.

Taking advantage of recent technological advances, the second option preserves the integrity of each linguistic arrangement by creating independent relational structures and providing a bridge to all other potential arrangements of nodes around the same or related concepts. This option has been adopted in the EuroWordNet (EWN) project, with its Interlingual index used to jump from one relational structure to others. At this time closer to a termbank than to a thesaurus, the EWN database is considered as a potential tool for the improvement of natural language processing in electronic resources and even for straightforward information retrieval.

The searchers and practitioners at EuroWordNet have observed and described four typical situations, all of which will be familiar to multilingual thesaurus designers:

- A set of word-meanings across languages has a simple equivalence relation and parallel language-internal relations.
- A set of word-meanings across languages has a simple equivalence relation but diverging language-internal relations.
- A set of word-meanings across languages has complex equivalence relations but parallel language-internal relations.
- A set of word-meanings across languages has complex equivalence relations and diverging language-internal relations (Vossen, Diez-Orzas, & Peters, 1997)

The number of occurrences of the second and fourth situations have been judged high enough to justify a decision to maintain cultural and linguistic differences in parallel monolingual wordnets. In this optimal model, language-independent data is shared and language specific properties are maintained (Vossen, Diez-Orzas, & Peters, 1997), permitting more than one view of the world to coexist.

Technology may allow us finally to discard the belief that compatibility of linguistic versions in a multilingual thesaurus must of necessity be equated with identity of relational structures. In so doing, it leaves us free to concentrate on usability and efficiency, on cultural representativeness, and on user-friendliness.

## References

Aitchison, J., Gilchrist, A., & Bawden, D. (1997). *Thesaurus Construction and Use: a Practical Manual* (3rd ed.). London: Aslib.

Bianucci, G., Martino, A. A., Coco, G., Moscati, G., & Rossi, L. F. (1992). L'usage de relations sémantiques dans l'élaboration de thesauri: L'expérience du PTP (Petit Thesaurus Politique). *Cahiers de Lexicologie*, 61, 2, 59-84.

Chaffin, R., & Herrmann, D. J. (1984). The similarity and diversity of semantic relations. *Memory & Cognition*, 12, 143-141.

Herrmann, D. J., & Raybeck, D. (1981). Similarities and differences in meaning in six cultures. *Journal of Cross-Cultural Psychology*, 12, 194-206.

International Organization for Standardization. (1985). *Documentation—Guidelines for the Establishment and Development of Multilingual Thesauri*. [Geneva:] ISO. (ISO 5964-1985(E))

Iyer, H. (1995). *Classificatory Structures: Concepts, Relations and Representations.* Frankfurt am Main: INDEKS Verlag.

Maniez, J. (1997). Fusion de banques de données documentaires et compatibilité des langages d'indexation. *Documentaliste—Sciences de l'Information,* 34, 212-222.

Merilaïnen, O. (1997). Descriptor equivalence in the context of bilingual indexing. *Libri,* 47, 107-113.

Oard, D. W. (1997, December). Serving users in many languages: Cross language information retrieval for digital libraries. *D-Lib Magazine* [Online], 20 paragraphs. Available: <http://www.dlib.org/dlib/december97/oard/12oard.html> [2000, February 9].

Oard, D. W., & Dorr, B. J. (1996). *A Survey of Multilingual Text Retrieval* [Online]. Available: <http://www.ee.umd.edu/dlrg/filter/papers/mlir.ps> [2000, February 9].

Otman, G. (1996). *Les Représentations Sémantiques en Terminologie.* Paris: Masson.

Peters, C., & Picchi, E. (1997, May). Across languages, across cultures: Issues in multilinguality and digital libraries. *D-Lib Magazine* [Online], 56 paragraphs. Available: <http://www.dlib.org/dlib/may97/peters/05peters.html> [2000, February 9].

Raybeck, D., & Herrmann, D. (1990). A cross-cultural examination of semantic relations. *Journal of Cross-Cultural Psychology,* 21, 452-473.

Romney, A. K., Moore, C. C., & Rusch, C. D. (1997). Cultural universals: Measuring the semantic structure of emotion terms in English and Japanese. In *Proceedings of the National Academy of Sciences of the United States,* 94, 5489-5494.

Sedelow, W. A., Jr., & Sedelow, S. Y. (1994). Multicultural/multilingual electronically mediated communication. *Social Science Computer Review,* 12, 242-249.

Soergel, D. (1997). Multilingual thesauri in cross-language text and speech retrieval. In *AAAI Spring Symposium on Cross-language Text and Speech Retrieval, Stanford University, March 24-26, 1997* [Online]. Available: <http://www.clis.umd.edu/dlrg/filter/sss/papers/soergel.ps> [2000, February 15].

Vossen, P., Diez-Orzas, P., & Peters, W. (1997). The multilingual design of the EuroWordNet database. In *IJCAI-97: Workshop on Ontologies and Multilingual NLP, Nagoya, Japan, August 23, 1997* [Online]. Available: <http://crl.nmsu.edu/Events/IJCAI/vossen.rtf.gz> [2000, February 9].

Wellisch, H. (1973). Linguistic and semantic problems in the use of English-language information services in non-English-speaking countries, or, How to install an elevator in the Tower of Babel. *International Library Review,* 5, 147-162.

Chapter 6

# Relationships among Knowledge Structures:
# Vocabulary Integration within a Subject Domain

Olivier Bodenreider
*National Library of Medicine, Bethesda, MD, USA*

Carol A. Bean
*School of Information Sciences, University of Tennessee, Knoxville, TN, USA*

Abstract:
   The structure of terminology systems can be seen as one way to organize knowledge. This paper focuses on three types of relationships among terms: synonymy, hierarchical relationships, and explicit mapping relationships. Examples drawn from various medical vocabularies illustrate each type of relationship. The integration of disparate terminological knowledge structures in the Unified Medical Language System is presented and discussed.

## 1. INTRODUCTION

   There are a large number of terminology systems used in medicine. Recent reviews present the scope and the structure of the major medical vocabularies (Cimino, 1996), and evaluate their content coverage (Chute et al., 1996) or their features (Campbell et al., 1997). While some vocabularies have been used for more than a century (e.g., the International Classification of Diseases), others are still very much works in progress (e.g., GALEN, SNOMED-RT).[1] Often vocabularies are designed to serve one particular purpose: For example, the U.S. National Library of Medicine (NLM) develops and uses the Medical Subject Headings (MeSH) as its controlled vocabulary for subject cataloging and to index articles from medical journals. Conversely, the International Classification of Diseases (ICD) is not only used world-wide to record causes of death or to register diseases in health statistics, but many adaptations of it (e.g., ICD-9-CM) are also used to record diagnoses or contact with health services for billing purposes.

   Despite recently-formed partnerships between the producers of some major vocabularies (e.g., between SNOMED and LOINC, or between SNOMED-RT and Clinical Terms Version 3[2]), most vocabularies are usually developed independently from one another. Several studies have examined principles for the construction of medical vocabularies (Chute, Cohn, & Campbell, 1998; Cimino, 1998; Evans et al., 1994; Rada et al., 1993; Rossi Mori et al., 1993). Nonetheless, emerging standards such as those defined by the European Committee for Standardization (CEN) have not yet been widely adopted. (For an overview,

81

*C. A. Bean and R. Green (eds.), Relationships in the Organization of Knowledge, 81–98.*

see Rossi Mori, Consorti, & Galeazzi, 1998).

No single vocabulary offers both a coverage broad enough to encompass the whole biomedical domain and a granularity suitable for the description of patient conditions in applications such as electronic patient records (Chute et al., 1996). In the last fifteen years, two major projects[3] using different approaches have been developed towards such a goal.

A top-down approach has been used in the European Union GALEN project. GRAIL, the "GALEN Representation and Integration Language," was designed prior to defining the CORE model for the representation of medical concepts (Rector & Nowlan, 1994). Putting such an emphasis on the conceptual model has enabled GALEN's success in developing language-independent terminology services to exploit the knowledge representation (Rector et al., 1995), but it still lacks broad coverage (Rector et al., 1998).

The Unified Medical Language System (UMLS) was developed at the U.S. NLM using a bottom-up approach. It provides a common interface to about 40 existing medical vocabularies and reduces the ambiguity inherent in large bodies of content (Humphreys et al., 1998; Lindberg, Humphreys, & McCray, 1993). The structure of a semantic network strengthens the limited knowledge model inherited from each vocabulary and refined by the UMLS editors. With more than 600,000 medical concepts, the UMLS now has reasonably broad coverage, but its knowledge representation is weaker than GALEN's.

The role played by terms is very different in the two systems: The UMLS can be described as a system that organizes terms, while terms are a by-product of the GALEN system. In other words, the UMLS makes heavy use of lexical knowledge to link precoordinated terms together, while terms are generated from the combination of atomic concepts under the GALEN model.

The identification of relationships among knowledge structures inherited from medical vocabularies was an early goal in the UMLS project and has been long been recognized for contributing added value in the UMLS Metathesaurus (Bodenreider, Nelson, et al., 1998; Cimino et al., 1993; Dessena, Rossi Mori, & Galeazzi, 1999). It is thus quite natural to use the UMLS to illustrate how these relationships are discovered through lexical knowledge, heuristics, and the knowledge of human editors. Numerous journal articles and presentations at international conferences have already described the structure (Nelson et al., 1992) and formal properties (Tuttle et al., 1994) of the UMLS Metathesaurus, as well as the methodology used for its creation and maintenance (Sherertz et al., 1990; Sperzel et al., 1992; Suarez-Munist et al., 1996; Tuttle et al., 1995); interested readers are referred to this literature. However, key elements of UMLS Metathesaurus construction and editorial processes will be briefly discussed as needed to illuminate the relationships among knowledge structures in this particular context.

To show how underlying knowledge structures may be connected through relationships, this chapter focuses on three types of relationships among terms: synonymy, hierarchical relationships, and explicit mapping relationships. Background information and examples from various medical vocabularies are provided for each type of relationship, and specific implications for integration among knowledge structures are discussed.

## 2. SYNONYMY

### 2.1 Vocabulary Terms and UMLS Concepts

Except for systems that focus mainly on knowledge representation such as GALEN and SNOMED-RT (and to some extent SNOMED International and Clinical Terms Version 3), the design of medical vocabularies, including the UMLS Metathesaurus, is enumerative rather than compositional. Enumerative terminologies represent each concept by one or more term, regardless of the concept's complexity. Enumerative description is independent of language-surface forms and results in lists of precoordinated terms whose validity and consistency are difficult to test computationally. In contrast, compositional models produce a formal and often complex representation for the concepts that is suitable for manipulation by computer programs. They are usually more difficult to design and labor-intensive to populate (Rassinoux et al., 1997).

In the UMLS, concepts are defined by extension: that is, by a list of terms that are equivalent in meaning. The concept is a sort of virtual entity, identified by a unique identifier (CUI). The concept has no name directly associated with it: By convention, a term is selected from the list of preferred terms in each vocabulary to be the preferred name for this concept, according to a precedence table based on the source (Campbell, Oliver, et al., 1998; McCray & Nelson, 1995). Terms in languages other than English, translated from one vocabulary already integrated in the UMLS, are part of the same concept as their English source. The 1999 edition of the UMLS Metathesaurus includes 1,134,891 terms corresponding to 626,313 concepts. UMLS concepts are of varying complexity and granularity.

Numerous concepts are named using but a few words (e.g., "Head," "Allergic reaction," or "Screening for diabetes"). However, other concepts bear long names resulting from verbose descriptions of medical procedures (e.g., "Electrocardiographic monitoring for 24 hours by continuous computerized monitoring and non-continuous recording, and real-time data analysis utilizing a device capable of producing intermittent full-sized waveform tracings, possibly patient activated; physician review and interpretation," from the Physicians' Current Procedural Terminology) or complex structures such as chemical compounds (a name for the anti-asthmatic drug called "Theophylline" is "3,7-Dihydro-1,3-dimethyl-1H-purine-2,6-dione").

Short names may hide complex concepts. "Transurethral prostatectomy," although a fairly simple name, describes a surgical procedure where prostatic tissue surrounding the urethra is removed using a special kind of endoscope inserted through the urethra. An "Open prostatectomy," on the other hand, differs from the former by more than just one qualifier: In this surgical procedure, an incision is made in the lower abdomen through which the whole prostate is removed by means of surgical instruments.

### 2.2 Synonyms

Synonymy is based on equivalence in the meaning of terms, so that one term can be interchanged with another, with no change in meaning. Formal definitions of synonymy involve the mutual entailment of sentences containing synonym terms. For example, "Pyrosis" and "Heartburn" are synonyms, both referring to the retrosternal sensation of burning often associated with the reflux of the acid stomach contents into the oesophagus.

In practice, however, such a strict definition is rarely used, and looser definitions are preferred. The UMLS Metathesaurus uses such a loose definition for practical reasons, so that closely related terms are considered synonyms, even though they don't necessarily have the formal properties of strict synonyms (McCray & Nelson, 1995). For example, "Renal cell carcinoma" (RCC) and "Kidney cancer" are considered synonyms, which might reflect that RCC is the most common form of kidney cancer in adults. "Kidney cancer," however, is actually broader in meaning than RCC since it also includes, among others, the most common form of kidney cancer in children (nephroblastoma), and kidney metastases.

In enumerative vocabularies, lexical resemblance is the major technique used to detect possible semantic closeness among lexical items (e.g., McCray, 1998). Lexical matching techniques include case normalization, removal of genitive markers, removal of punctuation, and word sorting among other techniques (McCray, Srinivasan, & Browne, 1994).

Another source of synonyms is the vocabularies themselves. Some medical vocabularies provide a list of synonyms (e.g., SNOMED International). Vocabularies such as MeSH append to each descriptor (or Main Heading) a list of entry terms. Entry terms are not necessarily synonyms of the main heading, but since they are expected to play an identical role in information retrieval, they are closely related to, and are at least possible candidates for, synonymy.

Whether discovered through lexical resemblance techniques or contributed by a source vocabulary, synonymy among terms in the UMLS Metathesaurus is assessed after a review by human editors. Synonymous terms represent the different possible names for a concept.

## 2.3 Integration Issues Related to Synonymy

### 2.3.1 Granularity

Synonymous relationships that are valid in the context of one vocabulary, according to its granularity, may become invalid or misleading when several vocabularies of different granularity are used simultaneously or merged. For this reason, the UMLS Metathesaurus may not incorporate all synonyms suggested by the source vocabularies. For example, "Ornithosis" and "Psittacosis" are two clinical forms of the same disease, an infection transmitted by contact with infected birds and marked by a respiratory infection and flu-like symptoms. Although "Ornithosis" and "Psittacosis" are often considered synonyms, they are represented by two distinct concepts in the UMLS Metathesaurus.

The quasi-synonymous relationship between "Renal cell carcinoma" and "Kidney cancer," presented earlier is found in PDQ, the National Cancer Institute's cancer database, and has been integrated in the UMLS Metathesaurus. Another example is the synonymous relationship between "Fetal cephalhematoma" and "Cephalohematoma" provided by SNOMED International. While "cephalhematoma" and "cephalohematoma" are spelling variants, the qualifier "fetal" suggests that "Fetal cephalhematoma" is narrower than "Cephalohematoma." Practically, however, the two terms are synonyms, since cephalhematoma refers to a condition seen almost exclusively in the newborn.

## 2.3.2 Implicit Contextual Knowledge

As mentioned above, natural language processing techniques are used to compute lexical resemblance among terms as a means of identifying potential synonyms. These techniques assume that terms are both syntactically correct and fully specified entities. While most terms found in medical vocabularies are correct noun phrases (without an initial determiner), some of them are not fully specified, but rather defined by comparison to a parent term. This is especially true of vocabularies that were not designed to be used computationally, such as the International Classification of Diseases (ICD).

In ICD, choices made for the presentation of terms include tabulation and the use of dashes to avoid repeating the part of a term used in several derived terms. For example, the different forms of "Alcoholic hepatic failure" listed below the term include, among others, "- acute," "- chronic," and "- subacute." The alphabetical index can appear even more obfuscated at first sight with terms such as "- - - - cervix." The term "Female infertility of cervical origin" has to be reconstructed by finding the parts corresponding to each dash (here, Infertility / female / associated with / congenital anomaly / cervix), sometimes several pages earlier. This convention makes the index much smaller and therefore somewhat easier to read, but also renders it almost impossible to manipulate computationally.

For the same reasons, the context of a chapter or a group of terms is not always present in every term of this chapter or group. For example, the term "Prostate" (D07.5) doesn't refer to the prostate gland as an organ, but rather to a location for the condition "Carcinoma in situ of other and unspecified genital organs." A fully specified term for D07.5 would be "Carcinoma in situ of prostate."

ICD is by no means the only vocabulary where implicit knowledge of the context is necessary. Such a design is common and is beneficial as long as the vocabulary is not used for natural language processing or knowledge representation. However, since numerous UMLS-based applications take advantage of lexical processing and would be confused by multiple meanings for the same term, Metathesaurus editors often restore meaningful terms from the context prior to integrating them into the UMLS.

## 2.3.3 Evolution over Time

Synonyms in the loose definition often change over time; this is especially true for synonyms across knowledge structures (Cimino & Clayton, 1994). Some terms once considered synonyms may be split into several distinct concepts, such as what occurs when a finer grained vocabulary is encountered (refinement), or when terms showing the same surface form actually have different meanings (disambiguation). Conversely, terms originally not considered to be synonyms and assigned to different concepts may be merged into one concept, with one or more concepts being deleted. The CONCORDIA model (Oliver et al., 1999) addresses the issue of such changes in medical terminologies.

The UMLS Metathesaurus keeps track of merges, splits, and deletions. These vocabulary maintenance issues make it difficult for data encoded using one version of the Metathesaurus to be used consistently with later versions.

Concepts deleted following a merge process must be given the identifier of the concept they have been merged into. For example, in the UMLS Metathesaurus, the term "Abnormal electrocardiogram" (formerly a name for the C0000752 concept) was merged into the C0522055 concept ("Abnormal electrocardiographic finding") in 1999.

Conversely no simple solution exists for splits. To decide whether the original concept C (named by term T), now split into $C_1$ (named by term $T_1$) and $C_2$ (named by term $T_2$), should be coded $C_1$ rather than $C_2$ would require additional information about its original meaning. The original concept C should be retained and be renamed "$T_1$ or $T_2$," to ensure compatibility with older data. For example, an earlier version of the UMLS used a single concept for "Cryptorchidism" and "Ectopia testis." Both terms suggest that the testicle failed to descend into the scrotum. However, in cryptorchidism the testicle is located at some point on its migration path, which is not the case in ectopia testis. Because of this distinction, the treatment for these two conditions can be quite different, and thus the two terms are not synonyms to a urologic surgeon. This was corrected in a subsequent version of the UMLS by removing "Ectopia testis" from the synonyms of "Cryptorchidism," and by creating a new concept for it. As a consequence, the meaning of the original concept drifted from "Cryptorchidism or Ectopia testis" to "Cryptorchidism [only]," making it difficult to compare data coded with different versions of the UMLS (Bodenreider, Burgun, et al., 1998).

This problem, although more likely to occur across heterogeneous data structures, can also occur within a single vocabulary family (e.g., the evolution of the ICD, from the 9th to the 10th revision).

## 3. HIERARCHICAL RELATIONSHIPS

Hierarchical relationships present a powerful means for structuring knowledge. Three primary structural models are commonly used in medical vocabularies: trees, graphs, and conceptual structures.

Traditional medical classifications are monohierarchical; that is, they have a simple single-tree architecture and use the position in the tree to identify concepts. The ICD is organized according to this architecture.

Other vocabularies allow concepts to have several parent concepts and do not use concept identifiers directly to describe their architecture. Concepts are usually given a unique identifier, while the structure is described either by independent identifiers or by a list of parent-child pairs based on the unique identifiers. MeSH descriptors, for example, have both one unique identifier and one or more tree numbers. Clinical Terms Version 3 and GALEN also use polyhierarchical structures. Such a data structure is called a directed acyclic graph (DAG).

Conceptual graphs (Sowa, 1984) have been used in the biomedical domain to address issues as diverse as clinical concept and data representation, classification systems, information retrieval, and natural language understanding and processing (Volot, Joubert, & Fieschi, 1998); however, few medical vocabularies actually use them. Medical terminology systems based on conceptual structures and description logic formalisms include GALEN (Rector et al., 1997), using the GALEN Representation and Integration Language (GRAIL), and SNOMED-RT (Spackman, Campbell, & Cote, 1997), using the Knowledge Representation System Specification (KRSS).

## 3.1 UMLS Metathesaurus

Since it preserves the original structure of its source vocabularies, some of which allow multiple inheritance, the UMLS Metathesaurus has a *de facto* graph structure. Moreover, by combining hierarchies (or contexts) from different sources, the UMLS Metathesaurus not only allows but also favors multiple inheritance. The UMLS Metathesaurus structure is thus compatible with the definition of a directed acyclic graph. UMLS concepts have unique identifiers and pairs of concept identifiers, associated by relationship qualifiers, which are used to describe the structure of the UMLS Metathesaurus.

Compared to that of any given source vocabulary, the context offered by the UMLS Metathesaurus is both broader and deeper. A broader context means that the ancestors of a concept are not necessarily constrained to any single particular representation of the world or ontology. A deeper context means that the granularity of the UMLS Metathesaurus is usually much finer than that of any source vocabulary.

Hierarchical relationships account for roughly half of the relationships represented in the UMLS Metathesaurus, excluding those, such as siblings, that are derived from other relationships. Some hierarchical relationships found in the UMLS Metathesaurus come from the source vocabularies. By convention, these relationships are called parent/child relationships. Even if these relationships were originally defined at the term level (i.e., among terms in a particular vocabulary), they are recorded at the concept level in the UMLS Metathesaurus, in the form of pairs of concept identifiers associated with a PAR (parent) or CHD (child) relationship type.

The UMLS Metathesaurus has another type of hierarchical relationship, called "broader in meaning" and "narrower in meaning," identified by the "RB" and "RN" relationship types. These hierarchical relationships differ from the former only by virtue of their origin. Instead of being inherited form the source vocabularies, the RB/RN relationships are added to the original structure using different methods. A relationship between two terms is first suggested by lexical analysis of the terms, refined through a facts database, and possibly reviewed by human editors (Sperzel et al., 1992). Equivalent strategies have been used outside the UMLS context to build SNOMED-RT (Campbell, Tuttle, & Spackman, 1998) or to merge overlapping terminologies such as SNOMED International and LOINC (Dolin et al., 1998). As with synonymy, hierarchical relationships can also be established by human editors in the absence of any common lexical features (e.g., the relationship of "Hypoadrenalism" to "Severe adrenal insufficiency").

Some of the RB/RN relationships are redundant with their PAR/CHD counterparts (e.g., the relationship of "Adrenal Gland Diseases" to "Adrenal Cortex Diseases" is recorded with both PAR and RB identifiers). However, allowing the term comparison process to be performed independently from the context of a given vocabulary permits the discovery of relationships among concepts coming from different sources that by definition cannot be inherited from the sources. For example, the ICD-10 term "Other disorders of adrenal gland" is considered narrower than the MeSH term "Adrenal Gland Diseases," although "Adrenal Gland Diseases" does not appear in ICD-10 hierarchies nor does "Other disorders of adrenal gland" in MeSH's.

Figure 1 provides the hierarchical context (ancestors and descendants) for "Addison's Disease" in the UMLS Metathesaurus. Although for practical reasons only part of the context is represented, the graph demonstrates some of the following advantages of the UMLS Metathesaurus structure. The granularity in the UMLS Metathesaurus is finer than in any other source vocabulary. For example, the five-level C19 MeSH hierarchy for "Addison's Disease" expands to ten levels in the UMLS. The structure also shows that an autoimmune disorder is only one possible causal mechanism for Addison's disease by making "Addison's disease due to autoimmunity" a child of "Addison's Disease." Finally, even the ICD-10 hierarchy, although comprising classification-specific terms with little meaning outside the classification itself (e.g., "Disorders of other endocrine glands"), is linked to meaningful concepts through relationships added by the Metathesaurus editors.

### 3.2    Nature of Hierarchical Relationships

Hierarchical relationships are based on subsumptive principles and include two major kinds of relationships (McCray & Nelson, 1995). Hyponymy (or the generic relation) is represented by the "isa" relation (is a kind of) or by "narrower than." "X isa Y" means that X and Y share essential features (called genus), while X has some special feature(s) (called differentia) that makes it different from Y and from other hyponyms of X. The generic relation is transitive. Concepts such as diseases, findings, and procedures can be organized by a generic relation. Meronymy (or the partitive relation) is represented by the "part_of" relation, that is, the part to whole relation. The partitive relation is not necessarily transitive. Spatial, temporal, and functional concepts may be organized by a partitive relation.

Informally, a composite concept description can be subsumed to another one for any of the following reasons (Bernauer, 1994):

- Introduction of a specializing criterion to the base concept, or the generic refinement of a concept element;
- Introduction of a partitive criterion to the base concept, or the partitive refinement of a concept element; or
- Introduction of a conjunctive coordination to the base concept, or to a concept element.

For example, the UMLS hierarchy for "Aortic Aneurysm" (the dilatation of the aorta), is organized by "isa" relations. The actual subsumptive principle, however, is not explicit in the UMLS (fig. 2).

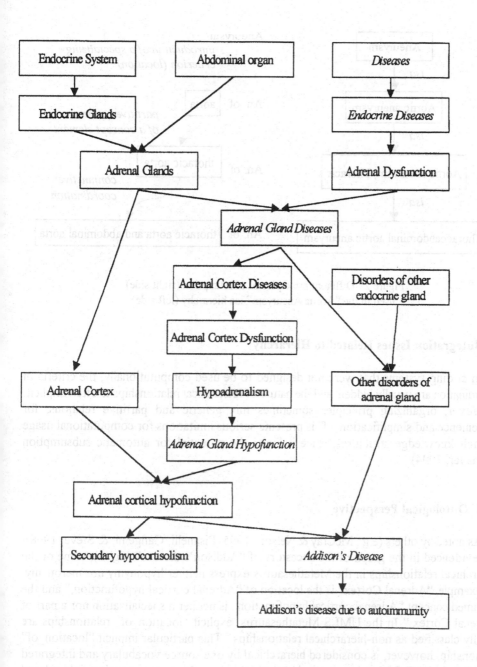

Figure 1. UMLS context for "Addison's Disease" (partial).
Concepts in italics belong to the C19 MeSH hierarchy.

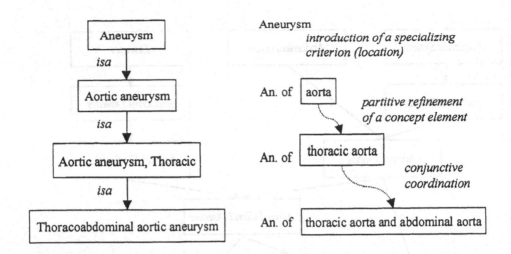

Figure 2.  Different principles of subsumption (right side)
used in the "Aortic Aneurysm" isa hierarchy (left side)

## 3.3  Integration Issues Related to Hierarchy

In coding systems that were not designed to be used computationally, the criteria of subordination are usually hidden, and the nature of hierarchical relationships is often implicit. Moreover, organizing principles sometimes mix generic and partitive relations, for convenience and simplification. This presents serious limitations for computational usage of such knowledge structures, since it limits the potential for automatic subsumption (Bernauer, 1994).

### 3.3.1  Ontological Perspective

As noted by others (e.g., McCray & Nelson, 1995; Pisanelli, Gangemi, & Steve, 1998), and evidenced in the graph of the ancestors of "Addison's disease" (fig. 3), some of the hierarchical relationships in the Metathesaurus express neither hyponymy nor meronymy. For example, "Adrenal Cortex" is the location of "Adrenal cortical hypofunction," and the subsumed concept "Adrenal cortical hypofunction" is neither a specialization nor a part of "Adrenal Cortex." In the UMLS Metathesaurus, explicit "location_of" relationships are usually classified as non-hierarchical relationships. This particular implicit "location_of" relationship, however, is considered hierarchical by one source vocabulary and integrated as such in the UMLS Metathesaurus. Although clearly in the same semantic neighborhood as "Addison's disease," "Adrenal Cortex" cannot be considered an ancestor of "Addison's disease" from an ontological point of view.

In contrast, many hierarchical relationships whose nature is not made explicit are indeed true "isa" relationships and could contribute to defining an ontology for the biomedical domain from the UMLS or from some combination of its source vocabularies. For example, although unqualified in the UMLS, the relationship of "Addison's disease due to autoimmunity" to "Addison's Disease" is actually an "isa" relationship (specialization). Making it explicit would allow "Addison's disease due to autoimmunity" to inherit properties from "Addison's Disease."

### 3.3.2 Granularity, Redundancy, and Simplification

Owing to differences in granularity among medical vocabularies, terms considered siblings in one vocabulary might be hierarchically related in a finer-grained vocabulary. This does not cause problems so long as the hierarchical relationships from different vocabularies are consistent, which is usually the case. For example, "Addison's Disease" and "Addison's disease due to autoimmunity" are two direct children of "Adrenal Gland Diseases" in SNOMED International, while other vocabularies provide a more detailed representation (Figure 3).

Using graph theory parlance, several possible paths exist from "Adrenal Gland Diseases" to "Addison's Disease," including a direct one provided by SNOMED International and an indirect one coming from MeSH. This redundancy, although useful for certain purposes, also makes it more difficult to process the knowledge, for example to visualize the concepts hierarchically related to a given concept. One solution to simplify the knowledge structure is to remove the relationships that can be inferred from other relationships by transitivity. Performed on graphs, this operation is known as transitive reduction. The graph representing the UMLS context for "Addison's Disease" (fig. 1 shows 19 vertices connected by 20 edges; there were 46 edges in the graph prior to the transitive reduction.

### 3.3.3 Implicit Knowledge

As is the case for synonymy, the lack of fully specified terms in certain vocabularies can be a source of erroneous relationships. For example, the term "Infection" found as a child of "Pulmonary disorders" and parent of "Pneumonia" is unambiguously understood as "Lung infection" by a human reader, since it belongs to the "Pulmonary" chapter of COSTAR. For natural language processing tools, however, there is no reason to consider the term "Infection" in COSTAR differently from the same term in any other vocabulary or in another chapter of the same vocabulary.

Inter-concept relationships, particularly those discovered by lexical techniques, also suffer from problems of implicit knowledge. In this example, "Infection" incorrectly becomes a synonym of "Lung infection," making "Pneumonia" a sibling of "Otitis media" (ear infection). Assuming that the parent/child relationships are "isa" relations, "Pneumonia isa Infection" remains true, whereas "Otitis isa Lung infection" does not.

### 3.3.4 Circular Hierarchical Relationships

As noted in other studies of inter-concept relationships in the UMLS Metathesaurus (e.g., Pisanelli, Gangemi, & Steve, 1998), the graph of UMLS concepts described by pairs of hierarchically related concepts contains cycles. In other words, some concepts happen to be both ancestors and descendants of themselves (loop), or of another concept (circular hierarchical relationship).

Most circular hierarchical relationships result from the way terms are integrated in the UMLS, rather than from conflicting organizations of the knowledge among medical vocabularies; that is, conflicts at the concept level come from relationships defined at the term level. Certain medical vocabularies use underspecified terms, containing qualifiers such as "unspecified" or "not otherwise specified," that are clustered by convention together with their specified equivalent in the UMLS. This results in loops if the two terms are in direct hierarchical dependence in one vocabulary, and in circular hierarchical relationships otherwise. Examples of loops include ICD-10 terms "Hodgkin's disease" (C81) and its child "Hodgkin's disease, unspecified" (C81.9), both names for the same UMLS concept C0019829. The following hierarchy extracted from the Clinical Terms Version 3 results in a direct circular hierarchical relationship when integrated in the UMLS. "Ligament reconstruction" is a parent of "Other reconstruction of ligament," which is a parent of "Reconstruction of ligament NOS." Here, the first and the last term in the hierarchy are clustered into the same UMLS concept.

Some cycles involve three concepts or more. Term ambiguity and the use of non-hierarchical relations in hierarchies (e.g., the relations between a disease and its symptoms, or the relations among chemical compounds) are responsible for a large number of these cycles. Other causes include inconsistencies among vocabularies, for example in the semantics of the "and" and "or" conjunctions, as also noted by other authors (Mendonca et al., 1998).

## 4. EXPLICIT MAPPING RELATIONSHIPS

Some medical vocabularies explicitly include mapping relationships in their structure. The target terms or concepts are either part of the vocabulary itself (internal mapping) or part of another vocabulary (external mapping). Although most mapping relationships come from or are endorsed by the developers of at least one of the vocabularies involved, some are provided by institutions unrelated to either vocabulary.

### 4.1 External Mapping Relationships

External mapping relationships have been developed for practical reasons: While there is no standard or common structure for medical vocabularies, there is a strong need for terms to be translated from one coding system to another one. Some vocabularies include mapping relationships to other vocabularies, allowing users to produce reports based on a mandatory coding system while using a more clinically oriented terminology instead (Read,

Sanderson, & Drennan, 1995).

For example, the International Classification of Primary Care (ICPC), the Clinical Terms Version 3 (CTV3), SNOMED International, and GALEN provide mapping relationships to the International Classification of Diseases (ICD). CTV3 also provides mapping relationships to OPCS-4, the coding system used in the United Kingdom for procedures. Mapping relationships have also been established from one version of ICD to the next or to the previous one. More generally, major coding systems provide cross-references to other coding systems.

Here again, mapping relationships are seldom one-to-one relationships. More often, due to differences in structure and/or granularity between the source and target vocabularies, they are one-to-many or even many-to-many relationships, which makes them difficult to use in an automated coding process. For example, ICPC-2 code P74 ("Anxiety disorder / anxiety state") is mapped to several ICD-10 codes. The ICD terms mapped to (including "Panic disorder" and "Generalized anxiety disorder") are actually narrower than the ICPC-2 term mapped from. As a consequence, the ICPC-2 term can not be translated into an ICD term other than "Anxiety disorder, unspecified" without additional clinical information. For one-to-many mappings, CTV3 provides a list of potential matches in the target coding system and highlight the most likely, to be used as default.

These mapping relationships are often produced manually. GALEN, however, automatically maps terms from different sources, as soon as these terms have been mapped manually to GALEN.

## 4.2 Mapping Relationships in the UMLS

Among its 626,313 concepts, the UMLS Metathesaurus acknowledges 328,145 mapping relationships (i.e., relationships whose attribute is "mapped_to"). The major source (89%) of mapping relationships is the Medical Subject Headings (MeSH) whose mapping from supplementary concepts to Main Headings is fully preserved in the UMLS. SNOMED International provides an additional 6% of the Metathesaurus mapping relationships.

Although all of them bear the same "mapped_to" relationship attribute, distinctions can be seen among mapping relationships from different source vocabularies. Mapping relationships inherited from MeSH are considered hierarchical relationships. The source concept is considered subsumed by the target concept, which usually holds true since the granularity of the supplementary concepts tends to be finer than that of the main headings. SNOMED International provides the mapping of SNOMED concepts to ICD-9-CM concepts. In this case, the source and target concepts are considered near-synonyms, or at least very close in meaning. In some cases, the terms naming the SNOMED and the ICD concepts are true synonyms and belong to the same UMLS concept. Mapping relationships from other sources are considered "other relationships," meaning that their nature is not necessarily hierarchical and not further specified. Mapping relationships account for 31% of the total number of hierarchical relationships, 15% of the near-synonyms, and 6% of the "other relationships."

In addition to mapping relationships, the UMLS Metathesaurus also provides some 7,000 "associated expressions" (ATXs) to map terms, mostly from ICD-9-CM to MeSH.

ATXs are created by human indexers from elementary concepts combined with both logical operators (i.e., AND, OR, NOT) and from relationships between MeSH Main Headings and subheadings. For example, the term "Mumps pancreatitis" has the associated expression "Mumps/complications AND Pancreatitis/etiology" in which the two MeSH main headings "Mumps" and "Pancreatitis" are qualified by a subheading.

## Endnotes

1. A list of the medical vocabularies mentioned in this chapter is given in the Appendix.

2. Formerly called "Read Codes."

3. Announced recently, the merging of SNOMED-RT and Clinical Terms Version 3 should create SNOMED-CT, a comprehensive language of health to support the computerized patient record.

## Acknowledgments

We would like to thank Geneviève Botti, Anita Burgun, Stuart Nelson, Jeremy Rogers, and Pierre Zweigenbaum for thoughtful comments on earlier versions of this manuscript.

## Appendix

Clinical Terms Version 3 (**CTV3**, formerly called "Read Codes"). England: National Health Service Centre for Coding and Classification, March, 1998. For information: <http://www.nhsccc.exec.nhs.uk> [2000, July 27].

Computer-Stored Ambulatory Records (**COSTAR**). Boston: Massachusetts General Hospital, 1995.

Physicians' Current Procedural Terminology (**CPT**). 4th ed. Chicago: American Medical Association, 1999. For information: <http://www.ama-assn.org/med-sci/cpt/coding.htm> [2000, July 27].

Generalised Architecture for Languages, Encyclopaedias, and Nomenclatures in medicine (**GALEN**). Manchester, Eng.: *Open*GALEN. For information: <http://www.opengalen.org> [2000, July 27].

International Classification of Diseases: 9th revision, Clinical Modification (**ICD-9-CM**). 6th ed. Washington, DC: Health Care Financing Administration, July, 1998. For information: <http://www.hcfa.gov/stats/pufiles.htm> [2000, July 27].

International Statistical Classification of Diseases and Related Health Problems (**ICD-10**). 10th rev. Geneva World Health Organization, 1998. For information: <http://www.who.int/whosis/icd10/index.html> [2000, July 27].

International Classification of Primary Care (**ICPC**). Denmark: World Organisation of Family Doctors, 1993. For information: <http://www.wonca.org/wonca_home.htm>

[2000, July 27].

Logical Observation Identifiers, Names and Codes (**LOINC**). Version 1.0j. Indianapolis: The Regenstrief Institute, 1997. For information: <http://www.mcis.duke.edu/standards/termcode/loinc.htm> [2000, July 27].

Medical Subject Headings (**MeSH**). Bethesda, MD: National Library of Medicine, 1999. For information: <http://www.nlm.nih.gov/mesh/meshhome.html> [2000, July 27].

Physician Data Query Online System (**PDQ**). Bethesda, MD: National Cancer Institute, August, 1998. For information: <http://cancernet.nci.nih.gov/pdqfull.html> [2000, July 27].

Systematized Nomenclature of Human and Veterinary Medicine: **SNOMED** International. Version 3.5. Northfield, IL: College of American Pathologists; Schaumburg, IL: American Veterinary Medical Association, 1998. For information: <http://www.snomed.org> [2000, July 27].

Systematized Nomenclature of Human and Veterinary Medicine-Reference Terminology: **SNOMED-RT**. Northfield, IL: College of American Pathologists. For information: <http://www.snomed.org> [2000, July 27].

Unified Medical Language System (**UMLS**). Bethesda (MD): National Library of Medicine, 1999. For information: <http://www.nlm.nih.gov/pubs/factsheets/umls.html> [2000, July 27].

## References

Bernauer, J. (1994). Subsumption principles underlying medical concept systems and their formal reconstruction. *Proceedings of the 18th Annual Symposium on Computer Applications in Medical Care,* 140-144.

Bodenreider, O., Burgun, A., Botti, G., Fieschi, M., Le Beux, P., & Kohler, F. (1998). Evaluation of the Unified Medical Language System as a medical knowledge source. *Journal of the American Medical Informatics Association,* 5(1), 76-87.

Bodenreider, O., Nelson, S. J., Hole, W. T., & Chang, H. F. (1998). Beyond synonymy: Exploiting the UMLS semantics in mapping vocabularies. *Proceedings of the 1998 AMIA Annual Fall Symposium,* 815-819.

Campbell, J. R., Carpenter, P., Sneiderman, C., Cohn, S., Chute, C. G., & Warren, J. (1997). Phase II evaluation of clinical coding schemes: Completeness, taxonomy, mapping, definitions, and clarity. CPRI Work Group on Codes and Structures. *Journal of the American Medical Informatics Association,* 4(3), 238-251.

Campbell, K. E., Oliver, D. E., Spackman, K. A., & Shortliffe, E. H. (1998). Representing thoughts, words, and things in the UMLS. *Journal of the American Medical Informatics Association,* 5(5), 421-431.

Campbell, K. E., Tuttle, M. S., & Spackman, K. A. (1998). A "lexically-suggested logical closure" metric for medical terminology maturity. *Proceedings of the 1998 AMIA Annual Fall Symposium,* 785-789.

Chute, C. G., Cohn, S. P., & Campbell, J. R. (1998). A framework for comprehensive health terminology systems in the United States: Development guidelines, criteria for selection, and public policy implications. ANSI Healthcare Informatics Standards Board

Vocabulary Working Group and the Computer-Based Patient Records Institute Working Group on Codes and Structures. *Journal of the American Medical Informatics Association,* 5(6), 503-510.

Chute, C. G., Cohn, S. P., Campbell, K. E., Oliver, D. E., & Campbell, J. R. (1996). The content coverage of clinical classifications. For The Computer-Based Patient Record Institute's Work Group on Codes & Structures. *Journal of the American Medical Informatics Association,* 3(3), 224-233.

Cimino, J. J. (1996). Review paper: Coding systems in health care. *Methods of Information in Medicine,* 35, 273-284.

Cimino, J. J. (1998). Desiderata for controlled medical vocabularies in the twenty-first century. *Methods of Information in Medicine,* 37, 394-403.

Cimino, J. J., & Clayton, P. D. (1994). Coping with changing controlled vocabularies. *Proceedings of the 18th Annual Symposium on Computer Applications in Medical Care,* 135-139.

Cimino, J. J., Johnson, S. B., Peng, P., & Aguirre, A. (1993). From ICD9-CM to MeSH using the UMLS: A how-to guide. *Proceedings of the 17th Annual Symposium on Computer Applications in Medical Care,* 730-734.

Dessena, S., Rossi Mori, A., & Galeazzi, E. (1999). Development of a cross-thesaurus with Internet-based refinement supported by UMLS. *International Journal of Medical Informatics,* 53, 29-41.

Dolin, R. H., Huff, S. M., Rocha, R. A., Spackman, K. A., & Campbell, K. E. (1998). Evaluation of a "lexically assign, logically refine" strategy for semi-automated integration of overlapping terminologies. *Journal of the American Medical Informatics Association,* 5(2), 203-213.

Evans, D. A., Cimino, J. J., Hersh, W. R., Huff, S. M., & Bell, D. S. (1994). Toward a medical-concept representation language. The Canon Group. *Journal of the American Medical Informatics Association,* 1(3), 207-217.

Humphreys, B. L., Lindberg, D. A., Schoolman, H. M., & Barnett, G. O. (1998). The Unified Medical Language System: An informatics research collaboration. *Journal of the American Medical Informatics Association,* 5(1), 1-11.

Lindberg, D. A., Humphreys, B. L., & McCray, A. T. (1993). The Unified Medical Language System. *Methods of Information in Medicine,* 32, 281-291.

McCray, A. T. (1998). The nature of lexical knowledge. *Methods of Information in Medicine,* 37(4-5), 353-360.

McCray, A. T., & Nelson, S. J. (1995). The representation of meaning in the UMLS. *Methods of Information in Medicine,* 34, 193-201.

McCray, A. T., Srinivasan, S., & Browne, A. C. (1994). Lexical methods for managing variation in biomedical terminologies. *Proceedings of the 18th Annual Symposium on Computer Applications in Medical Care,* 235-239.

Mendonca, E. A., Cimino, J. J., Campbell, K. E., & Spackman, K. A. (1998). Reproducibility of interpreting "and" and "or" in terminology systems. *Proceedings of the 1998 AMIA Annual Fall Symposium,* 790-794.

Nelson, S. J., Fuller, L. F., Erlbaum, M. S., Tuttle, M. S., Sherertz, D. D., & Olson, N. E. (1992). The semantic structure of the UMLS Metathesaurus. *Proceedings of the 16th Annual Symposium on Computer Applications in Medical Care,* 649-653.

Oliver, D. E., Shahar, Y., Shortliffe, E. H., & Musen, M. A. (1999). Representation of change in controlled medical terminologies. *Artificial Intelligence in Medicine,* 15, 53-76.

Pisanelli, D. M., Gangemi, A., & Steve, G. (1998). An ontological analysis of the UMLS Methathesaurus. *Proceedings of the 1998 AMIA Annual Fall Symposium,* 810-814.

Rada, R., Ghaoui, C., Russell, J., & Taylor, M. (1993). Approaches to the construction of a medical informatics glossary and thesaurus. *Medical Informatics (London),* 18, 69-78.

Rassinoux, A. M., Miller, R. A., Baud, R. H., & Scherrer, J. R. (1997). Compositional and enumerative designs for medical language representation. *Proceedings of the 1998 AMIA Annual Fall Symposium,* 620-624.

Read, J. D., Sanderson, H. F., & Drennan, Y. M. (1995). Terming, encoding, and grouping. *Medinfo,* 8 (Pt 1), 56-59.

Rector, A., Rossi Mori, A., Consorti, M. F., & Zanstra, P. (1998). Practical development of re-usable terminologies: GALEN-IN-USE and the GALEN Organisation. *International Journal of Medical Informatics,* 48, 71-84.

Rector, A. L., Bechhofer, S., Goble, C. A., Horrocks, I., Nowlan, W. A., & Solomon, W. D. (1997). The GRAIL concept modelling language for medical terminology. *Artificial Intelligence in Medicine,* 9, 139-171.

Rector, A. L., & Nowlan, W. A. (1994). The GALEN project. *Computer Methods and Programs in Biomedicine,* 45, 75-78.

Rector, A. L., Solomon, W. D., Nowlan, W. A., Rush, T. W., Zanstra, P. E., & Claassen, W. M. (1995). A terminology server for medical language and medical information systems. *Methods of Information in Medicine,* 34, 147-157.

Rossi Mori, A., Bernauer, J., Pakarinen, V., Rector, A. L., De Vries-Robbe, P., Ceusters, W., Hurlen, P., Ogonowski, A., & Olesen, H. (1993). Models for representation of terminologies and coding systems in medicine. *Studies in Health Technology and Informatics,* 6, 92-104.

Rossi Mori, A., Consorti, F., & Galeazzi, E. (1998). Standards to support development of terminological systems for healthcare telematics. *Methods of Information in Medicine,* 37, 551-563.

Sherertz, D. D., Olson, N. E., Tuttle, M. S., & Erlbaum, M. S. (1990). Source inversion and matching in the UMLS Metathesaurus. *Proceedings of the 14th Annual Symposium on Computer Applications in Medical Care,* 141-145.

Sowa, J. F. (1984). *Conceptual Structures: Information Processing in Mind and Machine.* Reading, MA: Addison-Wesley.

Spackman, K. A., Campbell, K. E., & Cote, R. A. (1997). SNOMED RT: A reference terminology for health care. *Proceedings of the 1997 AMIA Annual Fall Symposium,* 640-644.

Sperzel, W. D., Tuttle, M. S., Olson, N. E., Erlbaum, M. S., Saurez-Munist, O., Sherertz, D. D., & Fuller, L. F. (1992). The Meta-1.2 engine: A refined strategy for linking biomedical vocabularies. *Proceedings of the 16th Annual Symposium on Computer Applications in Medical Care,* 304-308.

Suarez-Munist, O. N., Tuttle, M. S., Olson, N. E., Erlbaum, M. S., Sherertz, D. D., Lipow, S. S., Cole, W. G., Keck, K. D., & Davis, A. N. (1996). MEME-II supports the cooperative management of terminology. *Proceedings of the 1998 AMIA Annual Fall*

*Symposium*, 84-88.

Tuttle, M. S., Olson, N. E., Campbell, K. E., Sherertz, D. D., Nelson, S. J., & Cole, W. G. (1994). Formal properties of the Metathesaurus. *Proceedings of the 18th Annual Symposium on Computer Applications in Medical Care*, 145-149.

Tuttle, M. S., Suarez-Munist, O. N., Olson, N. E., Sherertz, D. D., Sperzel, W. D., Erlbaum, M. S., Fuller, L. F., Hole, W. T., Nelson, S. J., Cole, W. G., & et al. (1995). Merging terminologies. *Medinfo*, 8 (Pt 1), 162-166.

Volot, F., Joubert, M., & Fieschi, M. (1998). Review of biomedical knowledge and data representation with conceptual graphs. *Methods of Information in Medicine*, 37, 86-96.

# Chapter 7

# Relationships in Classificatory Structure and Meaning

Clare Beghtol
*Faculty of Information Studies, University of Toronto, Toronto, ON Canada*

**Abstract:**
    In a changing information environment, we need to reassess each element of bibliographic control, including classification theories and systems. Every classification system is a theoretical construct imposed on "reality." The classificatory relationships that are assumed to be valuable have generally received less attention than the topics included in the systems. Relationships are functions of both the syntactic and semantic axes of classification systems, and both explicit and implicit relationships are discussed. Examples are drawn from a number of different systems, both bibliographic and non-bibliographic, and the cultural warrant (i.e., the sociocultural context) of classification systems is examined. The part-whole relationship is discussed as an example of a universally valid concept that is treated as a component of the cultural warrant of a classification system.

## 1. INTRODUCTION

The concept of "relationship," like those of "classification," "taxonomy," "ontology," and indeed "concept" itself, is transdisciplinary. No discipline or domain can claim these metalevel abstractions as its own. At the same time, the complexities of the world of knowledge mean that we may no longer consider any knowledge area to be unified or stable. The premise of this paper is that changing knowledge structures and the increased globalization of information exchange require rethinking of all aspects of bibliographic classification systems, including the kinds of relationships we habitually include in the systems. This paper builds on previous research (e.g., Beghtol, 1997b, 1998). Its general purpose is to raise questions, identify issues, and suggest potentially useful research areas. This broadly exploratory perspective is designed to help discern patterns in the treatment of relationships in bibliographic classification theory and systems, that is, how relationships are expressed and what types of relationships are commonly used. One potentially useful kind of exploration is the detailed discussion of specific kinds of relationships in order to assess their suitability for bibliographic classification. As an example of this kind of exploration, the part-whole relationship is examined. Some of the implications of these exploratory endeavors are described.

As many authors point out, "relation" was one of Aristotle's ten fundamental categories of existence, and it has been further asserted that "information is a relationship" (Barlow, 1994, p. 13). All possible relationships, however, have not been discovered or utilized in

*C. A. Bean and R. Green (eds.), Relationships in the Organization of Knowledge,* 99–113.

information retrieval systems (Weinberg, 1995), and no taxonomy of all kinds of relationships has been published (Soergel, 1998). In his major study of general types of relationships, Perreault identified 120 relationships grouped and notated in a triad structure. For example, his Subsumptive triad contained Type-Kind, Whole-Part, and Subject-Property (1994, p. 193, fig. 6). Perreault based his study on writers in various fields from Aristotle to the present (p. 191, fig. 3). One of his objectives was to supply potentially useful relationships that could replace the non-specific relationship expressed by the colon in *Universal Decimal Classification* (UDC) notation and that could be used for electronic information retrieval.

A number of other studies of kinds of relationships and their various potential uses for information retrieval have been carried out, and a few examples can be given. Coates identified twenty relationships that could obtain between the three components Thing, Material, and Action and tabulated how these compounds were usually described in subject headings (1960, ff. 54, Relationship Table). Stephens (1991) developed a classification of semantic relations for 5100 relations identified in the CYC system, which attempts to encode common sense knowledge about the world for computer manipulation. Byrne and McCracken (1999) broke down the usual hierarchical, equivalence, and associative relations found in thesaural systems into various subtypes, and added the capability of "relational inheritance" in order to increase retrieval precision. Four relations could be inherited: has_semantic_role, has_measurement, has_subject_category, and has_component.

In a working draft, the Relations Working Group of the Dublin Core Metadata Initiative (1997) identified six relationship pairs: Part-Whole relations, Version relations, Format relations, Reference relations, Creative relations, and Dependency relations. Some pairs are reciprocal. For example, the Reference relation contains two sub-relations (References and IsReferencedBy) designed to express the referral relationship from either of the two resources to the other. In this case, it is possible for one resource both to cite and to be cited by another, so the relation is potentially symmetrical as well as reciprocal. In other cases, however, the relationship is not normally symmetrical. For example, values for Creative relations are IsBasedOn and IsBasisFor. It seems unlikely that two resources would both be based on and the basis for each other at the same time, although it is possible that over time a kind of "dialogue relation" might obtain between two such resources if each was used by the other either consecutively or simultaneously. The Cross-Domain Working Group of the Dublin Core Metadata Initiative noted that a relation might have a semantic qualifier to clarify the relationship of one resource to another (LeVan, 1998), but these qualifiers were not specified.[1] The difficulty of identifying and expressing relationships has thus been recognized in recent metadata work, which exploits only a few of the variety of relationships that we can find in natural and artificial languages. Nevertheless, these and other studies are valuable and may prove productive for information retrieval in general.

## 2.  STRUCTURE AND MEANING IN
##     BIBLIOGRAPHIC CLASSIFICATION SYSTEMS

It is usually said that classification systems show topics and their relations, but research into the nature(s) and purpose(s) of these relationships has been undertaken less often than research into the topics that are to be established in the system. The only classification system based on relationships is Farradane's Relational Indexing system (e.g., Farradane, 1980), which was derived from the psychological theories of J. P. Guilford. Farradane's system included nine relationships, specifically Concurrence, Self-activity, Association, Equivalence, Dimensional (time, space, state), Appurtenance, Distinctness, Reaction, and Functional dependence (causation). These were combined to express any relationship(s) that might obtain between document subjects, and Farradane invented a way of diagramming these nine relations so they could be retrieved by computer.

In general, relationships in bibliographic classification systems are functions of both the syntactic (i.e., structural) and the semantic (i.e., meaning) axes of the systems (Coates, 1978; Beghtol, 1986a). In this paper, no distinction is drawn between syntax and structure or between semantics and meaning (cf. Tranöy, 1959). Structure and meaning are not mutually exclusive in either natural or artificial languages, but like many similarly artificial theoretical distinctions, this one provides a useful basis for organizing discussion.

## 2.1 Structural Relationships in Bibliographic Classification Systems

Bibliographic classifications are generally organized hierarchically. Although enumerative and faceted classification systems are often seen as opposing types, hierarchical structure is present in both at various levels of subdivision. In both types, the sub-groups (i.e., sub-classes in enumerative and sub-facets or foci in faceted systems) are most often conceptualized and presented hierarchically. In addition, classes and sub-classes are enumerated in both types. What usually differs more radically between the two types of systems is how the hierarchy is displayed (Beghtol, 1997a), and whether and how notational synthesis can be carried out. Notational synthesis is always available in faceted systems, but is not necessarily possible in enumerative ones. The distinction between allowing notational synthesis or not is thus a more salient difference between enumerative and faceted classifications than the presence or absence of hierarchy.

The function of notational synthesis is to allow the expression of topic combinations that have not been listed in the schedules. Theoretically, the greater the potential for synthesis, the shorter the schedules become. Particularly in conjunction with facet analysis, notational synthesis economically allows precise specification of topics because possible topic combinations do not have to be identified in advance and listed in the schedules. Thus, in theory any combination of topics, even those that were not needed or perhaps not even imagined when the classification was created, can be formulated through notational synthesis.[2]

Such synthetic notations, however, do not allow precise expression of the relationships between the topics for which a notation, whether enumerated or synthesized, has been developed. In general, joining notational elements implies that the notated topics exist in the document in question. When a standardized facet formula with facet indicators (such as Ranganathan's PMEST formula with its indicators) exists for the classification, the role of a certain topic element in the overall subject can be ascertained.[3] In some cases, this role implies a certain relationship between topics. For example, a space facet notating France and a time facet notating the nineteenth century implies that the document treats a certain topic in nineteenth-century France. Such a relationship is understood by convention. These space and time facets do not imply, for example, that the document was written in France during the nineteenth century. Geo-political and temporal elements of the document itself are assumed to be treated by the bibliographic description of the document.

Implied relationships also exist by virtue of the hierarchical structure of bibliographic classification systems. Usually the hierarchy is a taxonomic one, that is, one in which an array of coordinate sub-classes is made up of separate kinds of the entity named in the superordinate class. For example, in the *Library of Congress Classification* (LCC) Class HD, the hierarchy Economic History and Conditions, Labor, Wages, Methods of Remuneration, By Method is subdivided alphabetically by, for example, Annual wage, Bonus, Checkweighting, Cost-of-Living adjustments. These are all kinds of remuneration, and these enumerated coordinate classes have a syntactic "kind of" relation to the superordinate class. In some classification systems, such as the *Dewey Decimal Classification* (DDC), the notation for a concept often expresses the hierarchical level of the concept. In other systems, however, particularly ones with a retroactive notation (e.g., *Bliss Bibliographic Classification*, 2nd ed., BC2), the notation does not reflect the hierarchical level of a concept within the classification system.[4]

These kinds of syntactic structural relationships exhibit the relationship of sub-classes to their immediately superordinate classes. By following the hierarchy upward, one arrives eventually at the most general statement of the topic for that main class. Sometimes notational synthesis allows one to notate the relationship of a certain topic in one main class to a topic(s) in another main class. For example, the use of the colon in UDC allows one to express the existence in the document of topics from more than one main class, although the colon does not specify their exact relationship (cf. Perreault, 1994, as discussed above). Sometimes auxiliary tables allow one to notate a subordinate document topic that also appears in its own main class (e.g., Table 2 in DDC expresses geo-political areas that have their primary expression in the 900 class for History). In these cases, convention again dictates the interpretation one may give to the synthesized notation.

Ranganathan described relationships in order to explicate some of the syntactic devices in the *Colon Classification* (CC), but did not explicitly identify his discussion as one concerning relationships. A facet formula is a syntactic device that is roughly analogous to a grammatical sequence and that specifies a certain citation order for notational elements. In addition, discussion of the principles for facet sequence are discussions of relationship. For example, the Wall-Picture Principle states that "if two facets A and B of a subject are such that the concept behind B will not be operative unless the concept behind A is conceded, even as a mural is not possible unless the wall exists to draw upon, then the facet A should precede the facet B" (Ranganathan, 1965, p. 68). This passage describes a joint relationship between two concepts and seems to postulate a kind of context dependency similar to that developed later for PRECIS (e.g., Curwen, 1985). This example illustrates the tenuousness of the distinction between syntax and meaning because a syntactic discussion of structure turns on how meaning(s) can be conveyed to users of the system.

## 2.2 Semantic Relationships in Bibliographic Classification Systems

Like structural information containing both explicit and implicit relationships, explicit and implicit semantic information is found at various positions within a bibliographic classification system, but the semantic component is less well understood than the structural component. At the lowest level of meaning, an explicitly hierarchical structure provides much of the meaningful context for the enumerated topics and therefore reduces linguistic ambiguity. For example, "Cancer" in the superordinate class "Diseases" distinguishes the concept from "Cancer" in the superordinate class "Astrology." Thus, in classification systems, as in language in general, individual words describing topics attain meaning through their relation to a context.

In addition, a context beyond that of individual classes contributes broader meaning. The concept of "warrant" refers to fundamental decisions a classificationist has made about the foundation for the classification system. The warrant provides the semantic basis for a classification system. Such a warrant encompasses whatever rationale or authority is used to justify decisions about what concepts are included in the system, how they are ordered, and what relationships exist among them. These decisions are based on conscious or unconscious assumptions about, for example, how deeply a certain class should be subdivided and what the appropriate levels and units of analysis for a certain class are. The first and subsequent subdivisions of the whole universe of knowledge (or of a less inclusive knowledge domain) into constituents are based on assumptions and presumptions about what kinds of major groupings are "important" and "appropriate" for the particular purpose the classification has been created to serve. All classification systems, both bibliographic and non-bibliographic, are created to fulfill a particular purpose(s) (cf. Marco and Navarro, 1995). It appears to be impossible to invent a classification system of any kind that is neutral regarding purpose. This purpose may be ultimately practical, as in bibliographic classifications, or without direct practical application, as in philosophical divisions of knowledge. Nevertheless, some purpose is always discernable if one studies the system and its genesis. Kipfer's *The Order of Things* (1997) provides multiple lists of classes and categories for testing this view.

Like theories, classification systems advance arguments for a particular point of view (cf. Kwašnik, 1993). The assumptions that govern each system provide the overall meaningful context for that system and are part of its semantic foundation in the same way that the assumptions underlying theories provide meaning for the theory. For example, Hulme's concept of "literary warrant" is the rationale for basing subject access systems on topics that are written about in the literature. Literary warrant assumes that a library classification should reveal book topics that already exist and should not therefore try to enumerate all possible or potential topics (Hulme, 1911-1912). This assumption underlies all the semantic and syntactic elements of a classification system based on literary warrant by providing a *raison d'etre* for decisions that are made in the course of the system's creation. Similarly, systems based on other kinds of warrants partake of the assumptions made in decisions about them and advance a classificatory argument for which the system itself also provides evidence (Beghtol, 1986b).

At a higher level of generality, the sociocultural domain in which the classification is designed and for which it operates is also closely related to and deeply influences the development of any system. Although the intense debate on the best order for main classes has largely died out, this debate stressed the meaningfulness of different orders for different users at different times and places. The influence of sociocultural factors in the semantic relationships of classification systems has been called "cultural warrant." Lee coined the term when he pointed out that the semantic basis of a classification system is a product of the culture in and for which it was created (1976, p. 111). Earlier, the same idea was expressed by Hulme as "[book classification] presents for each period a bibliographical counterpart of the corresponding growth of the activities of the human mind" (1923, p. 5). Later, de Grolier pointed out that classification systems can be analyzed as "cultural artefacts" that reflect the culture from which they arise (1982, p. 34). A number of important recent papers take essentially the same view of the influence of sociocultural factors on classification systems (Bowker & Star, 1998).

In a discussion of social relations as meaning, Markus provided the example of the spatial arrangement of the Glasgow lunatic asylum (1993, p. 21, fig. 1.9, originally published in 1807). This spatial arrangement took the form of a classification system with three dimensions or facets: gender, social class, and mental state. The first subdivision was on the basis of gender. Male patients were housed in the right hand wing of the asylum and female patients were housed in the left hand wing. Both genders were further subdivided as belonging to either the Higher Rank (i.e., nobility) or to the Lower Rank (i.e., commoners). Higher Rank patients were housed at the front of their gender-specific wing and Lower Rank patients were at the back of their gender-specific wing. Four mental conditions for both genders and both social ranks were recognized: Frantic, Incurable, Convalescent, and In an ordinary state. People exhibiting each of these mental states were placed in a specific location in each social class of each gender-specific wing. For example, Frantic patients occupied the ground story of the remote ward of their respective gender- and class-specific wings, while Incurable patients were also housed on the ground floor of the same wing, but nearer the center. Thus, a spatial classification with facets for gender, class, and mental condition was mapped directly into the overall architecture and interior arrangement of the asylum.

One interesting point is that gender and social class are easily recognized categories today, even though we may not want to plan buildings on such a basis. In contrast, the categories for mental condition are unfamiliar and not self-explanatory. For example, what does "In an ordinary state" mean? Does it mean that the patient is ready to leave the asylum because he/she is now considered to be behaving normally? Does it mean that the patient is "In an ordinary state" of insanity, that is, not Frantic, Incurable, or Convalescent, but behaving in such a way as to not have to move to another section of the building? This classification mirrors exactly the culture from which it arose, and the assumptions on which it is based are its cultural warrant. The physical arrangement of mental patients in an asylum might be compared to the physical arrangement of documents in a library based on a classification system that is, like the classification of mental patients, based on the assumptions of the particular culture from which it arose and in which it is used.

When the cultural warrant of a classification system is ignored by subsequent authors, serious intellectual problems result. For example, Barley (1974) compared color classifications in old English and in modern English. The most common current way of classifying color is with the Munsell color chart, which classifies color on two dimensions:

the color itself and its hue. Old English speakers also classified color on two dimensions, but in that case the two dimensions were the color itself and its brightness, i.e.,

Our own modern English colour classification is firmly biased towards the differentiation of hues, so much so in fact, that we even term extremely light surfaces "white" and extremely dark surfaces "black" and treat them as hues. [Similarly] we reserve the noun category for their designation and use "pale" and "dark" as [adjectival] qualities to express the brightness dimension. Hue names are thus the fixed points on which we hang our whole colour system. Once we appreciate how lopsided and idiosyncratic is our own colour system, we shall not be surprised to find that the Anglo-Saxon approach to colour was quite different and that attempts to treat the latter as a hue-stressing system have resulted in a rare confusion. The main stress of the Old English [colour classification] falls firstly, not upon hue, but upon brightness. (Barley, 1974, pp. 16-17)

Thus, according to Barley, modern scholars trying to understand the old English color system have made the basic mistake of neglecting to take into account the cultural warrant of the classification system. In modern English, the meaning of color terms is biased toward the concept of hue, while in old English the meaning of color terms was biased toward the concept of brightness. Trying to translate the color terms of old English into the color terms of modern English is fraught with insoluble problems because the cultural warrants of the two systems were not identified and taken into account in the translation. This mistake can be likened to trying to compare temperatures measured in Fahrenheit with temperatures measured in Celsius without acknowledging that the measuring systems are based on different units.

Thus, "the classificatory landscape" (Fairthorne, 1985, p. 359) is infused with the entire sociocultural character of the domain (whether it is, for example, a geo-political area, a research domain, or a professional or institutional culture) that developed it for a specific purpose and found it useful. A system not based on an appropriate cultural warrant would not be useful and would not therefore be implemented, just as we would not implement the classification of mental patients that was appropriate for the Glasgow asylum. The semantic foundation of any classification system relies on shared assumptions and conventions that are not value-neutral. Instead, the system presents a syntactic and semantic argument for its own view of the world and justifies this bias on the basis of some expressed or unexpressed cultural warrant. In addition, the classification system itself provides evidence both for its own argument and for the biases of the culture in question. In this sense, one can "read" a classification system as a document that reveals preoccupations, opinions, and beliefs of the culture that created it.[5] The relationship of a system to its culture means that no system is an innocent expression of self-evident universal relationships. "Epistemological chauvinism" (Bousfield, 1979, p. 195) exists in all classification systems. The topics and their relationships that are deemed for some reason to be "useful," "important," "significant," or "fruitful" are those chosen for deployment in the system, and "the criteria of fruitfulness are beyond the analysis itself" (Tranöy, 1959, p. 27). That is, decisions about which kinds of relationships belong in a system are taken outside the system and thus of necessity reside, more or less obviously, in both the syntactic and semantic devices of the system that are in turn derived from its cultural warrant.

## 3. PARTS AND WHOLES: A UNIVERSAL RELATIONSHIP

This paper has argued that specific classification systems are bound to their cultures in identifiable ways and that this relationship provides the syntactic and semantic bases for the system. In spite of the cultural point of view that permeates a specific system, however, some general types of relationships appear to be cultural universals. Whether or not such a universal relationship is appropriate for and invoked by a certain system, as well as the exact form it takes in the system, are inevitably tied to cultural warrant, but the kind of relationship itself appears to be recognized in most, if perhaps not all, human thinking. Such a relationship is that of a part of an object or concept to the whole of the same object or concept. This relationship has various names (e.g., part-whole relationship, whole-part relationship, partition relationship, mereology) that are used interchangeably in this paper (see also Pribbenow, companion volume).

The part-whole relationship has been considered a "fundamental ontological relation" since Ancient Greece (Gerstl and Pribbenow, 1995, p. 865), and the apparent universality of the relationship in human languages has been verified empirically (e.g., Goddard, 1994). The relationship has been studied in numerous disciplines,[6] and has been recognized for subject access and analysis systems (e.g., Dahlberg, 1995; Schmitz-Esser, 1999). An extended attempt to base a general bibliographic classification system on the part-whole relationship occurred when the Classification Research Group (CRG) attempted to use the laws arising from the biological theory of integrative levels to develop a general classification system (e.g., Needham, 1943). This theory and its laws stipulate how parts combine into wholes to create living entities. The theory proved to be an unsuitable basis for a general classification system for various reasons, among them its inability to account appropriately for the non-biological creations of human beings, that is, "artifacts" such as architecture and books and "mentefacts" such as philosophy and fiction (e.g., Austin, 1976).

Part-whole relationships can be studied from a cognitive-linguistic perspective and/or from a logico-philosophical perspective (Guarino, Pribbenow, & Vieu, 1996). The relationship can be explained either from the standpoint of a theory of parthood or from the standpoint of a theory of wholeness. The relationship can be described as follows (Varzi, 1996):

- Parts and wholes are independent but related entities.
- Parthood can be explained in terms of wholeness.
- Wholeness can be explained in terms of parthood.

Thus, a number of sub-literatures about the part-whole relationship have developed based on different domain needs, preoccupations, and assumptions.[7] This part of the paper examines some notions about the part-whole relationship as it is used in and might in the future pertain to bibliographic classification systems and theories. The part-whole relation seems particularly germane to bibliographic classifications because their fundamental purpose is to subdivide the whole world of knowledge in order to provide access to its parts.

In the various part-whole literatures, consensus has arisen that, in order to understand complex concepts (including, but not limited to, abstract ideas, actions, tasks, events, and situations), people subdivide the concept into smaller units. Two methods of subdivision are commonly recognized: taxonomic subdivision into "kinds of" the thing and partitioning subdivision into "parts of" the thing. Both these types of subdivision express a certain relationship between the higher and lower level groupings and are capable of hierarchical arrangement. The "kind of" hierarchy is called a taxonomy, and the "part of" hierarchy is a partonomy. The hierarchies produced by both methods of subdivision are asymmetric. That is, an oak is a kind of tree and a tree is a kind of plant, but while an oak is thus a kind of plant, a plant is neither a kind of tree nor a kind of oak. Similarly, the hands of a clock are part of the face and the face is part of the clock, but while the hands are thus part of the clock, a clock is neither part of its face nor part of its hands.

In spite of these similarities, the two methods of subdivision have different characteristics. According to Tversky, partonomies and taxonomies are "products of different but complementary modes of investigation" (1989, 1990). In her view, the partonomic relationship usually:

- Can be established from a single instance (e.g., one apple has seeds, therefore all apples have seeds),
- Is a top-down analytic method (e.g., starts with the whole apple as the top level concept and proceeds downward to partonomic subdivision), and
- Reveals subcomponents and their relationships (e.g., seeds are found inside the central core of the apple).

In contrast, the taxonomic relationship usually:

- Is established by comparing and contrasting instances (e.g., apples and oranges have enough similarities to each other to make them kinds of fruit and enough dissimilarities from potatoes and carrots to exclude them from being kinds of vegetables),
- Is a bottom-up synthetic method in which low-level instances form groups (e.g., a number of products are examined, and certain significant features allow them to be divided into fruits and vegetables), and
- Reveals the features shared by the instances and the range of variability allowed in the group (i.e., one looks at the group of things that are called "fruit" and observes which features are necessary and which are allowed variability in determining membership in the class).

These generalizations seem broadly valid for explicating the distinction between taxonomic and partonomic subdivision, although further research into the general characteristics of these types of subdivision is needed.

Several points are interesting about both taxonomies and partonomies. Like all classificatory activities, the formation of "kind of" and "part of" hierarchies is not neutral but is culturally determined. For example, the human body is partitioned differently in different cultures (e.g., Burton & Kirk, 1979). Similarly, kinds of government departments will determine taxonomic subdivision on a culturally salient basis. In addition, the specific purpose for subdividing an entity determines which kinds of a thing and/or which of its parts are considered significant. For example, for the purpose of analyzing sentences, nouns and verbs are parts of speech, but if one's purpose is to create a dictionary, then nouns and verbs are kinds of words (Tversky, 1990). This example illustrates clearly that one thing (i.e., a noun) can be part of the partonomy of one higher level concept (i.e., a sentence) and also a member of the partonomy of a different, although related, higher level concept (i.e., a dictionary). It also emphasizes the importance of the purpose of a classification system, as discussed above. Thus, "types of hierarchy imply types of model" (Bainbridge, 1993, p. 1399), just as types of context imply types of subdivision. That is, useful subdivision is determined by the larger context, including the overall culture. Similarly, each smaller domain within a single culture may require different forms and content of subdivision.

The somewhat limited discussion of the part-whole relationship in the bibliographic classification literature is mirrored in the classification systems. Part-whole subdivision is used routinely in some parts of the systems. Geo-political subdivisions are normally based on a hierarchical spatial partition relationship, for example, Europe–United Kingdom–England–London. In this case, it makes no sense to subdivide on the taxonomic basis of a "kind of" relationship because, for example, England is not a "kind of" United Kingdom but is a "part of" it. In contrast, geographic subdivision can also be appropriately subdivided by kinds. For example, DDC Table 2 provides notation for types of geographic areas (e.g., Frigid zones, Islands, Coastal regions, Deserts).

Sometimes both "kind of" and "part of" relationships are used at one place. In LCC Class NK Interior Decoration, House Decoration, both kinds of relationships appear. Special Elements in House Decoration is generally subdivided on the basis of kinds of decoration (e.g., Audio-visual equipment, Ceramics, Christmas decorations, Collectibles). In Special Rooms in House Decoration, however, subdivision is only partially based on parts of a house (e.g., Attics, Basements). Other enumerated Special Rooms in House Decoration are kinds of rooms (e.g., Bathrooms, Bedrooms, Children's rooms). A further complication is that kinds of rooms are also, of course, parts of a house. Since LCC is based on literary warrant, we may assume that literature exists to justify both kinds of subdivision, but the same characteristic of division has not been used to arrive at the coordinate sub-classes. Thus, the non-mutually exclusive nature of parts and kinds needs to be taken into account during subdivision.

Some research has shown that basic level categories (e.g., chair) can be subdivided into either parts or kinds, but that partonomies for superordinate categories (e.g., furniture) are not as easy to create as taxonomies. Subordinate categories (e.g, kitchen chair) share the parts of their basic category, but are less amenable to subdivision by kind (Tversky, 1990). Bibliographic classifications often enumerate topics at the superordinate level and subdivide into kinds of basic categories, and different principles of subdivision often apply at different levels of subdivision. Research is needed to show whether these types and levels of specification are adequate. In general, both taxonomic and partonomic subdivision seem more appropriate to relatively concrete concepts than to relatively abstract ones. For example, houses or documents can be subdivided into kinds and/or parts with some ease. It is less easy, however, to establish either the kinds or the parts of abstractions like justice, truth, or event (Beghtol, 1997c). These intangibles may need different kinds of subdivision based on different kinds of analyses. Nevertheless, this discussion of the part-whole distinction provides an example of the kind of investigation of specific kinds of relationships that is needed to strengthen subdivision and specification in bibliographic classification systems.

# 4. CONCLUSIONS

Like other theoretical units such as words and sentences, every classification system is a postulated construct imposed on "reality" for some express purpose. A classificatory fabrication of reality is structured and rendered meaningful on a variety of levels within the classification system. We need to be able to supply a "mechanism for context effects" (Bainbridge, 1993, p. 1400) with each system in order to be able to move easily from one system to another, to map systems for different domains to a central system, or to account usefully for different cultural orientations of systems. We need to be able to incorporate point of view in the systems. Suggestions for these kinds of devices for thesauri were made by Schmitz-Esser (1999).

This paper makes no claim to completeness. Broad generalizations have been used to detect basic syntactic and semantic relationship patterns embedded in bibliographic classifications, but more specific research is needed into:

- The particular kinds of relationships used or implied in classification systems,
- The detailed syntactic and semantic relationships of a classification system both internally to itself and externally to other systems, and
- Methods of detecting and comparing the overall cultural warrant of systems to each other.

This research should be conducted without "methodological anxiety" (Richards, 1963, p. 169) using all the means at our disposal.

## Endnotes

1. Neither of the Dublin Core Working Group documents discussed here has the status of a Recommendation or a Proposed Recommendation.

2. Ranganathan's concept of seminal unscheduled mnemonics (e.g., Neelameghan, 1970) postulated that classifiers would be able to create notations for entirely new topics on the basis of cognitive universals. Although Ranganathan's particular examples have not been accorded much discussion, the idea is one that needs exploration.

3. Unlike thesaural systems, general classification systems have not used weights in the specification of topics, probably because the most "important" topic is assumed to be the one expressed by the main class from which the initial notation is taken.

4. A table showing kinds of notational systems used in bibliographic classifications and their characteristics appears in Foskett (1996, pp. 194-195, table 11.1).

5. Similar examples of the cultural warrant of classification systems may be taken from many fields. For example, Farago (1991) described the Renaissance debate over whether the visual arts were part of the sciences or part of "eloquence" (i.e., whether they should be considered to arise from nature or from artifice) and related this culturally-charged debate

to the relegation of non-western art to the status of "artifact." Ritvo (1997) described the relationship between nineteenth-century English zoological classifications and the then-established social classes and intellectual categories. In these cases, the biases of the classification systems both reflect and reinforce their sociocultural environments. Without such culturally meaningful relationships, no useful classification appears to be possible.

6. For example, fiction (Stevick, 1970); education (Niemi, 1996); computer science (Varzi, 1996); literature and the arts (Kritzman, 1981); anthropology (Witkowski & Brown, 1978; Casson, 1983); neuropsychology (Robertson & Lamb, 1991); philosophy (Fine, 1998); sociology (Scheff, 1997). It has also been the subject of multidisciplinary enquiries including the sciences and the arts (e.g., Lerner, 1963).

7. These sub-literatures and others like them (e.g., classification sub-literatures) incidentally provide us with an example of the operation of cultural warrant in different research fields.

## Acknowledgments

The research for this paper has been partially supported by the Canadian Social Sciences and Humanities Research Council (File No. 410-96-0024).

## References

Austin, D. (1976). The CRG research into a freely faceted scheme. In A. Maltby (Ed.), *Classification in the 1970s: A Second Look*, 158-194. London: Bingley.
Bainbridge, L. (1993). Types of hierarchy imply types of model. *Ergonomics*, 36, 1399-1412.
Barley, N. F. (1974). Old English colour classification: Where do matters stand? *Anglo-Saxon England*, 3, 15-28.
Barlow, J. P. (1994). A taxonomy of information. *Bulletin of the American Society for Information Science*, 20 (June/July), 13-17.
Beghtol, C. (1986a). Bibliographic classification theory and text linguistics: Aboutness analysis, intertextuality and the cognitive act of classifying documents. *Journal of Documentation*, 42, 84-113.
Beghtol, C. (1986b). Semantic validity: Concepts of warrant in bibliographic classification systems. *Library Resources & Technical Services*, 30, 109-125.
Beghtol, C. (1997a). Graphic representations of hierarchical systems: Preliminary study. In P. Solomon (Ed.), *Advances in Classification Research, Proceedings of the 7th ASIS SIG/CR Classification Research Workshop*, 22-43. Medford, NJ: Learned Information.
Beghtol, C. (1997b). Stories: Applications of narrative discourse analysis to information storage and retrieval problems for works in the arts, humanities, and other disciplines. *Knowledge Organization*, 24, 64-71.

Beghtol, C. (1997c). What is an event? Domain analysis of narrative documents. In *Knowledge Organization for Information Retrieval*, Proceedings, 6th International Study Conference on Classification Research, pp. 57-59. The Hague: FID (International Federation for Information and Documentation).

Beghtol, C. (1998). Knowledge domains: Multidisciplinarity and bibliographic classification systems. *Knowledge Organization*, 25, 1-12.

*Bliss Bibliographic Classification* (2nd ed.). (1977- ). J. Mills & V. Broughten (Eds.). Boston: Butterworths.

Bousfield, J. (1979). The world seen as a colour chart. In R.F. Ellen & D. Reason (Eds.), *Classifications in Their Social Context*, 195-220. London: Academic Press.

Bowker, G. C. & Star, S. L. (Eds.). (1998). How classifications work: Problems and challenges in an electronic age [Special issue]. *Library Trends* 47(2).

Burton, M. L. & Kirk, L. (1979). Ethnoclassification of body parts: A three culture study. *Anthropological Linguistics* (21), 377-399.

Byrne, C. C. & McCracken, S. A. (1999). An adaptive thesaurus employing semantic distance, relational inheritance and nominal compound interpretation for linguistic support of information retrieval. *Journal of Information Science*, 25, 113-131.

Casson, R. W. (1983). Schemata in cognitive anthropology. *Annual Review of Anthropology*, 12, 429-462.

Coates, E. J. (1960). *Subject Catalogues: Headings and Structure*. London: Library Association.

Coates, E. J. (1978). Classification in information retrieval: The twenty years following Dorking. *Journal of Documentation*, 34, 288-299.

Curwen, A. G. (1985). A decade of PRECIS, 1974-84. *Journal of Librarianship*, 17, 244-267.

Dahlberg, I. (1995). Conceptual structures and systematization. *International Forum on Information and Documentation*, 20(3), 9-24.

De Grolier, E. (1982). Classifications as cultural artefacts. In I. Dahlberg (Ed.) *Universal Classification I*, v. 2, 19-34. Frankfurt am Main: INDEKS Verlag.

Dewey, M .(1876- ). *Dewey Decimal Classification and Relative Index*. Albany, NY: Forest Press.

Dublin Core Metadata Initiative. Relations Working Group (1997). *Relation Element Working Draft 1997-12-19* [Online]. Available: <http://purl.org/dc/documents/working_drafts/wd-relation-current.htm> [2000, February 10].

Fairthorne, R. A. (1985). Temporal structure in bibliographical classification. In L. M. Chan, P. A. Richmond, & E. Svenonius (Eds.), *Theory of Subject Analysis: A sourcebook*, 359-368. Littleton, CO: Libraries Unlimited.

Farago, C. J. (1991). The classification of the visual arts in the Renaissance. In D. R. Kelley & R. H. Popkin (Eds.), *The Shapes of Knowledge from the Renaissance to the Enlightenment*, 23-47. Norwell, MA: Kluwer.

Farradane, J. (1980). Relational indexing. *Journal of Information Science*, 267-276 and 313-324.

Fine, K. (1998). Mixing matters. *Ratio* (new series), XI: 278-288.

Foskett, A. (1996). *The Subject Approach to Information* (5th ed.). London: Library Association Publishing.

Gerstl, P. & Pribbenow, S. (1995). Midwinters, end games, and body parts: A classification of part-whole relations. *International Journal of Human-Computer Studies*, 43, 865-889.

Goddard, C. (1994). Semantic theory and semantic universals. In C. Goddard & A. Wierzbicka (Eds.), *Semantic and Lexical Universals: Theory and Empirical Findings*, 7-29. Philadelphia: John Benjamins.

Guarino, N., Pribbenow, S., & Vieu, L. (1996). Guest editorial: Modeling parts and wholes. *Data & Knowledge Engineering*, 20, 257-258.

Hulme, E. W. (1911-1912). Principles of book classification. *Library Association Record*, 13, 354-358, 389-394, and 444-449 and 14, 39-46 and 174-181.

Hulme, E. W. (1923). *Statistical Bibliography in Relation to the Growth of Modern Civilization*. London: Butler and Tanner.

Kipfer, B. A. (1997). *The Order of Things: How Everything in the World Is Organized into Hierarchies, Structures, & Pecking Orders*. New York: Random House.

Kritzman, L. D. (1981). Preface. In L. D. Kritzman (Guest Ed.), *Fragments: Incompletion and Discontinuity*, vii-x. New York: NY Literary Forum.

Kwašnik, B. H. (1993). The role of classification structures in reflecting and building theory. In R. Fidel, B. H. Kwašnik, & P. J. Smith (Eds.), *Advances in Classification Research, Proceedings of the 3rd ASIS SIG/CR Classification Research Workshop*, 63-81. Medford, NJ: Learned Information.

Lee, J. M. (1976). E. Wyndham Hulme: A reconsideration. In W. B. Rayward (Ed.), *The Variety of Librarianship: Essays in Honour of John Wallace Metcalfe*, 101-113. Sidney: Library Association of Australia.

Lerner, D. (1963). Introduction: On parts and wholes. In D. Lerner (Ed.), *Parts and Wholes: The Hayden Colloquium on Scientific Method and Concept*, 1-9. New York: The Free Press of Glencoe.

LeVan, R. (1998). *A Cross-domain Attribute Set (Version 1.1 1998-10-09)* [Online]. Available: <http://www.oclc.org/oclc/research/projects/core/documents/notes/notes-levan-19981009.htm> [2000, February 10].

*Library of Congress Classification*. (1901- ). Washington, DC: Library of Congress, Cataloging Distribution Service.

Marco, F. J. G. & Navarro, M. A. E. (1995). On some contributions of the cognitive sciences and epistemology to a theory of classification. *International Information, Communication and Education (INICAE)*, 14, 178-192.

Markus, T. A. (1993). *Buildings and Power: Freedom and Control in the Origin of Modern Building Types*. London: Routledge.

Needham, J. (1943). *Time: The Refreshing River: Essays and Addresses, 1932-1942*. London: George Allen & Unwin.

Neelameghan, A. (1970). Seminal mnemonics as a pattern for system analysis. *Library Science with a Slant Toward Documentation*, 4, 353-364.

Niemi, D. (1996). A fraction is not a piece of pie: Assessing exceptional performance and deep understanding in elementary school mathematics. *Gifted Child Quarterly*, 40, 70-81.

Perreault, J. M. (1994). Categories and relators: A new schema. *Knowledge Organization,* 21, 189-198.

Ranganathan, S. R. (1933–). *The Colon Classification.* [India]: [various publishers].

Ranganathan, S. R. (1965). *The Colon Classification.* Rutgers Series on Systems for the Intellectual Organization of Information, v. IV. S. Artandi (Ed.). New Brunswick, NJ: Rutgers Graduate School of Library Service.

Richards, I. A. (1963). How does a poem know when it is finished? In D. Lerner (Ed.) *Parts and Wholes: The Hayden Colloquium on Scientific Method and Concept,* 163-174. New York: The Free Press of Glencoe.

Ritvo, H. (1997). *The Platypus and the Mermaid and Other Figments of the Classifying Imagination.* Cambridge, MA: Harvard Univ. Press.

Robertson, L. C. & Lamb, M. R. (1991). Neuropsychological contributions to theories of part/whole organization. *Cognitive Psychology,* 23, 299-330.

Scheff, T. (1997). Part/whole morphology: Unifying single case and comparative methods. *Sociological Research Online* [Online], 2(3), 101 paragraphs. Available: <http//www.socresonline.org.uk/socresonline/2/3/1.html> [2000, February 9].

Schmitz-Esser, W. (1999). Thesaurus and beyond: An advanced formula for linguistic engineering and information retrieval. *Knowledge Organization,* 26, 10-22.

Soergel, D. (1998). Framework for data element standardization. In R. Schwartz (Ed.), *Advances in Classification Research, Proceedings of the 6th ASIS SIG/CR Classification Research Workshop,* 115-126. Medford, NJ: Information Today.

Stephens, L. M. (1991). The classification of semantic relations based on primitive properties. In S. M. Humphrey & B. H. Kwašnik (Eds.), *Advances in Classification Research, Proceedings of the 1st ASIS SIG/CR Classification Research Workshop,* 159-168. Medford, NJ: Learned Information

Stevick, P. (1970). *The Chapter in Fiction: Theories of Narrative Division.* Syracuse, NY: Syracuse University Press.

Tranöy, K. E. (1959). *Wholes and Structures: An Attempt at a Philosophical Analysis.* Copenhagen: Munksgaard.

Tversky, B. (1989). Parts, partonomies, and taxonomies. *Developmental Psychology,* 25, 983-995.

Tversky, B. (1990). Where partonomies and taxonomies meet. In S. L. Tsohatzidis (Ed.), *Meanings and Prototypes: Studies in Linguistic Categorization.* London: Routledge.

*Universal Decimal Classification* (International med. ed. English). (1994- ). The Hague: UDC Consortium.

Varzi, A. C. (1996). Parts, wholes, and part-whole relations: The prospects of mereotopology. *Data & Knowledge Engineering,* 20, 259-286.

Weinberg, B. H. (1995). Complexity in indexing systems—Abandonment and failure: Implications for organizing the Internet. In *ASIS '95, Proceedings of the 59th ASIS Annual Meeting,* 84-90. Medford, NJ: Information Today.

Witkowski, S. R. & Brown, C. H. (1978). Lexical universals. *Annual Review of Anthropology,* 7, 427-451.

# Chapter 8

# Relevance Relationships

Carol A. Bean
*School of Information Sciences, University of Tennessee, Knoxville, TN, USA*

Rebecca Green
*College of Information Studies, University of Maryland, College Park, MD, USA*

**Abstract:**
   Relevance arises from relationships between user needs and documents/information. In the quest for relevant retrieval, some content-based relationships are best used initially to cast a net that emphasizes recall, while others, both content- and non-content-based, are best used subsequently as filtering devices to achieve better precision. Topical relevance, the primary factor in the initial retrieval operation, extends far beyond topic matching, as often assumed. Empirical studies demonstrate that topical relevance relationships are drawn from a broad but systematic inventory of semantic relationships.

## 1. INTRODUCTION

   Relevance is widely acknowledged to be both the most fundamental issue of information science as a discipline and the most central concern of information and document retrieval systems as applications. From a practical point of view, the purpose of such systems is commonly considered to be the retrieval of relevant information or at least the retrieval of citations to documents in which relevant information can be found. But from a theoretical point of view, about the only aspect of relevance that is agreed upon is how difficult it is to predict what information or documents will be found relevant to a given user need.

   Let us take the goal of an ideal information/document retrieval system to be the identification of information, documents, and/or texts that have the potential of helping the user who makes a reasonable effort to resolve some need. What characteristics of a document or information source affect whether or not it is relevant to a given user need? In other words, what relationships between users and user needs, on the one hand, and knowledge and information sources, on the other hand, account for relevance? Given the almost infinite variety included on both sides, it is not surprising that many different factors—dozens of them, in fact—play a role in the degree to which an information source is relevant to a user need (see, for example, Cuadra & Katter, 1967; Schamber, 1994, p. 11). Some of these factors play a contributory role and increase the likelihood that a document or information source will be found relevant to a user need, while others play an

115

*C. A. Bean and R. Green (eds.), Relationships in the Organization of Knowledge*, 115–132.

inhibitory role and decrease that likelihood. This distinction between types of relevance factors is best taken into account in what is envisioned as a two-step retrieval process: In the first step, the contributory relevance factors are used to cast a wide net for potentially relevant documents or information sources, thus promoting recall; in the second step, the inhibitory relevance factors are used to narrow the retrieval set, thus promoting retrieval precision. This model partakes of the same spirit as the two-stage view of relevance and retrieval put forth in Boyce (1982). Of course, the actual retrieval process may involve more than two steps, in which case the two-step process of first retrieving and then filtering will also recur multiple times. Not only does this retrieve-then-filter pattern hold for well-defined searches, but it also mirrors a phenomenon of information need refinement that occurs commonly in less-well-defined searches: Users often begin the search process with a broad notion of what they are seeking. As the process continues and users interact with information sources, their perception of their information need often tightens into a much sharper focus (Hirsh, 1999, p. 1280; Kuhlthau, 1991).

## 2. TOPICALITY AND RELEVANCE

In large part, contributory relevance factors are content-based, where content includes the various components constituting the subjects of document. According to Langridge (1989), subject components include topic, form of knowledge, disciplinary specialization, form of writing, ideological perspective, and audience. Of these, topic is the prototypical contributory relevance factor. Indeed, topicality has long been perceived as a primary factor in accounting for relevance. In introducing a special topic journal issue on relevance research, Froelich (1994, p. 129) reflected this consensus when he wrote: "The nuclear sense of relevance is topicality. . . . Most of the articles in this issue acknowledge that it is a [sic] important aspect of relevance, a necessary but not sufficient condition: if the citation is not on the topic, how could it be relevant for that topic?" Consistent with the characterization of relevance as the property of a text's being potentially helpful to a user in the resolution of a need, logical relevance of some sort (although not necessarily deductive) is assumed (Cooper, 1971; Wilson, 1973); by its nature, such relevance is content-based. Indeed, in one major study various aspects of information content (including topic, spatial and temporal contexts, methodologies used, etc.) accounted for the *only* factors mentioned by users in assessing relevance 62% of the time (Barry, 1998, pp. 1296-1297); how often such aspects were included among other types of factors is not known. In another study examining document selection, topicality was the criterion most frequently used and was explicitly mentioned by all users in the study (Wang & Soergel, 1998, pp. 122-123).

Content-based components can also operate as inhibitory relevance factors. In a search using Boolean logic, the NOT operator might be applied to certain topical elements to limit the scope of the retrieval. If not applied at the search stage, the same topical elements could be used by the user (or an intermediary) to filter out presumably unwanted sources retrieved by an overly-broad search. Moreover, non-topical, content-based components may be used to focus the retrieval set by filtering on form of writing, ideological perspective, or audience.

A variety of non-content-based factors, amply documented in studies examining user relevance variable studies (e.g., Barry, 1994) also come into play and interact with the retrieval set as selected on the basis of content-related factors. Say, for example, that the retrieval set contains a document that would, by itself, enable the user to resolve his or her need fully, if only it were written in English, rather than being written in a language the user neither knows nor knows any speakers/readers thereof. In such a case, the inherent logical relevance of the document would be tempered by the user's cognitive ability, within the limits of reasonable effort, to make use of the text. We might say that such a text, although relevant, was not pertinent to the user; alternatively, the text had no utility for the user.

On occasion rhetoric overwhelms thoughtful consideration in the relevance 'debate,' and attempts to set up topical relevance and user relevance in opposition to each other. This appears to stem back to the classic review article by Saracevic (1976), which summarizes a number of views of relevance. Subsequent reference to Saracevic's work often projects two diametrically opposed views of relevance, an objective system view, based on topicality or aboutness, and a subjective user view, based on contextual factors, including, for example, novelty, source characteristics, and availability. The retrieval model proposed above suggests that topicality (and other content-based factors) and the various user-oriented contextual factors work in tandem: It's not a case of either/or, but of both/and. The current ascendancy of the user view represents an appropriate move away from a strictly objective view of relevance based on aboutness, but if it ignores the importance of topicality to relevance, it is simply throwing the baby out with the bath water. On the one hand, user relevance variables are typically used as precision devices and presuppose that other factors have been used to define the initial retrieval set. The user is unlikely to want to see *all* novel information sources, *all* sources available in the local library collection, etc., but may well want to see *only* novel information sources and *only* sources available in the local library collection. When we characterize the ideal retrieval system as retrieving all and only what the user would select (Doyle, 1963, p. 199), the *all* side of the statement represents the recall-oriented retrieval step, largely steeped in topicality, while the *only* side of the statement represents the precision-oriented filtering step, in which myriad other user variables are taken into account. As Sievert et al. found, "The pursuit of topical features is still an important first step in finding information . . .; quality filters should be used after all the topical aspects of an information need have been addressed" (1996, p. 355). On the other hand, the user relevance view could have it all simply by embracing topicality as the ultimate user variable, since topicality, more than any other single factor, corresponds to what the user is looking for, another point supported by the study by Sievert et al.

## 3. TOPICAL RELEVANCE AS A RELATIONSHIP

The user relevance community rightly demands that factors beyond topicality/aboutness enter into assessments of relevance. This is now widely recognized and accepted. Another misconception stemming from the system relevance view has, however, not been widely recognized and is at least as detrimental as the exclusion of user variables had been to our designing improved retrieval systems. This is the premise that topical relevance begins and ends with topic matching. Typical of statements that espouse this premise are the following:

"The clearest and most persistent definition of relevance is one of matching or *topicality*: whether the topic of the information retrieved matches the topic of the request" (Eisenberg & Schamber, 1988, p. 164); "Objective relevance is usually measured as *topicality*—how well the topic of the information retrieved matches the topic of the request" (Harter, 1992, p. 602). This premise of near synonymy between topicality, the measure for topical relevance, and topic matching is closely related to what Belkin (1980, p. 188) calls the 'best match' hypothesis and which he suggests "underlies all traditional IR theory and practice." He argues that while some relationship exists between the representation of a request (which is typically topical) and the actual information need, "it should . . . be clear that it is not terribly direct" (p. 190).

Why would the assumption that "Topical relevance = Topic matching" be considered detrimental? The crux of the argument is this: Given the retrieve-and-filter model proposed above, a retrieval system can never be more effective (only more efficient) than its retrieval mode. Since the assumption of topic matching places severe limitations on what is initially retrieved, it forever thereafter limits what is made accessible to the user. The alternative view presented here is that topical relevance must be characterized relationally. A retrieval system based on a relational view of topical relevance would potentially result in higher recall retrieval, since additional relationships between the subject of the need/query and the subject of information sources would be taken into account. (Note that topic matching is one possible relationship, so the retrieval results of a system based on a relational view of topical relevance could easily be a superset of the results in a conventional, topic-matching system.)

The argument is sometimes made that recall failures do not affect the user, that if the user is unaware of the existence of certain (relevant, even pertinent) sources, the user will not be dissatisfied by not having retrieved them. But this takes too narrow a view of user satisfaction: The user will not be satisfied if a competitor finds the missed relevant documents and is then able to bring a superior product to market or to bring an equivalent product to market in a more timely fashion. The user will not be satisfied when a debilitating medical condition is endured for years because the complementary information from non-bibliographically coupled literatures is never brought together and an effective remedy found. That the user may remain unaware of the source of his or her dissatisfaction is not equivalent to claiming that the user is not affected by the recall failure.

It has been suggested above that higher recall would result naturally from building a relational view of topical relevance into retrieval systems. Many would argue—despite the scenarios just offered, which support the idea that recall failures can matter a great deal—that higher recall is the last thing we need, when we often find ourselves drowning in retrieval sets numbering in the hundreds, thousands, even millions (but this latter magnitude of retrieval presumably occurs only in situations where results are ranked). The need for higher precision is paramount. But a relational view of topical relevance can be used just as easily to tighten the belt of precision as to let out the belt of recall (and perhaps can be used to do both simultaneously). For instance, rather than just searching on topic A and topic B in the same document, a relational view of topic searching could limit retrieval to only those documents in which A and B stand in some particular relationship or set of relationships to each other.

Aside from the potential for controlling recall and precision tantalizingly put forth above, are there any reasons to suppose that a relational view of topical relevance is a more accurate view than the traditional topic matching standby? In fact, there are numerous reasons to doubt the validity of the topic-matching hypothesis and/or to adopt a relational topical relevance stance. These reasons pertain to the potentially "anomalous state of knowledge" of users with their information needs, the inconsistencies inherent in the indexing/subject representation process, citation analysis, and the interaction between literature use and the production of knowledge.

## 3.1 Users and Information Needs

Users often turn to information and document retrieval systems because they want to solve some type of problem for which they currently lack adequate information and/or skills. In a turn of phrase propelled into the LIS community's vernacular by Belkin, Oddy, and Brooks (1982), the user may be in an "anomalous state of knowledge" (ASK). In some cases, the user has a reasonably clear model of the context of the information need and can specify very precisely what will fill that need, but in many and in more sophisticated situations, the user is far removed from knowing how to resolve his or her need. The resolution of the need may well be a multiple-step process, where the user might be able to anticipate at the beginning of the search process some of the characteristics of information or of documents that will prove to be relevant, but where the user, because of the very state of ignorance that has brought him or her to the retrieval system in the first place, is unable to recognize immediately many items that ultimately will be found relevant. Thus, relevance is not always a matter of "I'll know it when I see it." Moreover, unless both the problem and its solution are previously known, it may be that no one could anticipate in advance what would be found relevant to the resolution of the need. In such cases, we cannot reasonably suppose that relevant documents are simply those on the same topic as the information need. But we also do not want to suppose that the subject matter of various bodies of relevant literature and the overall topic of the information need bear no relationship to each other. We sense that their subjects should be related, but that they may not just match.

By way of illustration, we turn to Harter (1992), who relies heavily on Sperber & Wilson (1986) for his sense of "psychological relevance." After noting that the equation of relevance with "on the [same] topic" diverges from the everyday meaning of *relevance*, he gives two quite apt examples that hammer home the point: "That there was a drought in South Dakota in 1985 was relevant to my vacation plans there that year. Developments in computer technology are relevant to the future careers of students enrolled in schools of library and information science" (pp. 602-603). Clearly the topics of the two parts of each of the examples are conceptually related, but do not match. Harter's piece gives a number of examples of documents that are relevant to a single query, but which are not about the topic of the query. He notes that their topics "are all related to one another in the mind of the requester" (p. 610), implying perhaps that the relationships are idiosyncratic, but if numerous readers are able to follow those relationships, then the relationships must be at least somewhat conventional and/or systematic.

## 3.2 Subject Representation

Documents often fully indicate such objective attributes as their authorship or facts of publication, but the announcement of their topical nature is often limited to what is conveyed by the title. A title will often, but not always, shed light on the overall subject matter of a document; however, only the rare title will adequately convey all the topics covered by a document. In response, indexers/subject catalogues assign descriptors/subject headings to documents, potentially as many as can be anticipated to reflect reasons a user might find the document relevant. And herein lies a significant reason why topic matching is too narrow a notion on which to base topical relevance: Perceptions of the topic(s) of any given document varies across different persons, and varies even for a single person across time and situational context.

Interindexer inconsistency (which has been found to range from 4% to 82% [Markey, 1984, pp. 157-160]), and by extension intersearcher inconsistency, poses a significant challenge to the topic matching premise: If trained indexers cannot agree on the topic(s) of documents, how then can it be assumed that effective retrieval can be achieved with topic matching, when this depends on which indexers produced index term assignments, as well as on which searchers select index terms for the query. Relevant documents will be missed and non-relevant documents retrieved simply because indexers and/or searchers (or moving further backward or forward in the chain, writers and/or users) perceive topicality differently from each other.

The celebrated retrieval study reported in Blair & Maron (1985) also sheds light on the limitations inherent in topic matching. This evaluation of free-text searching in a full-size, operational text database demonstrates that "it is impossibly difficult for users to predict the exact words, word combinations, and phrases that are used by *all* (or most) relevant documents and *only* (or primarily) by those documents (p. 295)." Free-text searching is an operational substitute for topic matching in which the major effort—after the question negotiation and subject analysis stages that must first occur in all searching—is to determine the multiple ways in which the subjects or topics identified may be expressed. The examples of recall failure discussed in the Blair & Maron study show that the problem is not, however, limited to synonym control, as would be true if topic matching were sufficient. For instance, one particular issue under investigation corresponded to a number of phrases found in relevant documents: "trap correction," "wire warp," "shunt correction system," "Roman circle method," and "air truck." These are not just synonymous phrases. Instead they vary in how they are related to each other and thus in how they are related to the user's need.

## 3.3 Citation Relationships

A major premise of citation analysis is that the relationships between citing and cited documents are worthy of examination. For one document to cite another is *prima facie* evidence that the cited document is relevant to some aspect of the citing document, a recognition which dates back at least to Martyn (1975). Further, although citation indexes may serve many different functions, their most general function is to use documents that have already been identified as being relevant to a user need as stepping stones to other relevant documents.  It follows that the relationships between citing and cited documents are relevance relationships.

Of especial interest here are topical relationships between citing and cited documents. Unfortunately, there have been but few investigations into this issue.  On the one hand, Ali (1993) and Trivison (1987) examined term co-occurrence between the titles (and abstracts, in the latter case) of citing and cited documents; documents bound by a citation relationship were found to have a significantly higher number of co-occurring terms than those without a citation relationship to each other.  This result provides mild support for the topic-matching hypothesis.  On the other hand, in a study by Harter, Nisonger, & Weng (1993), which examined semantic (i.e., topical) relationships between citing and cited documents, the overall similarity between the sets of index terms assigned to citing and cited documents was relatively low, the union overlap similarity coefficient averaging in the 0.15-0.20 range. However, this measure may not reflect the nature or the degree of semantic relatedness, because it is based solely on the degree to which two sets of index terms match exactly. Since different indexers will almost always have been involved in assigning the sets of terms, a citing and a cited document with a high degree of semantic/topical similarity may not have been assigned the same index terms.  Indeed, in cases where documents have inadvertently been re-indexed, the similarity score between the multiple sets of index terms has been only about 50% (p. 548), even though the "two" documents, being one and the same document, were perfectly similar semantically.  Add to this that index terms that are semantically related (e.g., as hypernyms/hyponyms, synonyms, antonyms, related terms) contributed nothing to the similarity score: Only exact matches were counted.  Thus, the low average similarity coefficient reflects only that exact matches are not prevalent between the index terms of citing and cited documents.  The degree to which such documents are topically related, and the identity of the topical relationships between them, is still largely unknown.

Another reason that the topic of a citing document and the topic of a cited document might not match has been pointed out by Weinberg (1994), referring back to Martyn (1964, 1975): A citation is not a consistent unit of information.  A citation need not be to a whole work, but may be to a small part of it, as is often the case when a paper is cited for methodological reasons; therefore the topic of the overall work being cited may not account for the topical relationship between that document and the document that cited it. Conversely, a citation may appear within a part of the citing work whose topicality is tangential to that of the overall document.  A similar situation may apply in the literature retrieval situation.  A document may be relevant to only a specific facet of the user need, and/or only a portion of a document may be relevant to the overall user need.  In either case, the overall topicality of the user need may not match the overall topicality of the relevant document, even though the citation may be made for reasons of topical relatedness.

## 3.4 Knowledge Synthesis

Concomitant with the current information explosion is an increasing trend toward specialization.  As a result, knowledge fragmentation occurs: Elements of knowledge conceptually linked to each other may occur in disjoint (i.e., isolated) literatures. For example, Swanson (1990) describes a cluster of documents ("AB") supporting the argument that dietary fish oil increases red blood cell deformability and reduces blood viscosity and a second cluster of documents ("BC") reporting that some sufferers of Raynaud's syndrome experience red blood cell rigidity and high blood viscosity. The two literatures are non-interacting: with rare exception, they do not have authors in common; they do not cite each other; they do not cite the same literature; and they are not cited by the same literature. Despite their bibliographic isolation, the two literatures are conceptually linked: From their two findings, the hypothesis that dietary fish oil may benefit Raynaud's patients can be inferred. Once identified, this literature-based hypothesis becomes subject to empirical verification as do other hypotheses. If confirmed, knowledge will have been advanced through the synthesis of a chain of premises, each from a distinct literature.

The knowledge synthesis problem can be readily recast as an information need. In the above setting the user's information need is: What treatment options exist for Raynaud's syndrome? Swanson reports that some drug therapies have met with a degree of success, "although neither cause nor cure is known" (p. 31). Moreover, at the time Swanson began and subsequently published his literature-based knowledge discovery exercise, there was no intersecting ("AC") literature suggesting the use of dietary fish oil to treat Raynaud's syndrome. Given those circumstances, the user would want to learn of the possibility of dietary fish oil's benefit for Raynaud patients by being directed to literatures AB and BC. In the terms of Cooper (1971) and Wilson (1973) respectively, these literatures are logically, or better, evidentially relevant to the user's information need. But they are not on the same topic as the user need, that is, treatment options for Raynaud's syndrome. Literature BC comes the closer, as it is on the topic of conditions correlated with Raynaud's syndrome. Literature AB's topic, the effects of dietary fish oil, does not appear to match the topic of the user need at all; yet that literature, coupled with BC, is highly relevant.

Literature-based knowledge synthesis has been viewed as a phenomenon distinct from general literature retrieval because the topic matching criterion traditionally assumed by retrieval theory is so obviously inappropriate for the knowledge synthesis context. The advancement of knowledge presupposes seeing the world in new ways, discovering new connections, going beyond what is currently accepted. Topic matching alone cannot effectively support such discovery.

The distinction between knowledge synthesis and literature retrieval dissolves when the comparison is made from the other direction, that is, by comparing literature retrieval to knowledge synthesis. Swanson has addressed situations where an objectively new hypothesis—a hypothesis previously undocumented and perhaps previously unnoticed—is generated. But for an individual to adopt a subjectively new hypothesis as a result of literature retrieval, no matter how many other persons are already conversant with it, is no less a matter of knowledge synthesis. If we think of knowledge synthesis as the desired outcome of all literature retrieval, then we quickly recognize the need to discard the topic matching straitjacket as the only mode in which topical relevance is manifest. As the example discussed above suggests, user needs and literature topically relevant to those needs may be conceptually linked through other—more complex and more sophisticated—relationship types. For instance, Swanson's knowledge discoveries are based on inferences from transitive causal relationships of the form, 'A causes B' and 'B causes C.'

A final reason to be discussed as to why topic matching may fail to capture topical relevance adequately is that relevant documents sometimes are not on the same topic of the user query, but may be related inferentially, or more specifically, by analogy. For example, Gillaspie (1992, p. 258), in identifying reasons why relevant documents might be missed in legal document retrieval, names this as one such reason. Since analogy is a mechanism for inference in legal reasoning, it may account for the relevance of a document to a legal query, but a system based on topic matching will likely fail to retrieve the document. Analogical relevance is thus cast as operating within the context of knowledge synthesis: The user must be able to recognize that the set of relationships functioning in one context, as recorded in some body of literature, can be profitably applied to another context. This application may produce new insight, such as spurring the generation of a solution to a problem. Whole literary genres (e.g., parables, fables) are based on their potential to be analogically relevant to situations quite unlike those incorporated in their exposition. But analogical relevance is not limited to the literature of the humanities. Many theories in the natural and social sciences are based on metaphorical models borrowed from other domains (see, for example, Gentner & Gentner, 1983).

Retrieval based on analogical or inferential relevance obviously cannot be effected on the basis of topic matching. What possibility exists for providing systematic access to analogically or inferentially relevant literature? Presumably, if such is possible at all, it will be based on the network of relationships that the user creatively maps from a source context to a target context.

## 4. EMPIRICAL SUPPORT

If, as argued above, using content similarity as the predominant retrieval criterion is inadequate, a clear need exists for new and different approaches to the study of relevance and its assessment. Two avenues are immediately apparent: Investigate non-topical relationships or investigate non-matching topical relationships. While these approaches may be orthogonal, they need not, and indeed must not, be seen as antagonistic. In the user-centric environment currently dominating the information science field, the former has held overwhelming sway. Far less attention has been directed to the latter; indeed, investigations of any aspect of topicality are almost nonexistent. The reader should have no trouble finding numerous studies of non-topical user-centered relevance, and is thus referred to the extensive literature on this topic that has emerged over past years. Instead, this section will present empirical investigations undertaken to identify and characterize topical relevance relationships, that is, to determine what relationship types actually account for topical relevance.

Two lines of research have examined topical relationships between user needs and relevant texts, that is, relationships between the topics of user needs and the topics of texts previously judged to be relevant to those needs. One approach deals with potential rather than actual user needs, while the other deals with a priori determinations removed from any experimental relevance assessment. Thus, whether or not a document is relevant to a query is not at issue; it is assumed to be relevant in context. Further, issues of making the relevance judgements are avoided. What is of interest is the reason for the assumed relevance: specifically, how or why a document is relevant to a query. To tease this out requires a good sense of the query and the underlying information need that generated it. Both are then considered in context of the setting or environment in which they occurred, as well as the nature and structure of knowledge in the domain, which may be general or specialized to some degree, or organized by subject such as in medicine or by body of literature such as scripture. This line of research also presumes that if a query expressing an information need contains a topical component, then any text satisfying that need will also contain topical elements in some identifiable relationship to those of the query. That is, topic will be a necessary and recognizable component of any document that is relevant to the information need. Note that this says nothing about the sufficiency of topicality.

First we describe an exploratory study that aimed to identify enough topical relevance relationships to organize a typological framework sufficient to demonstrate the nature and scope of topical relevance. Subsequently, these topical relevance relationships were compared with an inventory of general semantic relationships in an independently-generated frame thesaurus. We then describe preliminary results drawn from a study of the relationships among relevant query-document pairs in a test collection used for information retrieval system evaluation.

## 4.1  Typology of Topical Relevance Relationships

The topics of thirty user needs were compared with the topics of 611 texts relevant those needs to determine the relationships between them (Green & Bean, 1995). Our goal was to establish a basic typology of topical relevance relationships by identifying the relationship types that occur most commonly. In operational terms, this may be expressed as: Given a set of user needs and a set of texts relevant to those needs, what relationships occur between the topic(s) of each user need and the topic(s) of each text segment relevant to that need? We made the a priori assumption that some large number of relationship types would account for topical relevance, but that a reasonably small percentage of relationship types from the total inventory would account for a significantly greater proportion of relationship occurrences.

The original paper explains the methodology in detail, but briefly, relationships between user needs and relevant texts were identified as follows. User needs were represented by the subject headings in a topical concordance: *A Topical Guide to the Scriptures of the Church of Jesus Christ of Latter-day Saints* ("Topical Guide"). Relevant texts were cited under each heading and consisted of passages from the Bible, King James Version. A set of plausible user needs that would potentially be satisfied from the cited texts was back-generated from the sample of thirty Topical Guide headings.

For example, the following set of user needs emerged when the cited passages were considered in the context of the Topical Guide heading, "Meetings":

When should we meet? (On what occasions? How often? On what day of the week?)
Under what conditions should we meet?
Why should we meet?
Who is to meet? (With whom do we meet? Is God present at our meetings?)
What activities are appropriate during meetings?

Likewise, the heading, "God, Mercy of" spawned these user needs:

Is God merciful?
Under what conditions is God merciful?
To whom is God merciful?
How is God's mercy manifest?
Why is God merciful?
What is the relationship between God's mercy and man's righteousness?
What does God's mercy do for us?

A total of thirty-three content-based relationship types were identified and organized into three larger relationship groups. Topic matching accounted for less than a third of all relationships identified; a third of the topic-matching occurrences expressed adjectival or adverbial modification of some aspect of the user need topic (ex. 1), and the rest were about equally divided between referential and definitional assertions (ex. 2). Hierarchical relationships accounted for fewer than ten percent of all types observed; about two-thirds of these were taxonomic (ex. 3) and a third meronymic (ex. 4). Well over half of the relationship types observed were what we termed "structural relationships." This group comprises either entire complex conceptual structures or gestalts (ex. 5), or their intra-structural components (ex. 6), or such specialized complex structures as metaphorical devices (ex. 7). The following examples are drawn from the typology of topical relevance relationships that was generated from the total set of relationships identified in the study.

- Example 1. Topic matching relationships: Attributes, Adjectival, Characteristics
  *User need:* What is the intelligence of God like?
  *Topical Guide heading:* God, Intelligence of
  *Cited passage:* "But the wisdom that is from above is first pure, then peaceable, gentle, and easy to be intreated, full of mercy and good fruits, without partiality, and without hypocrisy." (James 3:17)

- Example 2. Topic matching relationship: Definition
  *User need:* What is faith
  *Topical Guide heading:* Faith
  *Cited passage:* "Now faith is the substance of things hoped for, the evidence of things not seen." (Hebrews 11:1)

- Example 3. Hierarchical relationship: Taxonomy, Type/token
  *User need:* What (who) is an example of a translated being?
  *Topical Guide heading:* Translated beings
  *Cited passage:* "And Enoch walked with God: and he was not; for God took him." (Genesis 5:24)

- Example 4. Hierarchical relationship: Partonomy, Activities involved
  *User need:* What do (religious) meetings consist of?
  *Topical Guide heading:* Meetings
  *Cited passage:* "And . . . when the disciples came together to break bread, Paul preached unto them . . .; and continued his speech until midnight." (Acts 20:7)

- Example 5. Syntagmatic relationship: Complex structures: Balance/equilibrium
  *User need:* Should I give money to panhandlers?
  *Topical Guide heading:* Laziness
  *Cited passage:* "For even when we were with you, this we commanded you,
  that if any would not work, neither should he eat." (2 Thessalonians 3:10)

- Example 6. Syntagmatic relationship: Structural components: Recipient
  *User need:* To whom is God merciful?
  *Topical Guide heading:* God, Mercy of
  *Cited passage:* ". . . I the LORD thy God am a jealous God, . . . shewing mercy
  unto thousands of them that love me, and keep my commandments."
  (Exodus 20:5-6)
  This passage says that God is merciful to those who satisfies the stated
  conditions. (Note that this passage also satisfies the User need regarding
  "Under what conditions is God merciful?" by stating the precipitating conditions
  for God's mercy.)

- Example 7. Syntagmatic relationship: Complex structures: Metaphorical device
  *User need:* How can I get out of and stay out of spiritual debt?
  *Topical Guide heading:* Debt
  *Cited passage:* "And forgive us our debts as we forgive our debtors." (Matthew
  6:12)

This study revealed that topical relevance relationships include a wide variety of
relationships, only some of which, perhaps only a relatively small proportion, are matching
relationships.   Others are examples of paradigmatic relationships or syntagmatic
relationships. Indeed, there appear to be no constraints on the kinds of relationships that
can function as topical relevance relationships. They are distinguishable from other types
of relationships only on functional grounds.

Because these findings strongly suggested that the set of topical relevance relationships
is coextensive with the set of all relationship types instead of being fundamentally distinct
in some inherent way, we subsequently assessed (Bean & Green 1997) how well these
topical relevance relationships corresponded to those in a structured frame thesaurus of
general semantic relationships created independently (Green 1997). Almost all of the topic-
matching and structural component relationships mapped directly to specific frames or frame
slots in the general relational thesaurus. For example, meronomy mapped to the Whole-Part
relationship frame, and the structural component Object mapped to the Patient slot of the
Process frame.  While only half of the gestalt structures had complete frame thesaurus
correspondents (e.g., Balance as compared to Debt), well over two-thirds of the elements
of such complex structures could be mapped into the frame thesaurus. It is likely that a
more extensive sample for the typology would have a correspondingly greater representation
in the frame thesaurus. Discrepancies such as these are a natural limitation in comparisons
of taxonomies generated by top-down and bottom-up approaches.

## 4.2 A Priori Relevance Relationships in an Information Retrieval Test Collection

Another promising area for empirical investigation of topical relevance relationships lies in identifying the nature of the topical associations between queries and relevant documents in test collections used for information retrieval system evaluation. The very emphasis in such systems on topical relevance, which has been criticized as a weakness by the user relevance community, here becomes a strength to exploit empirically.

The most common means of assessing information retrieval systems employs test collections as the primary tool and uses the metrics recall and precision. The basic task can be summarized as finding all but only those items in a given collection known to be relevant to a set of specific queries. In a traditional technical system evaluation, a set of information needs is used to formulate a corresponding set of queries, which are addressed to the system and used to retrieve a set of documents. The retrieved documents are reviewed and judged for topical relevance to the corresponding queries. The test collection comprises the combination of the sets of documents, queries, and relevance assessments. Despite numerous problems and unresolved issues in the use of test collections, many centering around the limitations of topical relevance, it has remained the de facto "gold standard" for technical evaluation of system performance for over thirty years.

Recently, a new large-scale biomedical test collection for information retrieval testing was developed using a nontraditional approach (Bean et al., 1999). This test collection, based on the Current Bibliographies in Medicine (CBM) series of the National Library of Medicine (NLM), specifically targeted improvement of topical relevance assessment. Each CBM covers a distinct subject in biomedicine and was prepared by NLM's Reference Department in support of a specific NIH Consensus Development Conference (CDC). The scope and direction of each CDC are determined by a set of specific questions formulated by a planning committee and then addressed by a separate panel of experts, who synthesize the publicly available data and information into clear and accurate answers to the questions posed.

In preparing bibliographies in support of these consensus conferences, information professionals on the NLM staff work with NIH conference coordinators and other domain subject experts to define the scope and coverage of each bibliography. They then search a variety of online databases and combine the resulting citations with topical reference lists and other sources of citations. The final compilation of citations is examined for relevance by the team members and a draft bibliography subsequently forwarded to the subject experts for their review. Thus, the CDC questions represent a statement of information needs for a specific user group and purpose, and each CBM is custom-created by the NLM accordingly. As stated in the CBM series note since its inception in 1992, "The only criterion for the inclusion of a particular published work is its relevance to a topic being presented" (e.g., Conway & Cooper, 1997). In most of the bibliographies, the relevant citations are organized by topic.

In this study (Bean et al., 1999), test collection queries were derived from the original questions developed by the NIH planning committee for each CDC, and modified according to the topical structure of the corresponding CBM. That is, sets of unequivocal queries were reconstructed by mapping headings from the CBM Table of Contents to corresponding questions addressed by the CDCs. The headings and subheadings in the CBM Table of

Contents were examined to identify the most specific section or sections that corresponded exactly to the topic expressed in the questions or parts of questions.

Where citations were further organized into multiple subsections under the matched heading, the subheadings were disregarded. For example, the CBM Heading "Management of Advanced-stage and Recurrent Cervical Cancer," including its eight subheadings for specific therapies, was matched with the CDC Question "What is the appropriate management of advanced stage and recurrent cervical cancer?" CDC questions with multiple discrete parts were examined to determine where mapping was possible between parts of questions and headings. In these cases, the original questions were revised into well-formed sub-questions after eliminating the non-mapped phrasing. For example, the CBM Heading "Genotype/Phenotype Correlations in Cystic Fibrosis Patients" was matched to the sub-question "What is the current state of knowledge regarding genotype-phenotype correlations in cystic fibrosis?" that was derived from the CDC Question "What is the current state of knowledge regarding cystic fibrosis natural history, epidemiology, genotype-phenotype correlations, treatment, and genetic testing in various populations?"

In this manner, a set of baseline natural-language queries was "back-generated" by precise matching of questions with headings. Because only unequivocal mappings were accepted, each citation under a matched heading was deemed to have a priori relevance to the corresponding question. Each relevant citation thus identified was retrieved from the document test file. The topic of the query was compared to the topics of the cited texts to determine how they were related. One of the smaller query-relevant document sets will serve to demonstrate briefly the basic approach used to generate queries, map relevant citations to queries, and identify topical relationships between queries and relevant texts.

A 1997 CDC addressed issues around narcotic maintenance treatment for heroin addiction. The associated CBM is entitled *Effective Medical Treatment of Heroin Addiction* (Conway & Cooper, 1997). One of the specific questions posed to the panel of experts was: "What is the scientific evidence to support conceptualization of opiate addiction as a medical disorder including natural history, genetics and risk factors, and pathophysiology, and how is diagnosis established?" Organized according to the conference agenda, the CBM contains a main section entitled Molecular neurobiology and pathogenesis of opiate addiction; this section has four subsections, one on Genetic and other risk factors. The test collection query generated from the conference question and the bibliography headings was thus: "What is the scientific evidence regarding genetic and other risk factors to support conceptualization of opiate addiction as a medical disorder?" A shorter version of this query is: "What are the genetic and other risk factors underlying opiate addiction?"

The query may be defined by a conceptual structure containing the components "genetic factors" or "risk factors" in a direct evidentiary relationship with "opiate addiction." Further, the specification of opiate addiction as a "medical disorder" operationally constrains the species of interest to humans. Thus, the topic of the query may be expressed as "genetic risk factors for opiate addiction in humans," which has three main topical components: Genetic Risk Factors, Opiate Addiction, and Human Subjects.

The test collection document set contained five relevant documents for this query. The first tested a statistical model of two genetic pathways to drug abuse in humans. The second localized opioid receptor genes near the trait locus for high morphine consumption in mice. The third reported higher rates of dysfunction and psychopathology among children of parents with opioid dependance. The fourth found differences between rat strains in brain opioid levels and morphine tolerance and withdrawal. The fifth reported higher correlations for predictors associated with substance abuse in identical than in fraternal twins. In no case did the salient topics of the relevant document match in all respects the topical components of the query. However, each matched on one or more of the specific aspects, and where they did not match, their topics were related in other logical ways.

The topics substance abuse, drug abuse, opiate dependence, and morphine consumption, tolerance, and withdrawal are all relevant by virtue of participating in relationships that occur in a hierarchical context with Opiate Addiction. Substance and drug abuse are broader concepts while both morphine consumption and morphine tolerance and withdrawal are conceptually narrower than Opiate Addiction; opiate dependence can be seen as either a quasi-synonym or co-hyponym. Three of the five texts addressed Opiate Addiction indirectly through one of these hierarchically-related topics. Of the two documents that specifically addressed Opiate Addiction, one was about rats and the other dealt only indirectly with Genetic Risk Factors of addiction (i.e., dysfunctional behavior in children of opiate-dependent parents), topics related through inferential associations. Although three of the five documents dealt with rodent instead of Human Subjects, animal models are often used to provide extrapolative evidence for medical phenomena in humans. Two studies dealt directly with the topic of genetic mechanisms underlying Opiate Addiction. While neither of the human studies provided direct evidence, they used standard biomedical inferential associations of genetic mechanisms underlying heritable behaviors in close relatives, here, twins and parents and their children; similar inferences support genetic mechanisms underlying differences among different strains of rats.

Thus, even in this very brief example, the topical relationships between queries and relevant documents can be seen to comprise a variety of types other than exact matching, specifically hierarchical and complex associative relationships. This evidence further supports the conclusion that the domain of topical relevance relationships is limited only by the boundaries of human cognitive associations.

## 5. CONCLUSIONS

Relevance is a highly complex phenomenon, involving relationships on many different levels. These include, for example, the relationship between a text's language and a user's language abilities, the relationship between the substantive content expressed in the text and the depth and breadth of the user's own knowledge base, and, as we have been looking at, the relationship between the topic of a text passage and the topic of the user's need. The topical relevance relationship is, in turn, itself a highly complex phenomenon, much richer than the mere topic matching that has been its assumptive heritage.

The importance of topical relevance is sometimes downplayed because topic matching often fails to prove a reliable indicator of relevance. Clearly, topicality is only one factor contributing to relevance; it is unrealistic to assume that a broader and/or deeper understanding of topical relevance can ever obviate the need for a simultaneously broader and deeper understanding of other relevance factors. But it is now equally clear that topicality's contribution to relevance is not merely an issue of topic matching.

Topical relevance relationships include hierarchical and structural as well as topic-matching relationships, suggesting that every relationship imaginable can serve as a topical relevance relationship. Since such relationships are only functionally distinguishable from others, no distinct set of relationships can be singled out as topical relevance relationships. This means both that the study of topical relevance, in particular in literature retrieval, needs to be informed by work with relationships in other areas and that the results of our investigations should likewise inform other research and applications.

## References

Ali, S. N. (1993). Subject relationship between articles determined by co-occurrence of keywords in citing and cited titles. *Journal of Information Science*, 19, 225-232.

Barry, C. L. (1994). User-defined relevance criteria: An exploratory study. *Journal of the American Society for Information Science*, 45, 149-159.

Barry, C. L. (1998). Document representations and clues to document relevance. *Journal of the American Society for Information Science*, 49, 1293-1303.

Bean, C. A. & Green, R. (1997, July). Development of a structured inventory of relationships. Paper presented at Beyond Word Relations, ACM SIGIR '97 Workshop, Philadelphia, PA.

Bean, C. A., Selden, C. R., Rindflesch, T. C., & Aronson, A. R. (1999). From bibliography to test collection: Enhancing topical relevance assessment for bibliographic information retrieval system evaluation. *Proceedings of the 1999 AMIA Annual Fall Symposium*, 1022.

Belkin, N. J. (1980). The problem of 'matching' in information retrieval. In O. Harbo & L. Kajberg (Eds.), *Theory and Application of Information Research: Proceedings of the Second International Research Forum on Information Science, 3-6 August 1977, Royal School of Librarianship*, Copenhagen (pp. 187-197). London: Mansell.

Belkin, N. J., Oddy, R. N., & Brooks, H. M. (1982). ASK for information retrieval. *Journal of Documentation*, 38, 145-164.

Blair, D. C., & Maron, M. E. (1985). An evaluation of retrieval effectiveness for a full-text document-retrieval system. *Communications of the ACM*, 28, 289-299.

Boyce, B. (1982). Beyond topicality: A two stage view of relevance and the retrieval process. *Information Processing & Management*, 18, 105-109.

Conway, M. E., Cooper, J. R. (Comps.). (1997). *Effective Medical Treatment of Heroin Addiction* [bibliography]. Bethesda, MD: National Library of Medicine. Also available: <http://www.nlm.nih.gov/pubs/cbm/heroin_addiction.html> [2000, 5 May].

Cooper, W. S. (1971). A definition of relevance for information retrieval. *Information Storage and Retrieval*, 7, 19-37.

Cuadra, C. A. & Katter, R. V. (1967). Opening the black box of 'relevance.' *Journal of Documentation*, 23, 291-303.

Doyle, L. B. (1963). Is relevance an adequate criterion in retrieval system evaluation? *American Documentation Institute Proceedings*, 26th annual meeting, 199-200.

Eisenberg, M., & Schamber, L. (1988). Relevance: The search for a definition. *Proceedings of the 51st Annual Meeting of the American Society for Information Science*, 25, 164-

168.

Froelich, T. J. (1994). Relevance reconsidered—Towards an agenda for the 21st century: Introduction to special topic issue on relevance research. *Journal of the American Society for Information Science*, 45, 124-134.

Gentner, D. & Gentner, D. R. (1983). Flowing waters or teeming crowds: Mental models of electricity. In D. Gentner & A. L. Stevens (Eds.), *Mental Models*. Hillsdale, NJ: Lawrence Erlbaum.

Gillaspie, D. L. (1992). Why online legal retrieval misses conceptually relevant documents. *Proceedings of the 55th ASIS Annual Meeting*, 29, 256-259.

Green, R. (1997). A relational thesaurus: Modeling semantic relationships using frames. Unpublished manuscript; OCLC Library and Information Science Research Grant final report.

Green, R. & Bean, C. A. (1995): Topical relevance relationships. II. An exploratory study and preliminary typology. *Journal of the American Society for Information Science*, 46, 654-662.

Harter, S. P. (1992). Psychological relevance and information science. *Journal of the American Society for Information Science*, 43, 602-615.

Harter, S. P., Nisonger, T. E., & Weng, A. (1993). Semantic relationships between cited and citing articles in library and information science journals. *Journal of the American Society for Information Science*, 44, 543-552.

Hirsh, S. G. (1999). Children's relevance criteria and information seeking on electronic resources. *Journal of the American Society for Information* Science, 50, 1265-1283.

Kuhlthau, C. C. (1991). Inside the search process: Information seeking from the user's perspective. *Journal of the American Society for Information Science*, 42, 361-371.

Langridge, D. (1989). *Subject Analysis: Principles and Procedures*. London: Bowker-Saur.

Markey, K. (1984). Interindexer consistency tests: A literature review and report of a test of consistency in indexing visual materials. *Library & Information Science Research*, 6, 155-177.

Martyn, J. (1964). Bibliographic coupling. *Journal of Documentation*, 20, 236.

Martyn, J. (1975). Progress in documentation—Citation analysis. *Journal of Documentation*, 31, 290-297.

Saracevic, T. (1976). Relevance: A review of the literature and a framework for thinking on the notion in information science. *Advances in Librarianship*, 6, 79-138.

Schamber, L. (1994). Relevance and information behavior. *Annual Review of Information Science and Technology*, 29, 3-48.

Sievert, M., McKinin, E. J., Johnson, E.D., Reid, J. C., & Mitchell, J. A. (1996). Beyond relevance—Characteristics of key papers for clinicians: An exploratory study in an academic setting. *Bulletin of the Medical Library Association*, 84, 351-358.

Sperber, D. & Wilson, D. (1986). *Relevance: Communication and Cognition*. Cambridge, MA: Harvard University Press.

Swanson, D. R. (1990). Medical literature as a potential source of new knowledge. *Bulletin of the Medical Library Association*, 78, 29-37.

Trivison, D. (1987). Term co-occurrence in cited/citing journal articles as a measure of document similarity. *Information Processing & Management*, 23, 183-194.

Wang, P. & Soergel, D. (1998). A cognitive model of document use during a research project. Study I. Document selection. *Journal of the American Society for Information Science*, 49, 115-133.

Weinberg, B. H. (1994). [Letter to the editor]. *Journal of the American Society for Information Science*, 45, 317.

Wilson, P. (1973). Situational relevance. *Information Storage and Retrieval*, 9, 457-471.

# PART II

**Relationships in the Organization of Knowledge: Systems**

# Chapter 9

# Relationships in Library of Congress Subject Headings

Lynn M. El-Hoshy
*Library of Congress, Washington, DC, USA*

**Abstract:**

This chapter describes the expression of relationships in a traditional library subject heading system, Library of Congress Subject Headings (LCSH). Following an introductory section on the history and scope of LCSH, information is presented on its reference structure, documentation, and notation. The development and current use of references to express equivalence, hierarchical, and associative relationships are discussed. Other relational devices, such as scope notes and Library of Congress Classification numbers, are also covered. Changes to improve the reference structure of LCSH and facilitate its use in online catalogs are reviewed.

## 1. INTRODUCTION

The Library of Congress Subject Headings system, commonly referred to as LCSH, was begun in 1898 in order to assign headings that represent the contents of books and periodicals in the collections of the Library of Congress on printed cards filed in a new dictionary catalog. The Library acquired materials on all subjects but assigned headings only to materials on topics covered by the Library of Congress Classification, which began development at the same time. The range of topics for which headings were assigned broadened as schedules of the classification were completed. Headings were initially selected from a list of subject headings compiled by a committee of the American Library Association (1898) for use in small and medium-sized libraries. As Library of Congress catalogers encountered works on subjects not included in that list, they consulted additional sources and devised new headings to fit into the system. After the Library of Congress offered its catalog cards for purchase in 1902, other libraries began to use those headings in their own card catalogs. J. C. M. Hanson (1909, p. 389), Chief of the Catalogue Division of the Library of Congress from 1897 to 1910, stated that decisions regarding the subject catalog were made to enable the Library to cooperate with the largest possible number of American libraries. He concluded that the success of the card distribution service depended largely on the presence of subject headings on an increasing proportion of cards.

The first list of headings was prepared and issued in parts from 1909 to 1914 under the title *Subject Headings Used in the Dictionary Catalogues of the Library of Congress*. Supplements and cumulative editions appeared at irregular intervals in the following years as subject headings accumulated to parallel the growth in library acquisitions. With the

135

*C. A. Bean and R. Green (eds.), Relationships in the Organization of Knowledge,* 135–152.

eighth edition in 1975, the title was changed to *Library of Congress Subject Headings*. By that time, LCSH had grown beyond the catalogs of the Library of Congress to become the most widely used subject heading list in American libraries. Additionally, it served as a pattern for the development of other general subject heading systems and was translated and/or adapted for use in other countries (Chan, 1995, pp. 3-4; 1998). Thus, when the format for exchanging bibliographic data in machine-readable form was developed in the late 1960s and libraries implemented systems to make use of that data, subject headings that were originally developed for manual card catalogs became the means of subject access in new online public access catalogs. In 1986, subject heading data were converted to the MARC format for exchanging authority data, and a weekly tape distribution service of subject authority records was initiated. Since then, incorporating those authority records into online catalogs and making use of their features to facilitate subject searching have become concerns for librarians and system designers.

In addition to history, it is important to understand the scope of LCSH. It contains headings for topical concepts and phenomena of all types as well as headings for proper-named entities that are not capable of authorship, such as products, buildings, structures, and wars or other disastrous events. It also includes headings for family names and nonjurisdictional geographics, such as continents and regions, geographic features of all types, parks, and celestial bodies. LCSH is meant to be used in conjunction with the Library of Congress name authority file or national authority file, which contains headings for names of persons, corporate bodies (including jurisdictions), and uniform titles that may be assigned as subject headings to works about those entities. Subdivisions are widely used in LCSH to combine various aspects of a topic into one heading, and as a device for arranging entries that share the same main heading. Subdivisions may represent subtopics or topical aspects, geographics, time periods, or forms of materials (e.g., —**Economic aspects**; —**Washington (D.C.)**; —**20th century**; —**Bibliography**). Heading/subdivision combinations that represent unique concepts are included in LCSH. Subdivisions that represent geographics and common or frequently used topics and forms are "free-floating"; that is, they may be combined with designated categories of subject headings according to rules to synthesize headings that are not represented by subject authority records. Therefore, the universe of subject headings assigned to bibliographic records far exceeds the headings explicitly contained in LCSH.

## 2. REFERENCE STRUCTURE AND DOCUMENTATION

A structure of references connects the entries in LCSH and delineates their relationships. References lead from entry terms to authorized headings to express equivalence, for example, "Bakery products *use* **Baked products**." These serve to bring materials on the same subjects together in a library catalog. References link headings to express hierarchy, for example, "**Baked products** *search also under* **Muffins**," and to express other associations, for example, "**Birds** *search also under* **Ornithology**." These references enable searchers to broaden, narrow, or redirect searches systematically. The specific categories of equivalence, hierarchical, and associative relationships for which references are made are now defined and documented. That was not the case before the 1980s.

The nineteenth century dictionary catalog movement from which LCSH grew was based on the theories and rules of Charles Ammi Cutter, who recognized that alphabetically arranged, specific subject headings need to be tied together by references. Cutter's rules (1904, pp. 70-71) called for two types of references: from terms not chosen as headings to their selected forms and "from general subjects to their various subordinate subjects and also to coordinate and illustrative subjects" to form a "pyramid of references" (p. 79). Cutter served as a member of the committee that prepared the ALA list on which LCSH was based. Its introduction cited two difficult tasks confronting compilers of subject heading lists: choosing between synonyms and related headings and making necessary cross references. It noted that cross references should be liberally supplied to bring together in a catalog all books on a subject. Terms chosen as headings were those "under which it is supposed that the majority of educated Americans will look" with references from other forms. The list of *see also* references was "especially full" (American Library Association, 1898, p. iv).

Early editions of LCSH contained no explanation of the basis on which references were made. In an address near the end of his tenure, Hanson (1909) devoted more attention to justifying the forms of subject headings, particularly the use of inversion and subordination to collocate subjects, than to elucidating references. Speaking on the varying order of terms in headings that combined place and topic, he said, "Our chief consolation has been that references will presumably furnish the necessary clue to the location of entries, and thus disarm to some extent the criticisms sure to be hurled at us for inconsistencies, real as well as apparent" (p. 387). He also disclosed the closely intertwined relationship that existed between the dictionary catalog and Library of Congress Classification and the reliance placed on classed entries in the adjacent card shelflist to provide the complementary systematic arrangement of subjects. From the fourth edition on, introductions published with LCSH supplied some explanation of headings and references.

David Judson Haykin (1951), Chief of the Subject Cataloging Division of the Library of Congress from 1941 to 1952, provided in his practical guide the first public statement of the principles underlying LCSH and the policies in force at mid-century. He included information about references in a chapter on structure and integration in the subject catalog. Following that publication, the Library of Congress made announcements on specific policy issues and practices as needed. In 1984, a preliminary edition of a manual on constructing and applying headings was published in order to facilitate cooperation with other libraries. The loose-leaf *Subject Cataloging Manual: Subject Headings*, hereafter called SCM:SH (Library of Congress, 1996), is now in its fifth edition and is updated semiannually. The manual's instruction sheets on references are cited in the following sections of this chapter. In response to calls for a subject cataloging code during the 1980s and the perceived need for a contemporary statement on the basic principles of LCSH, the Library of Congress commissioned Lois Mai Chan (1990) to prepare a document on its principles of structure and policies of application. Chan (1995) also authored the basic textbook on LCSH, which is now in its third edition. Kirtland and Cochrane (1982) compiled a bibliography on critical evaluations of LCSH written from post-World War II to 1979 that is organized by categories, including syndetic structure, and that contains commentaries. Shubert (1992) critiqued their bibliographic essay and provided a similarly organized survey of the literature published on LCSH in the 1980s.

## 3.  REFERENCE NOTATION

A collateral aspect of the reference structure of a subject heading system is its notation. The system for denoting references in LCSH evolved and then underwent a major change in the 1980s. In early editions of LCSH, the terms used as headings and references were not distinguished by typography. Following some entry terms were instructions to *see* other terms; following other entries were instructions to *see also* other terms. Heading entries in the predecessor ALA list had included *refer froms*, or reversed references, terms from which *see* or *see also* references were made, although they were not differentiated. For the fourth edition of LCSH in 1943, the first volume continued the pattern of previous editions, while a second volume contained a separate listing of headings, each followed by *refer from* references in separate groups of *see* and *see also* reference tracings. With the fifth edition in 1948, these tracings were incorporated into the regular list of headings and entry terms with identifying symbols: *sa* for *see also*, *x* for *refer from (see)*, and *xx* for *refer from (see also)*. These symbols became a standard feature of later editions and supplements until they were replaced in the 1980s by the standard designations of BT, NT, RT, and UF used in thesauri.

At a conference on subject retrieval, Richard S. Angell (1972), who succeeded Haykin as Chief of the Subject Cataloging Division of the Library of Congress, described LCSH and enumerated his recommendations for improving the system. In the interest of making LCSH more intelligible to users and compatible with other indexing vocabularies, he recommended replacing the traditional designations of references and tracings with those commonly used in thesauri through the use of a computer program. He viewed such a conversion as an opportunity to conduct a systematic review and revision of the reference structure so that the resulting references would match their new designations. These issues were later considered by participants at a meeting on subject access convened by the Council on Library Resources (Russell, 1982). Although they recommended editing the reference structure of LCSH to make true hierarchical relationships explicit and evaluating whether headings could be rearranged and displayed hierarchically, the participants gave higher priority to creating and distributing a current machine-readable version of LCSH with regular updates. A subcommittee of the ALA Subject Analysis Committee (SAC) (1985) surveyed a random sample of librarians and library educators on suggested changes to the format of LCSH products and found a preference for using words instead of symbols to designate references in the printed and microfiche lists. A majority of survey respondents supported a possible future change to thesaurus-like terminology.

Meanwhile planning for bringing subject headings online was underway at the Library of Congress. When data on approximately 150,000 LCSH entries were converted to the MARC authority format in early 1986, an automatic substitution of designations occurred based on the fact that broader and related headings could be differentiated in tracings fields of authority records through the use of the value "g" in a control subfield. An official announcement explained,

> If a term appeared only in the listing of "xx" (refer from) tracings, it was coded "g" for broader term. If the term appeared both in the listing of "xx" and "sa" tracings, it was coded "n" for related term. Because no intellectual evaluation of the references was

done and because a new policy for making cross references was introduced in 1985, these designations in many cases will be incorrect ("Cross reference structure," 1986).

No systematic review of the reference structure was undertaken or planned at that time. The 1986 microfiche cumulation and the 11th printed edition of LCSH in 1988 were the first to display the new notation. Adoption of the thesaural codes was criticized by Dykstra (1988) as misleading and irresponsible because headings in LCSH are not single concepts constructed according to the national and international standards for thesauri.

Today the approximately quarter million subject authority records reside in a master database at the Library of Congress and serve as the source of the printed, microfiche, and CD-ROM editions of LCSH as well as subscription record distribution services. In those records, data about subject headings are encoded following the MARC 21 authority format. References are carried in those records as *see from* or *used for* (UF) terms in tracing fields tagged as 4XX, and as *see also from* broader term (BT) and related term (RT) headings in tracing fields tagged as 5XX. Because of the extra work that would be involved in maintaining authority records, the Library of Congress does not record narrower term (NT) headings in tracing fields, where they could be identified with the value "h" in a control subfield. Programs are required to translate field tags and codes in order to generate the reciprocal *use* and narrower term (NT) references in lists and thesaural displays. Systems that support online catalogs need to generate appropriate labels and reference instruction phrases, such as "Search under ..." or "Search also under ...." The ability to provide any further differentiation of references depends on the coding available in the authority format and the implementation of the format at the Library of Congress.

## 4. EQUIVALENCE RELATIONSHIPS

The principle of a uniform heading is applied in LCSH. One term or phrase is selected as the valid heading to represent a discrete subject. References are made from equivalent terms and phrases to valid headings. These references help catalogers to find and apply headings when they catalog items containing variant terminology and enable searchers to match their vocabulary with authorized headings. Haykin (1951, p. 13) wrote that *see* references tell the reader "That which you seek under this heading is to be found in this catalog under the heading referred to" or "Look for the subject matter you desire under the heading referred to."

Guidelines on making *use* references in LCSH are given in an instruction sheet in the SCM:SH (H 373). *Use* references are made for both semantic and lexical variants. Semantic variants are primarily synonyms and include technical versus popular terms for concepts and processes (e.g., "Parabolic antennas *use* **Satellite dish antennas**," and "Heart attack *use* **Myocardial infarction**") and scientific versus common names of organisms (e.g., "Galanthus *use* **Snowdrops**"). Foreign terms are given as *use* references only if they are in general use in English language sources (e.g., Aufklärung *use* **Enlightenment**). In those situations in which a foreign term has been accepted into widespread English use, it will generally be selected as the valid heading with references made from less frequently used English equivalents; for example:

**Tofu**
 UF        Bean curd
            Soybean curd

Regional or national variants of English can also be accommodated. With the growing availability and use of bibliographic records in databases of bibliographic utilities with international membership, LCSH is increasingly being applied in English language cataloging outside the United States, including the United Kingdom. In 1995 the British Library reinstated the use of LCSH on records in the *British National Bibliography* in response to demand from customers and cooperative partners (Elliot, 1994/5). Where there is a one-to-one correspondence between customary British English usage and the American usage reflected in LCSH, as with railways for **Railroads**, terms can be linked with a *use* reference. If these references were flagged, they could support the switching of headings and references to present users with their preferred terminology. However, difficulties arise when the same term has different meanings, as with football (MacEwan, 1996, p. 5). The current solution in LCSH is:

**Football**                          **Soccer**
 UF        American football      UF        Association football
                                              Football (Soccer)

The category of synonyms is extended to encompass near synonyms and narrower terms when they are not considered useful as separate headings. A pragmatic approach to making references was generally followed over the years. The introduction to the ninth edition of LCSH (Library of Congress, 1980, p. ix) stated, "See references are not necessarily statements of equivalence; they simply indicate to catalogers and catalog users that a particular word or concept does not have a separate file but is entered under another heading." Currently, upward references (*use* references from narrower terms) are made only when it is judged clearly impractical to establish and maintain separate headings.

Antonyms represent a special type of *use* reference that was made more frequently in the past, possibly because they could be viewed as poles on a continuum. Cutter (1904, p. 71) advised choosing one of two subjects exactly opposite and referring from the other, but granted exceptions. Angell (1972, p. 156) recognized antonyms as a valid type of *see* reference, and Chan (1995, p. 126) included them in the listing of types of *use* references that are found in LCSH. They are not mentioned in the current instruction sheet in the SCM:SH (H 373).

Problematic situations exist when concepts that were once considered vague or imprecise were not established as headings but instead were added as *use* references to two or more related headings; for example:

**Acoustics**
 USE       Hearing
            Sound

Such references are remnants of past practice that persist in LCSH because time and effort are required to sort out the necessary distinctions to establish a separate heading and to update the bibliographic entries that were cataloged over the years according to those references.

Lexical variants include spelling variations; singular/plural forms; variant word endings; alternative forms of expression, including phrases versus subdivisions; and rearrangements of terms to provide entry under significant words, particularly direct versus inverted order. Abbreviations, acronyms, and initialisms are made as *use* references only when they are in general use. Alphabetic adjacency is taken into consideration and preference is given to hierarchy. An inverted *use* reference is not made if it would begin with the same word as a hierarchical broader term reference. For example, on the heading **Talking birds** a *use* reference is not made from "Birds, Talking" because the heading has a broader term reference **Birds**.

Haykin (1951, p. 8) advocated a policy of constant change of headings to reflect current usage and to maintain an up-to-date catalog. When the form of a heading is changed or canceled in favor of another heading, the earlier form is included as a UF in the record for the later heading. These explicitly coded reference tracings are intended to aid in bibliographic file maintenance. In the printed editions of LCSH they bear the legend *[Former heading]*. After the coding was implemented in the Library of Congress subject authority file in 1988, retrospective projects were undertaken to add and code UFs for earlier forms on headings that were changed through the 1970s. There are three situations in which this type of reference cannot be made. The first is when the only difference between an earlier and later form of heading is the presence of a hyphen, diacritic, or upper or lowercase letter because these forms normalize to the same character string for computer filing. Another situation in which an earlier form of heading is not recorded occurs with the revision of a heading and associated headings constructed with subdivisions combined with that same heading. For example, when the previous headings **Implant dentures** and **Implant dentures—Complications** were revised to **Dental implants** and **Dental implants—Complications**, the reference from the earlier form of heading was added only to the unsubdivided heading **Dental implants** because a subdivision can only be attached to a valid heading in LCSH. The third situation in which a UF for an earlier form is not made is when a heading for a precoordinated concept is canceled in favor of two or more headings that represent that concept coextensively. Examples are headings of the type **[class of persons]—Education—[topic]** (e.g., **Gifted children—Education—Science**), which were replaced by two headings: **[class of persons]—Education** and **[topic]—Study and teaching** (e.g., **Gifted children—Education** and **Science—Study and teaching**). A change of this type generally occurs when the level of precoordination in a heading is reconsidered and judged to have been inadvisable.

When relationships exist between entry terms and headings or subdivisions that cannot be adequately conveyed by one or more simple references, LCSH allows the creation of complex or *general see* references as outlined in the SCM:SH (H 374). These references are made to a category of headings or subdivisions rather than to individual headings, and frequently list one or more individual headings as examples. *General see* references are made in three situations:

- From non-used variant forms of national and ethnic adjectival qualifiers to their preferred adjectival forms instead of making an explicit *use* reference to each heading established with that qualifier (e.g., Ecuadoran to Ecuadorian);
- From variant spellings of a common word used in several headings in preference to

making explicit *use* references to individual headings beginning with or including that same word (e.g., catalogue to catalog); and

- From a concept to a corresponding free-floating subdivision when no generic heading for that concept exists.

An example of the last case is the form subdivision —**Amateurs' manuals**, which may be added to headings for technical topics to designate a do-it-yourself manual on that topic, e.g., **Brewing—Amateurs' manuals**. No general heading for amateurs' manuals exists in LCSH, most likely because the Library of Congress has not yet cataloged a general item about such manuals that would require the heading. A *general see* reference is created to provide lead-in vocabulary from that phrase and to alert catalog users to the existence of the subdivision.

Enhancements to the entry vocabulary of LCSH are discussed in the last section on "Improving the reference structure of LCSH."

## 5. HIERARCHICAL RELATIONSHIPS

Haykin (1951, p. 14) called the system of *see also* references a substitute for logic in the alphabetic subject catalog and a device for binding related headings together. His rules for making them were

1) to more specific subjects or to topics comprehended within it, or to an application of the subject; and 2) to coordinate subjects which suggest themselves as likely to be of interest to the user seeking material under the given heading, because they represent other aspects of the subject, or are closely related to it.

He did not categorize the nature of specificity nor state whether references would be reciprocal in the latter case. Twenty years later, Angell (1972, pp. 154-155) outlined the process that had been followed for some time in adopting new headings in LCSH and that involved making *see also* hierarchical references in a downward direction from one level to the next lower level, reciprocal *see also* references between related headings, and *see* references in a lateral direction. That approach served as the grounds for his recommendation for a switch to thesaural reference notation. However, he also acknowledged that someone might not be able to discern that practice from looking at the published list of headings because references reflecting other practices survive in LCSH, judgments on the nature of relationships are subjective, and errors may be missed in editorial review. Indeed, over the years several authors have criticized the *see also* reference structure of LCSH or examined references in specific subject domains, pointed out deficiencies and inconsistencies, and suggested improvements or total restructuring (Richmond, 1959; Coates, 1960; Sinkankas, 1972; Wepsiec, 1978, 1982, 1991; Petersen, 1983; Weinberg, 1993).

In response to calls for a more rational reference structure, a staff committee met at the Library of Congress from 1983 to 1984 to determine the principles to be followed in making references among headings. The resulting principles, which stress hierarchical relationships, were adopted in 1985 and incorporated into an instruction sheet in the SCM:SH (H 370).

Headings established or revised after that date follow the new guidelines. They may be identified by a value "a" in a fixed field byte of the MARC authority format (008/29) that indicates whether references have been evaluated. At the time of the initial file conversion in 1986, that value was set either to "b" to indicate that references had not been evaluated and may not conform to the guidelines or to "n" for not applicable if no references were present. Efforts to review and revise the hierarchical references of LCSH are covered in the last section.

Following the new guidelines, hierarchical broader term/narrower term (BT/NT) references are made to indicate three types of relationships: genus/species or class/class member, whole/part, and instance or generic topic/proper-named example. Headings that belong to more than one logical hierarchy receive references from each hierarchy. Headings are linked only to the next broader heading in each hierarchy. Broader term/narrower term references are generally required for each heading, except in a limited number of situations in which orphan headings (headings without references) are allowed:

- Headings that represent a top term, or the broadest topic in a hierarchy,
- Headings for geographic regions,
- Headings for family names, and
- Inverted headings with adjectival qualifiers for language, nationality, ethnic group, or time period when the only appropriate broader term reference would be an identical heading without qualification (e.g., **Art, French**).

Headings are established to fill hierarchical "gaps" if a missing heading comes readily to mind or becomes apparent in the process of checking dictionaries, thesauri, etc., while carrying out the routine research required for proposing a new heading.

How a heading is formulated can affect its relationship to other headings and therefore the references that are made to it. Headings that are constructed by combining subdivisions with main headings occasionally express subordination in their basic structure. Although topical subdivisions are used most frequently to designate attributes, actions and processes, or aspects of a subject, some heading/subdivision combinations, particularly for equipment and vehicles, represent whole/part relationships (e.g., **Airplanes—Motors**). In addition, some older headings that include subdivisions represent past practice and embody hierarchical relationships (e.g., **Blood groups—ABO system**, **Blood groups—Lewis system**). Headings that are constructed with conjunctions, prepositions, or certain parenthetical additions to represent compound or complex topics do not necessarily fit neatly into hierarchical categories. Therefore, guidelines were adopted for linking compound headings on the basis of the words that they contain. As a general rule, the generic heading for the concept that is the second element in the heading is considered the broader heading, even if the resulting reference is not truly hierarchical; for example:

| **Camping with dogs** | | **Dogs as laboratory animals** | |
|---|---|---|---|
| BT | Dogs | BT | Laboratory animals |

In the past, complex or *general see also* references were made in many instances to categories of headings rather than to individual headings, frequently listing one or two as examples. They were made in situations in which it was not considered practical to make individual references to all specific headings encompassed by a broader heading. In some cases, specific references were present in the official catalog of the Library of Congress, but for reasons of economy, a *general see also* reference was included in the printed list. These references suggested the pattern of headings under which a group of topics was entered, and alerted searchers who may have entered the catalog at a level broader than intended to the existence of specific headings. Policies in place today favor making individual BT/NT references in such situations. *General see also* references continue to be made according to the guidelines given in the SCM:SH (H 371). They are made to refer from a generic heading to a corresponding free-floating subdivision, or to refer from a generic heading to a group of headings beginning with the same word, usually from a noun to its variant adjectival form, for example, "**Heart**, search also under headings beginning with the word **Cardiac**." *General see also* references are also made from a subject heading for a category of organizations to the comparable category of name headings, for example, "**Museums**, search also under names of individual museums." Until 1986, when they were abandoned because of maintenance problems, the Library of Congress made individual subject-to-name references for name headings of individual corporate bodies that had been assigned as subject headings. Wilson (1998) has traced the history of subject-to-name references for corporate bodies and argued for their reinstatement to provide better subject access to individual corporate bodies in online catalogs.

## 6. ASSOCIATIVE RELATIONSHIPS

Coates (1960, p. 69) analyzed the reference structure of LCSH and concluded that there were two distinct layers of references linking related headings. The first layer was a rather complete network of downward hierarchical references and horizontal coordinate references, apparently based on a classification scheme. "Superimposed upon this is a second layer of references, the content of which is unpredictable and apparently unrelated to any underlying principle." He stated that without precise definitions of what collateral subjects are, "the collateral relationship may be invoked to justify indiscriminate reference linkages" (p. 74). Angell (1972, pp. 157-158) echoed Coates' observation and advocated studying collateral *see also* references. In recommending a review of the entire reference structure of LCSH, he observed that "many NT tracings would be recognized as 'one-way collateral see also's' and removed or made reciprocal as the case required."

The reference policies that were put in effect in 1985 include restrictive rules for related term references. The intention of the policies is to focus attention on hierarchical relationships and to reduce the size and complexity of LCSH by minimizing the number of related term references. Those rules, which are given in the SCM:SH (H 370), first state the situations in which related term references should *not* be made:

- To link headings beginning with the same word or word stem unless they are top terms in the hierarchies of a discipline,
- To link two headings having a common broader term at any level of a hierarchy, or
- To link two headings if headings at higher levels of their respective hierarchies are already linked by related term references.

Related term references are allowed in three situations, but only if not covered by the prohibitions:

- To link a discipline and an object studied,
- To link headings for classes of persons and their fields of endeavor, and
- To link two terms that have overlapping meanings or that are needed to define each other.

Decisions on references in the latter category are made on a case-by-case basis as headings are reviewed and added to LCSH.

## 7. SCOPE NOTES

Selected scope notes were present in LCSH from the start. They were regarded as directions and definitions whose purpose was "to aid in maintaining proper distinctions between closely related and overlapping subjects" (Hanson, 1909, p. 392). Haykin (1951, pp. 18-19) included them with references in his discussion on structure and integration and wrote that a scope note

partakes of the nature of a definition on one hand and a "see also" reference on the other. It may, in fact, include both definitions and references. Its principal feature, however, is that it indicates the limits within which the subject entries under it fall and at what points other headings will serve the reader's needs.

Currently only 2 percent of subject headings have associated scope notes. An instruction sheet in the SCM:SH (H 400) describes the categories of headings for which scope notes have been made and outlines the procedures for making them. In addition to the first category of a single heading defined without reference to any other heading, the second category is a single heading described with reference to more specific headings. This type of note was supplied when it was felt necessary to state explicitly that a heading is used for the topic in its most general sense and that specific aspects are found under more specific headings. The instruction sheet remarks that this situation is more commonly handled by making a *general see also* reference or specific BT/NT references. An additional category is two or more closely related or overlapping headings in which reciprocal "mirror image" notes under each heading provide contrasting information regarding the scope and usage of superficially similar headings. In the current environment in which the provision of related term references is restricted, related headings that are differentiated in scope notes are generally not also linked by references. Indeed, the two headings used as examples in the instruction sheet, **Ageism** and **Age discrimination**, would not be candidates for such links because they begin with the same word stem. The unpredictability of whether information about related headings is found in scope notes or in references can hamper attempts to display that information consistently and to make use of it to expand searches in a systematic manner.

## 8. LIBRARY OF CONGRESS CLASSIFICATION NUMBERS

What a subject heading accomplishes with words, a classification number accomplishes with notation: to represent the subject contents of library items. Subject headings and classification numbers provide complementary access to subjects. Library of Congress Classification (LCC) numbers are carried in authority records for approximately 32 percent of the subject headings in LCSH and appear directly following those headings in LCSH products. They are added to individual subject headings when there is an identical or close correspondence between the scope, meaning, and language of the subject heading and the classification schedule caption associated with the classification number. Because LCC is an enumerative system based on disciplines or fields of knowledge, topics can be scattered by application or aspect. Therefore, a subject heading could have more than one corresponding class number. For example, works on corn as a plant are classified in subclass QK for Botany of class Q for Science, while works on corn as a field crop are classified in subclass SB for Plant Culture of class S for Agriculture. In such cases, both numbers are supplied with a qualifying term added to each, for example, **Corn [QK495.G74 (Botany)] [SB191.M2 (Culture)]**. Spans of numbers are provided for topics that have breakdowns or captions indented under them in the classification schedules, such as **Computer networks [TK5105.5-TK5105.9]**. It is not possible to provide a number for all headings because many areas of the classification do not provide the same level of specificity as LCSH does. Numbers for topics in the classification schedules that correspond to headings constructed with a free-floating subdivision added to a main heading will not be recorded unless an authority record has been made for that combination.

Class numbers were present following headings in the first edition of LCSH. In his history of the evolution of dictionary subject cataloging, Miksa (1983, pp. 216-221) described the influence that the developing classification system had on decisions regarding the structure of subject headings and contended that both systems embodied attempts to provide a useful collocation of subjects. Hanson (1909, p. 391) stated the purpose for supplying matching numbers with subject headings:

> The plan is to have numbers of the new classification fully represented, thus making the list of subjects in a measure an index to the classification. Further, systematic arrangement of the subjects for the dictionary catalog has generally been regarded as a more effective means of furnishing a survey of related headings than the usual array of references from general to specific subjects. Up to the present time it has been carried out by means of the card shelf list for a part of science, technology, bibliography and history. By printing the class mark opposite each subject the extension of the plan to other classes represented in the new classification will be much simplified. The main purpose of this systematic arrangement is naturally to aid the cataloger in the assignment of subjects, and to prevent the dispersion of books on the same or closely related subjects under different headings. It should also prove of assistance to users of the catalog.

Today LCSH and LCC are issued jointly in a quarterly cumulative CD-ROM publication called *Classification Plus*. Through hypertext links, one can jump directly from a class number associated with a subject heading to that number in a classification schedule and see its caption and placement in a classified array. The usefulness of this feature is limited only by the quality and quantity of the links. Currently, the Library of Congress provides accurate class numbers on newly established subject headings for which they can be supplied. In the past, however, there was no systematic attempt to keep the headings and class numbers in synchrony nor to review the assigned numbers in an organized manner. The introduction to the 22nd edition of LCSH (Library of Congress, 1999, p. ix) cautions that class numbers "should not be used without verification in the latest editions of the schedules and their supplements." Class numbers on existing headings are revised on a case-by-case basis as errors or omissions are discovered and reported to the Library of Congress.

In online catalogs with linked authority and bibliographic records, providing connections from subject headings with their associated references to class numbers assigned to items can be a powerful tool. Mitchell (this volume) reports on efforts and research to link LCSH and class numbers in the Dewey Decimal Classification.

## 9. IMPROVING THE REFERENCE STRUCTURE OF LCSH

One of the assumptions of the Council on Library Resources meeting on subject access in 1982 was that LCSH would be the controlled subject vocabulary in online public access catalogs (Russell, 1982, p. 68). Recommendations from the meeting addressed how subject access in online catalogs could be improved with the highest priority going to making LCSH available in machine-readable form. As Mandel and Herschman (1983, p. 153) summarized,

> In order to get the most from the controlled vocabulary used by the great majority of American libraries, efforts should be made to update and distribute LCSH in a useful machine readable form, to improve its cross-reference structure, and to consider means for displaying the hierarchical relationships among its terms.

An additional high priority was placed on establishing mechanisms for a set of libraries to contribute new subject headings to LCSH, and for reference librarians and catalogers at a larger group of libraries to suggest *see* references for inclusion in LCSH, possibly using transaction logs from online public access catalogs as a source of terms (Russell, 1982, pp. 69-70). That same year the Council funded a short-term project to address the second need. The LCSH Entry Vocabulary Project began with a nucleus of four libraries and had as its objective the development of procedures for outside libraries to propose new entry terms for consideration in the LCSH editorial review process. Cochrane (1983) outlined the procedures set up during the project and reported that they showed every sign of continuing for an indefinite period. Proposals made during the initial project filled gaps in the reference structure of LCSH and pointed out the need for new or revised headings in some cases, and for better and more explicit guidelines for making references. The project formed the basis for the establishment later that year of the Cooperative Subject Cataloging Projects (CSCP) at the Library of Congress to process proposals from libraries for additions and changes to LCSH. After the founding of the Program for Cooperative Cataloging, CSCP was renamed the Subject Authority Cooperative Program (SACO) in 1995. Through SACO more than 90 libraries of all types in the United States and other countries currently propose new headings and references for LCSH as well as changes to existing headings. Having a large and diverse pool of contributors ensures a constant stream of subject heading proposals that represent a variety of users. Enriching the lead-in vocabulary of LCSH requires constant vigilance on the part of catalogers to seek and identify variant terminology when they propose new headings, and to recognize the need to add missing entry terms as references to existing headings when they consult LCSH. Providing more entry vocabulary gives users a greater chance of matching their natural language search terms with the subject headings applied in a catalog. Bates (1986, 1989) proposed adding an expanded "superthesaurus" enriched with a vast number of entry terms as a user interface to controlled vocabularies like LCSH in online catalogs in order to help users orient themselves and to provide guidance in employing techniques like keyword searching and Boolean combinations.

Improving the references that link headings in LCSH has been a gradual process since the change in reference notation enabled the differentiation of hierarchical and related term references. The references of headings established after 1985 follow the guidelines that were put in place to emphasize hierarchical relationships and are coded as evaluated. References on older headings are evaluated, revised, and recoded on a case-by-case basis as headings are changed, or as workload permits. Fifty-one percent of headings now have references that are coded as evaluated, while 23 percent are coded as not evaluated. References are also added to existing headings that lack them unless a heading belongs to one of the categories for which orphan headings are allowed; currently, 26 percent of headings are orphan headings.

Online catalogs that include authority records and link headings in bibliographic records with those authority records can help users refine or redirect their searches by providing displays of headings and the relationships among them. Therefore, it is important to continue the intellectual work of revising the references of individual headings in LCSH so that displays of relationships will be conceptually sound. However, at some point, it will be necessary to evaluate the overall structure. Chan (1995, p. 403) noted that references are apparently created on a "heading-by-heading basis without attempting to fit concepts into a systematic structure." She suggested that a useful area of research would be the question of whether a classification scheme, either existing, to be adapted, or to be constructed, could function as a hierarchical guide to mapping the structure of LCSH.

At the 1994 annual meeting of the Subject Analysis Committee (SAC) of the Cataloging and Classification Section of the Association for Library Collections & Technical Services division of the American Library Association, two discussion issues prompted the formation of a subcommittee on subject relationships and references the following year. One issue was the restrictive policy on making related term references in LCSH; the other was the observation that while some online catalogs display narrower and related terms, few provide references to broader terms. Stone (1996) summarized the SAC deliberations and built a case for the utility of referring searchers up a hierarchy of headings when their original queries retrieve inadequate results.

The final report of the Subcommittee on Subject Relationships/Reference Structures (American Library Association, 1997) summarized its activities to investigate subject relationships likely to be of use to catalog users, options for recording those relationships, and options for presenting relationships to users. A subcommittee member, Dee Michel, demonstrated the wide variety of possible relationships by developing a taxonomy of 165 subject relationships that is included as Appendix B, Parts 1 and 2, of that final report. The subcommittee tested the taxonomy by characterizing the *see also* references of a multi-referenced heading from LCSH, and in a follow-up exercise examined the references of six additional headings, looking for clusters of similar relationships. Using the results of the exercises and the taxonomy, the subcommittee developed a checklist of candidate relationships that could be used to establish references systematically when proposing new headings, or to redirect searches and facilitate browsing. The associative relationships that the subcommittee identified as useful were field of study/object of study, field of study/practitioner, agent/process, causal relationships, position in time and space, and frequently interchangeable/near synonyms. As the number of headings with evaluated references now exceeds the halfway mark in LCSH, it might be time for the Library of Congress to consider whether to expand the categories of relationships for which related term references are made.

The subcommittee also looked at displays of references in online catalogs and stressed the importance and helpfulness of clear explanations and labels, meaningful ordering of subdivided headings, and categorical or clustered displays of relationships, which could require expanded coding of references. They noted that many systems do not display the currently encoded relationships of broader term/narrower term and related term references, and recommended that all systems should have that capability. Another subcommittee member, Greenberg (1997), provided an assessment of the state of reference structures in online public access catalogs in the mid-1990s that involved limited and inconsistent access to references overall with examples of progress occurring in prototype catalogs and in theoretical and practical research. A follow-on SAC subcommittee was established in 1998, which has sponsored discussion forums and a program at ALA meetings to promote the inclusion and display of references in online catalogs.

A recent improvement to LCSH is the addition of authority records for subdivisions. In 1999, the Library of Congress began to create and distribute authority records to control the more than 3,100 form and topical free-floating subdivisions that may be combined with various categories of headings according to rules in the SCM:SH. Because free-floating subdivisions are a basic structural element of LCSH, the need to include information about them in the online authority file was recognized by many groups and individuals over the years, including Cochrane (1986, pp. 58-59) and Drabenstott and Vizine-Goetz (1994, p. 257); the latter noted that "scope notes, *see* references, and the syndetic structure under subdivisions could be added to such machine-readable records to help both library catalogers and public users of online systems." All subdivision authority records contain a basic usage statement and coding to indicate the categories of headings with which they may be applied; some records contains UF and hierarchical references that will be enhanced in the future. The records initially will be useful for validating the forms of subdivisions, but their full potential will be realized only when corresponding headings are also categorized and coded, and when references are enhanced. Much experimentation and investigation will be needed to determine the best means of integrating subdivision authority records in online catalogs and of displaying the information that they contain.

Bates (1989, pp. 402-403) pointed out that when online searching capabilities, such as keyword searching of subjects and titles, Boolean logic, truncation, and multi-index searching are added to preexisting indexing, the result is not simply additive; the features can interact in a multiplicative way. Drabenstott and Vizine-Goetz (1994) described how system design and programming can capitalize on the desirable features of LCSH and overcome its limitations. They recommended the use of search trees to enable systems to select and carry out strategies that enlist the catalog's controlled vocabulary to produce successful retrievals. More recently, Yee and Layne (1998) discussed searches for subjects in online catalogs that involve effective file and index structures, indexing, and displays with recommendations for the best possible defaults and sophisticated options. Future sophisticated techniques might involve applying multiple strategies, adding graphical displays of terms, or supplementing reference structures with lists of co-occurrence terms generated from collections of indexed items.

Over the past century, an evolutionary and pragmatic approach has been taken to develop LCSH. With the advent of online catalogs, Mandel (1984) wrote, "The only constructive approach is to seek ways to work with the Library of Congress in modernizing LCSH." In 1995, Taylor wrote, "if it is true that we will continue to maintain online catalogs and that in these catalogs there is a need for controlled vocabulary, we will probably be using Library of Congress Subject Headings (LCSH) for the forseeable future" (p. 489). All libraries that use LCSH have an investment in its continued development and a stake in its future. They can now contribute to its development cooperatively. The constructive and pragmatic approach is to take advantage of evolving technology while identifying measures that could be undertaken to improve LCSH as a tool in online catalogs.

## Acknowledgments

The author would like to acknowledge the indispensable comments and suggestions received from Library of Congress colleagues who read the manuscript: Barbara Tillett, Mary Kay Pietris, and Tom Yee; as well as Lois Mai Chan, Pauline Cochrane, and Ahmed El-Hoshy.

## References

American Library Association. (1898). *List of Subject Headings for Use in Dictionary Catalogs* (2nd ed. rev.). Boston: Published for the A.L.A. Publishing Section by the Library Bureau.

American Library Association, Subject Analysis Committee. (1985). *Report of the SAC Format of LCSH Subcommittee*. S.l.: Author.

American Library Association, Subject Analysis Committee, Subcommittee on Subject Relationships/Reference Structures. (1997). *Final Report to the ALCTS/CCS Subject Analysis Committee* [Online]. Available: <http://www.ala.org/alcts/organization/ccs/sac/rpt97rev.html> [2000, February15].

Angell, R. S. (1972). Library of Congress subject headings—Review and forecast. In H. Wellisch & T. D. Wilson (Eds.), *Subject Retrieval in the Seventies: New Directions*, 143-162. Westport, CT: Greenwood Publishing and University of Maryland, School of Library and Information Services.

Bates, M. J. (1986). Subject access in online catalogs: A design model. *Journal of the American Society for Information Science, 37*, 357-376.

Bates, M. J. (1989). Rethinking subject cataloging in the online environment. *Library Resources & Technical Services, 33*, 400-412.

Chan, L. M. (1990). *Library of Congress Subject Headings: Principles of Structure and Policies for Application* (Annotated version). Washington, DC: Library of Congress, Cataloging Distribution Service.

Chan, L. M. (1995). *Library of Congress Subject Headings: Principles and Application.* Englewood, CO: Libraries Unlimited.

Chan, L. M. (1998). Still robust at 100: A century of LC subject headings. *Library of Congress Information Bulletin, 57*, 200-201.

Coates, E. J. (1960). *Subject Catalogues: Headings and Structure.* London: Library Association.

Cochrane, P. A. (1983). *LCSH Entry Vocabulary Project: Final Report to the Council on Library Resources and to the Library of Congress.* (ERIC Document Reproduction Service No. ED 234 780)

Cochrane, P. A. (1986). *Improving LCSH for Use in Online Catalogs: Exercises for Self-help with a Selection of Background Readings.* Littleton, CO: Libraries Unlimited.

Cross reference structure in the LC automated subject authority file. (1986, Summer). *Cataloging Service Bulletin, 33*, 62.

Cutter, C. A. (1904). *Rules for a Dictionary Catalog* (4th ed. rewritten). Washington, DC: U.S. Government Printing Office.

Drabenstott, K. M. & Vizine-Goetz, D. (1994). *Using Subject Headings for Online Retrieval: Theory, Practice, and Potential.* San Diego: Academic Press.

Dykstra, M. (1988, March 1). LC subject headings disguised as a thesaurus. *Library Journal, 113*, 42-46.

Elliot, J. (1994-1995, Winter). Subject headings come home to roost. *Select: Newsletter, British Library, National Bibliographic Service, 14*, 7.

Greenberg, J. (1997). Reference structures: Stagnation, progress, and future challenges. *Information Technology and Libraries, 16*, 108-119.

Hanson, J. C. M. (1909). The subject catalogs of the Library of Congress. *Bulletin of the American Library Association, 3*, 385-397.

Haykin, D. J. (1951). *Subject Headings: A Practical Guide.* Washington, DC: U.S. Government Printing Office.

Kirtland, M.. & Cochrane, P. (1982). Critical views of LCSH—Library of Congress subject headings: A bibliographic and bibliometric essay. *Cataloging & Classification Quarterly, 1*(2/3), 71-94.

Library of Congress, Subject Cataloging Division. (1980). *Library of Congress Subject Headings* (9th ed.). Washington, DC: Library of Congress, Cataloging Distribution Service.

Library of Congress, Cataloging Policy and Support Office. (1996). *Subject Cataloging Manual: Subject Headings.* Washington, DC: Library of Congress, Cataloging Distribution Service.

Library of Congress, Cataloging Policy and Support Office. (1999). *Library of Congress Subject Headings* (22nd ed.). Washington, DC: Library of Congress, Cataloging

Distribution Service.

MacEwan, A. (1996). LCSH and the British Library: An international subject authority database? *Catalogue & Index*, 120, 1-6.

Mandel, C. A. (1984). Helping LC improve LCSH only constructive approach. *American Libraries*, 15, 336.

Mandel, C. A. & Herschman, J. (1983). Online subject access: Enhancing the library catalog. *Journal of Academic Librarianship*, 9, 148-155.

Miksa, F. J. (1983). *The Subject in the Dictionary Catalog from Cutter to the Present.* Chicago: American Library Association.

Petersen, T. (1983). The AAT: A model for the restructuring of LCSH. *Journal of Academic Librarianship*, 9, 207-210.

Richmond, P. A. (1959). Cats: An example of concealed classification in subject headings. *Library Resources & Technical Services*, 3, 102-112.

Russell, K. W. (Ed.). (1982). *Subject Access: Report of a Meeting Sponsored by the Council on Library Resources, Dublin, Ohio, June 7-9, 1982.* Washington, DC: The Council.

Shubert, S. B. (1992). Critical views of LCSH—Ten years later: A bibliographic essay. *Cataloging & Classification Quarterly*, 15(2), 37-97.

Sinkankas, G. M. (1972). *A Study in the Syndetic Structure of the Library of Congress List of Subject Headings.* Pittsburgh: University of Pittsburgh, Graduate School of Library and Information Sciences.

Stone, A. T. (1996). Up-ending Cutter's pyramid: The case for making subject references to broader terms. *Cataloging & Classification Quarterly*, 23(2), 5-16.

Taylor, A. G. (1995). On the subject of subjects. *Journal of Academic Librarianship*, 21, 484-491.

Weinberg, B. H. (1993). The hidden classification in Library of Congress subject headings for Judaica. *Library Resources & Technical Services*, 37, 369-379.

Wepsiec, J. (1978). Inquiry into the syndetic structure of the Library of Congress subject headings in anthropology. *Library Resources & Technical Services*, 22, 61-80.

Wepsiec, J. (1982). Library of Congress subject headings pertaining to society. *Cataloging & Classification Quarterly*, 2(3/4), 1-29.

Wepsiec, J. (1991). Hierarchical structure of subject headings in the social sciences. *Cataloging & Classification Quarterly*, 13(1), 79-102.

Wilson, M. D. (1998). Specificity, syndetic structure, and subject access to works about individual corporate bodies. *Library Resources & Technical Services*, 42, 272-281.

Yee, M. M. & Layne, S. S. (1998). *Improving Online Public Access Catalogs.* Chicago and London: American Library Association.

# Chapter 10

# The Art and Architecture Thesaurus:
# Controlling Relationships through Rules and Structure

Pat Molholt

*Health Sciences Division, Columbia University, New York, NY, USA*

**Abstract:**

The Art and Architecture Thesaurus (AAT) staff developed a set of associative, interconcept relationships to interconnect terminology contained in 33 hierarchies. Each of the 20 relationships is tightly defined and is applied under strict rules. The result benefits the user by providing reliable, standardized links between concepts. This chapter describes the logic, methodology, and impact of the AAT approach to relationships.

## 1. BRIEF HISTORY OF THE AAT

The creation of the AAT grew out of a desire on the part of an architectural historian to find or create a single rational slide classification scheme. Repeatedly faced with mastering new numbering systems as she moved from collection to collection, the historian, Dr. Dora Crouch, wanted uniformity. Teaming up with Toni Petersen and Pat Molholt[1], the three women met with architectural historians and slide-collection curators to better understand the problem and quickly recognized that agreement on object and concept names must precede classification of those objects and concepts. Without agreeing on how to describe something or what to call it, agreement cannot be achieved on how to classify it. With this recognition, the focus of the work quickly turned away from classification and toward a search for the "perfect" vocabulary.

The group obtained a modest grant from the Council on Library Resources to evaluate existing relevant vocabularies. That investigation led to a report on a series of incompatible, incomplete, and imprecise word lists, none individually able to serve the descriptive needs of the broad art and architecture community (Crouch, Molholt, & Petersen, 1981). When taken together and modified, however, they could begin to address those needs. A subsequent planning grant was obtained from the National Endowment for the Humanities (NEH) in 1980 and another NEH grant to begin work on the architecture section was obtained in 1981. In 1993 support for the project was assumed by the J. Paul Getty Trust under its Art History Information Program.

*C. A. Bean and R. Green (eds.), Relationships in the Organization of Knowledge, 153–170.*

As the project underwent a transition through funding sources, its leadership changed to Petersen and Molholt as co-directors. The mission also changed, with the realization that, despite the tremendous advantage provided by the cooperative partners who allowed the team to incorporate their vocabularies, there remained a great deal of work to be done, not the least of which revolved around the structure of the vocabulary. [2] The purpose of the vocabulary became clearer as well.

> The thesaurus was envisioned as a set of terms that would include vocabulary for the history and the making of the visual arts; that is, it would form a hinge between objects and their replicas or representations and the bibliography about them. Its coverage would be geographically and historically comprehensive but would not include terminology for iconographical themes. The terminology would be hierarchically organized and optimized for computerized use. Scholars in the field would review the work at all stages. (*Art & Architecture Thesaurus*, 1994)

The result, 15 years and millions of dollars later, was the publication in 1994 by Oxford University Press of the second edition of the AAT in five volumes containing nearly 90,000 terms in 33 hierarchies; Oxford had also published the first edition in 1990.

In the context of the monograph in hand, the AAT is important because it introduced a rational scheme for the deployment of associative, non-hierarchical relationships into a complex, large-scale thesaurus. This effort took the notion of the unprincipled "see also" reference found in card catalogs and various vocabulary tools and converted it into a rule-based scheme that allows users to view information from predictable alternate perspectives. The AAT is also important for having created a set of explicit editorial guidelines that are available for use by others wishing to do similar work in other disciplines.

## 2. BRIEF DESCRIPTION OF THE AAT

### 2.1 Overview

The scope of the AAT began somewhat narrowly with art and architecture, initially omitting, among other things, the world of decorative or fine arts. In due time the scope broadened to encompass a much richer span of topics, including material culture and the built environment. These changes came slowly, prompted by needs from the field. The scope is now described in the Introduction to the AAT as including the "disciplines of fine arts, architecture, decorative art, material culture of the Western world from antiquity to the present" (*Art & Architecture Thesaurus*, 1994). It does not include iconography *per se*, although there are many object names that are commonly used for iconographic purposes. In addition, terms in the Associated Concepts hierarchy often serve to describe, for example, the content of art (e.g., satire).

The terms chosen as descriptors or main terms (as opposed to lead-in vocabulary or alternate terms) come primarily from the language used by scholars and researchers. In addition, terminology used by librarians, curators, archivists, registrars—those who organize and describe information in the fields of art and architecture—is also included. Warrant for a term's inclusion is its use in the literature of research and scholarship. Terms too new for that route of entry are given a provisional status and re-examined later to see if the term is the one used in scholarship, or if another term has arisen instead.

## 2.2 Vocabulary Structure

The key to the methodical deployment of associative relations in the AAT is the structure of the vocabulary. There are two primary aspects to that structure: First is the hierarchies and second is the organization of the hierarchies into facets. With this structure in place, one can write rules about the relationships of concepts that would be impossible to articulate, for example, in a simple alphabetical listing of concepts/terms. The 33 hierarchies listed below move from highly abstract (Associated Concepts or Styles and Periods) to highly specific (Containers or Information Forms). In all cases, however, the homogeneity of topics in a hierarchy is tightly defined. The hierarchies are made up of individual, non-overlapping concepts identified by a noun or noun phrase constructed according to national and international conventions (British Standards Institution, 1987; International Organization for Standardization, 1986; American National Standards Institute, 1980). Within each hierarchy the terms are ordered according to genus-species, or class-subclass, relationships between terms. This relationship yields the commonly understood BT/NT, or broader term/narrower term structure. This organizational concept is reinforced through the display of terms in an indented fashion, grouping siblings in the same relationship to the same "parent" concept at the same level of indention. Users of the printed AAT are further aided by shaded bands that help the user identify levels of indention which can be as many as 15 or so. The AAT makes special use of the whole/part relationship, reserving its use for listing constituent parts not "conceptual" parts. Thus, windows and the parts or components of windows are listed together in the Components hierarchy of the Objects facet, but the nave, aisles, etc., that might be thought of as components of a cathedral are NOT listed with cathedrals but under <religious building fixtures>.[3]

ASSOCIATED CONCEPTS
  Associated Concepts
PHYSICAL ATTRIBUTES
  Attributes and Properties
  Conditions and Effects
  Design Elements
  Color
STYLES AND PERIODS
  Styles and Periods

AGENTS
    People
    Organizations
ACTIVITIES
    Disciplines
    Functions
    Events
    Physical Activities
    Processes and Techniques
MATERIALS
    Materials
OBJECTS
    Object Groupings and Systems
    Object Genres
    Components
    (Built Environment)
    Settlements and Landscapes
    Built Complexes and Districts
    Single Built Works
    Open Spaces and Site Elements
    (Furnishings and Equipment)
    Furnishings
    Costume
    Tools and Equipment
    Weapons and Ammunition
    Measuring Devices
    Containers
    Sound Devices
    Recreational Artifacts
    Transportation Vehicles
    (Visual and Verbal Communication)
    Visual Works
    Exchange Media
    Information Forms

Facets are a kind of super structure imposed on both the order and the content of the hierarchies. The seven facets, shown in capital letters above, organize the hierarchies beginning with abstract concepts and ending with concrete objects, the latter being the bulk of the thesaurus. Membership of a concept is first to a facet and then to a hierarchy. Membership in a particular facet suggests the existence of shared properties or characteristics which the facet's definition attempts to make clear.

The two-part structure of hierarchies and facets enables two activities. First, it allows one to formulate and impose rules for the inclusion of non-hierarchical relationships, and second, it allows one to lay out rules for creating compound terms, for example, combining a term such as *marble* from the Physical Attributes facet with the term *benches* from the Objects facet resulting in *marble benches*. The rules for relationships will be dealt with below.

## 3. THE NEED FOR ASSOCIATIVE RELATIONSHIPS

The issue of related-term links arose for the AAT in mid-1990 for three reasons: the pressure applied by early users of the vocabulary for such links, the growing stability of the content and structure of the AAT allowing for them, and the availability of staff to address the problem.

In the first instance, users who had worked with draft versions of the AAT recognized when looking at the alphabetic portion of the terminology, that the usual feature of *see also's* that point to related terms was missing. In particular, they were looking to draw together *all parts of* or *all uses of* an object or a concept. Part of the users' concern was in fact addressed by the hierarchical display. However, because this was a wildly foreign feature compared to the subject-heading lists they were generally accustomed to, users did not readily accept its usefulness as a partial substitute for the familiar *syndetic* or cross-reference structure they were accustomed to. The second reason for not addressing related-term links was that the scope or subject coverage of the vocabulary was growing rapidly in both planned and unplanned ways. Planned expansion included the ongoing development of new hierarchies by the editorial staff. In addition, test users were calling for terminology needed for their collections and this terminology frequently pressed against the defined boundaries of the AAT domain, resulting in interesting meanderings into engineering, climatology, and a host of other seeming tangential subject areas, all representing unplanned growth. The base vocabulary needed to be relatively stable in order to efficiently apply a related-term structure and since the vocabulary was both expanding and hierarchies were in considerable flux, work on any overlay structure had been postponed.

Eventually, however, the stability of the AAT was sufficient to the task and the staff was freed up after completing an extensive project to write *scope notes* for much of the architecture section of the thesaurus. Scope notes are part of the alphabetic portion of the AAT and reflect the extensive research work that surrounds every term in the thesaurus, clarifying its meaning (definitional scope note) or providing guidance on its use (instructional scope note). It turns out that the instructional scope note, including such phrases as "includes...excludes" or "distinguished from...by..." contains critical clues to a term's relationships with other terms.

Work on determining a set of relevant links began with background research on associative links by Donald Sanders, the Architecture Editor. He examined the editorial policies of other thesauri and their use of related terms. He compiled lists of link types from sources such as Nutter (1989), Neelameghan & Rao (1976), Molholt (1990), and others. The commonly used technique for constructing related-term relationships, to this point, was the "rule" articulated by Soergel (1974), namely:

> Concept A is related to concept B (has an associative relationship to concept B) if the following holds: an indexer or searcher weighing the use of A should be reminded of the existence of B and there is no hierarchical relationship between A and B.

Application of this "rule" resulted in embedding the world-view of the individual doing the linking into the catalog or index being created. This was an unacceptable method that produced unacceptable results—results that provided the user with inconsistent and unpredictable links. The AAT editors tested the fallibility of this world-view approach by means of a simple exercise. The exercise demonstrated that the experiences of each individual were a key force in determining her or his concept of what it meant for one term or concept to be related to another term or concept. No two AAT editors saw the issue of relatedness in the same way. In this exercise Sanders gave the four AAT editors five terms —*authenticity, end users, meetings, campuses,* and *hammers*—and asked them to list all the AAT terms they felt were related to each of these terms. In analyzing the responses, he found not a single case where all five individuals listed a common related term and only two cases where four of the five editors listed the same term, namely, *universities* in response to *campuses* and *construction* in response to *hammers*. In a longer-term view, the problem of consistency in selecting associated terms was not only going to be difficult with a fixed set of editors, but would be compounded by the fact of normal turnover in any staff charged with both developing and maintaining a system of links throughout the life cycle of a vocabulary. In order to transcend these problems, it was clear that a system of rules must for the basis of the links.

It was also clear that the user deserved more assistance in navigating complex information resources. If the relationship link was part of a pre-defined set, and if the particular relationship being evoked in any instance was known to the user, then the user could choose to explore that link if it made sense in meeting her or his information needs. In addition, knowing *a priori* what possible links exist in a vocabulary can suggest to a user what appropriate search strategies might be employed in seeking out information.

## 4. FINDING THE RULES

### 4.1 The Group Process

The editors had used a highly collaborative method of knowledge structuring when gathering terms and assembling the hierarchies. This collaboration was carried through into the link-building process. One of the earliest "mistakes" made by the project directors was to allow individuals to work on the vocabulary alone. Early along the thesaurus construction learning curve, an editor would arrange a grouping of terms into a hierarchy by physically arranging sheets of paper, one per term, along a long table set up in a separate room. This physical manifestation of the hierarchy would be left there for others to see. Another editor would go into the room and, disagreeing with some parts of the arrangement, rearrange the hierarchy. This could happen several times, and there seemed to be no progress. Pretty soon the directors realized that, as long as no one was forced to declare their reasoning in making changes, no one was learning anything about what was happening as the terms were being moved about. Just what was it that was illogical, unpleasing, or awkward about the arrangement of the terms? To answer that question, and to begin building the editorial manual of rules for the construction process, a policy was instituted that no changes could be made without explanation to the editor responsible for that part of the vocabulary. The dialogue that ensued was constant and considerable. The tradition of exchanging points of view and actively challenging each other with examples resulted in consistencies unattainable when people work in isolation. When it came time to begin work on related terms, the patterns of collaboration and challenge for the betterment of the product were firmly in place.

The team that worked out the system of associative relations was, more or less, the team that assembled most of the hierarchies. They did not have any outside assistance except for one meeting with a panel of eight experienced lexicographers. This group was assembled in March of 1990 to see how much consensus there might be around the topic of related terms (the lexicographic label for associative relationships). There was significant disagreement within this group on the type of links appropriate for a hierarchically structured vocabulary as well as disagreement on the question of whether to identify for the user the nature of the link being made between concepts. After a long and difficult day, a bare majority agreed that structured links would be useful, as would be identifying the links to the users. No one, however, had advice on how to proceed to identify, structure, and validate the links. No one had set about these tasks in a collaborative way with the goal of getting around the world-view problem that was, *de facto*, embedded in other thesauri.

The task facing the editors was to take the vocabulary that was already structured into hierarchies, and find a necessary, although perhaps not complete, set of links or associative relationships to tie the hierarchies horizontally. Associative or interconcept links operate on the horizontal plane and join two distinct concepts or groups of concepts by means of a specific and labeled connection. The connection not only has a name, but it also has the property of directionality. An interconcept link may be unidirectional, symmetric, or complemented by a corresponding link operating in the opposite direction. These issues and others concerning how many links are sufficient, and how links will be recorded in the vocabulary were worked out in group sessions.

Editors were guided by a series of memoranda posing questions for discussion, and later, by tentative agreements that were reached. The sessions were filled with give-and-take challenge by one editor to another armed with examples from the parts of the vocabulary they held responsibility for. While some proposed link appeared to work in the more concrete hierarchies such as Tools and Equipment, it may not work at all in the Conditions and Effects hierarchy. That led to discussions about why, and often to the discovery of a corollary link in the more abstract hierarchies, or a modification to the link to fit both situations, or to a rule that the link only applied to certain hierarchies. However, there was a hidden assumption that if a link was to be considered valid, it could not be restricted to one subject area: that is, examples from both art and architecture had to work.

The group constantly worked from examples and there arose numerous cases where examples didn't fit the rule. Such "cross verification" among editors was part of the validation process. Over time, the group identified three possible causes for a "no-fit" situation:

- The rule is at fault and must be restated or modified.
- The terms in the example are idiosyncratic and not truly related by the rule in question.
- One in the pair of terms in the example is in the wrong place in the hierarchy and moving it will solve the problem.

A further consideration evolved—a term may actually fit equally well (or badly) in either of two hierarchical placements. As one of the editors put it, "When determining where a terms goes and if you find it could go in two places, then you know you need a link." This discovery turned out to be the 1A, Alternate Broader-Term Link, and 1B, Alternate Narrower-Term Link. This unusual pair of links was necessitated because the AAT does not allow polyhierarchies. When concepts can belong to several hierarchies, there is no need for this link type.

## 4.2 Whole/Part Links: A False Start

After five months of general discussion, testing of ideas, reading and working around the issue and trying to get a toe-hold, the editors began discussion of the whole/part link. This was chosen in desperation—one had to begin somewhere—and partly because this seemed to be one of the more concrete of the link types. The editors also made an early attempt in their work to examine links from the largest grouping of terms, the facet. That is, they looked at rules that would permit the linking of any term in one facet to any term in another facet. An obvious example of this was a link between objects and materials, for example, *desks* and *oak*. As the group worked on this idea, they realized what they were actually doing was building indexing strings or multiple concept phrases, such a *oak desks*, which were, in fact, specialized examples of a concept rather than an object-material link. This recognition was critical—one of two such discoveries that were based on the structure of the knowledge base itself. Because the AAT is divided into hierarchies and terms were de-coordinated, the temptation was to rebuild them using links:

> **chairs** *made of* oak
> **blouses** *made of* silk

On further study, the team recognized these would be false links. *Brick houses* are a type of *houses*, and in a vocabulary that was not de-coordinated, the concept of *brick houses* would appear under *houses* (if there was a hierarchical arrangement of concepts) or simply listed in a general alphabetic list.

As the editors examined the whole/part relationship, they began formulating procedures and subrules. In order to constrain the development of links, the group considered the uses to which the vocabulary would be put. For example, simply because an object had a set of parts, it was not automatically necessary to link them together from the point of view of an information search. Someone wanting information on fireplaces would not inherently benefit from a link to all the fireplace's component parts. In the pure and abstract sense there might be little question that all entities should be linked to all their constituent parts. In the pragmatic worlds of lexicography and artificial intelligence, one looks for the guidance of necessity in determining just how far to go in detailing whole/part relationships. Two subrules arose:

- **Subrule 1:** Is the part necessary and sufficient for an understanding of the whole?
- **Subrule 2:** Is the part in some way different by association with the whole, and would a link provide the user with more information about the part? In determining this, consider the value of the post-coordinated phrase using the two terms (e.g., *radio towers*).

If one's goal is to chronicle the usual or ordinary parts of certain objects, be they automobiles or apartment buildings, the issues just raised are moot. The practical necessity to set limits, however, lead to these *uniqueness* subrules as guidelines. Consider the following examples: *gardens* and *lenses*. *Gardens* are used in many settings and for many proposes, but under Subrule 1, the editor must ascertain if the association between *gardens* and, for example, *shopping centers* is unique—that is, is the concept *gardens* necessary or sufficient for understanding *shopping centers?* No, it is not. Nor are *gardens* fundamentally changed by association with *shopping centers*, so that Subrule 2 also yields a negative answer.

In the case of *lenses*, the result of applying these subrules is different. While *lenses* as part of *cameras* are neither necessary nor sufficient for understanding cameras, *lenses* do have unique properties when used in *cameras*. In addition, the test of post-coordination— does the phrase *camera lenses* tell us something more about *lenses* because of the association with *camera?*—is positive, so a whole/part link would be made between the two. The decision, however, is not easily implemented because of the vocabulary's structure. When you link to a term, you automatically link to the siblings under that term, some of which may hold the same relationship to the whole. Link-building caused terms to be moved because they violate the validity of a link among sibling terms. The notion is to always make the link at the highest level possible. When this doesn't work, the editor then commences a search for a more appropriate hook for that relationship.

## 4.3 The Role of Scope Notes

As mentioned above, the richness of the information in a term's scope note provided considerable clues to associated links. Another heuristic arose:

Terms appearing in scope notes should be considered for associative links. If there is no mention of a term in the scope notes, the editor must provide a basis whereby a third party can understand why a link was made.

The importance of this rule is twofold: It prevents an individual world-view from entering into link building, and it assumes the relationship is inherent in the definition of the term. For example, linking the concept of *security* by the function link 3R to objects such as *locks, alarms,* and *peepholes* is not allowed. (For a complete listing of the links, see below.) There is nothing inherent in the definition of any of these terms that indicates they are security devices. A particular culture may link the notion of lock and security, but the definition does not.

## 5. THE EFFECT OF LINKS ON VOCABULARY STRUCTURE

There are no empirical measures that can be applied to the intellectual task of building a vocabulary. That is not to say there are no rules for thesaurus construction. ANSI Z39.19-1980 and -1993 contain such rules, but it is not possible to construct measures of their application in what is in essence a highly abstract process. Despite this, the AAT team discovered that testing the validity of a link within the thesaurus provided a secondary test for the validity of the hierarchies. The measures of link validity are relatively subjective:

- Does the link work with all siblings? If not, why?
- Does the link work with like concepts? If not, why?
- Are there exceptions needed for some terms? If so, why?

Structuring and linking are closely related and the process of checking or validating links accomplishes a refinement of the vocabulary structure. In the implementation of links in the AAT, the staff discovered many examples of faulty hierarchical structures that they had not recognized before. For example, the recognition that *collar beams* was inaccurately placed under <beams by location or content> when it better fit under <*roof frame components*>, as a sibling of *rafters*. This discovery was based on the clear relationship between *collar beams* and *rafters* as expressed by the scope note for the former, "horizontal members which tie together and stiffen two opposite rafters, usually at a point about halfway up the rafters." The problem arose when the staff tried to make a related-term link between *collar beams* and *rafters* but could not find an appropriate link code, thus causing them to reexamine the location of the terms. The link building process, then, served as a welcome check on the accuracy of the hierarchies.

## 6. ELEMENTS OF A LINK FORMALISM

The notation for a link should:

- Indicate the direction of the link,
- Provide an identification of the link type (name), and
- Identify what concepts are joined, that is, single concepts or groups of concepts.

In a monohierarchically structured vocabulary such as the AAT, there are two levels of link formulation:

- A formalism that enables links to be made between specific groups of terms by linking the relevant broader terms found in two hierarchies. Such a formalism can be called an *authorization formalism.*
- A formalism that links specific individual concepts. Such a formalism can be called an *instantiation formalism,* as it instantiates a particular link.

The form of both formalisms, as given below, is the same. The difference is that an authorization formalism terminates at a Node 2 that has sibling terms, whereas an instantiation formalism has a Node 2 that is a single term with no siblings.

| Slot Name | Filler |
|---|---|
| Link Type Number | Numeric Designator |
| Link Name | Label of the link |
| Form | Alphabetic Designator |
| Node 1 | Hierarchy and Term or Unique Term Address |
| Node 2 | Hierarchy and Term or Unique Term Address |
| Reciprocity | Y/N |
| Corollary Link | Link Type Number and Form Designator |

Below is the completed formalism for the Type 1 Alternate Placement link, for the term *radio towers.*

| Slot Name | Filler |
|---|---|
| Link Type Number | 1 |
| Link Name | Alternate Placement |
| Form | A |
| Node 1 | <communication structures>  radio towers |
| Node 2 | towers  radio towers |
| Reciprocity | Y |
| Corollary Link | 1B |

All links have equal weight: They are either valid or not; that is, either they fit the link rule and can be created or they do not fit the rule and cannot be created. There is no notion in this system of weak or strong links as in some artificial intelligence systems.

## 7. WHAT ARE THE RULES?

Twenty links were identified as relevant to the art and architecture domain. They are listed below:

| Concepts Being Linked | Code |
|---|---|
| Alternate Broader Term | 1A |
| Alternate Narrower Term | 1B |
| Whole to Part | 2A |
| Part to Whole | 2B |
| Concept/User or Creator | 3A |
| Concept/Resulting or Causative Action | 3B |
| Concept/Locational Context or Setting | 3D |
| Concept/Documents or Products Resulting or Necessary | 3E |
| Agent/Field of Study or Resulting Action | 3F |
| Agent/Material Used or Needed | 3G |
| Agent/Locational Context or Setting | 3H |
| Agent/Equipment Needed or Produced | 3J |
| Agent/Documents or Products Used or Created | 3K |
| Activity/Resulting or Causative Action | 3M |
| Activity/Materials Required or Produced | 3N |
| Activity/Locational Context or Setting | 3P |
| Activity/Equipment Needed or Produced | 3Q |
| Activity/Documents or Products Used or Created | 3R |
| Materials/Objects | 3S |
| Distinguished From | 4 |

As an example of "Molholt's first rule of thesaurus construction," namely that a thesaurus can never be finished, there has been re-consideration of the Materials/Objects and Whole/Part links. In fact, since the time of the research underlying the doctoral thesis on which this chapter is based (Molholt, 1996), other changes may have occurred.

### 7.1 Is There a Core Set of Links?

There arises the question of whether there is a core set of links that are both adequate and sufficient to represent knowledge in general, or a domain in particular. Underlying this question are two issues: (1) the structure of the knowledge base to which the links will be applied and (2) the application driving the need for links. In the case of the knowledge base structure, it is absolutely clear that there is a close tie between how the core concepts of a domain are captured and structured and what links are needed to adequately fill in the knowledge framework. The fact that the AAT is built out of single concept terms (*houses* but not *brick houses*) could have a significant effect on the need for links. In fact, it doesn't. The 20 links, when strictly applied do not allow the almost intuitive joining of certain kinds of concepts, such as materials and objects, for example, *brick houses*. This is because such relationships are heavily dependent on the structure of the knowledge base being used. If the vocabulary had been structured differently, in particular if the various "kind of x" or *is-a* relationships that are reflected by the combination of object names with materials or with styles and periods were included in the knowledge base, then the entire question of wanting to link those concepts would be moot. It is nonetheless moot, but for a slightly more abstruse reason, namely that such combinations are simply a "kind of x" or generalization/specialization relationship that does not warrant linking. In a grammar parsing system, they are simply modifiers to a noun, not related by an inherent aspect of their definition.

## 7.2 The Influences of Guide Terms on Links

There is another element of thesaurus structure that influences the need for links: the convention of guide terms used in the AAT. Guide terms are used for the purpose of collocating, or grouping, terms when there is no applicable term under which to list the concepts. These nonpostable terms (i.e., which cannot be used for indexing) are enclosed in angle brackets (< >). For example, *<storage spaces>*, *<group dwellings>*, and *<corner buttresses>* have no terms that both meet the editorial guidelines for inclusion in the thesaurus and convey the same meaning as the guide term. Yet the grouping provided by these devices is useful in that it brings together concepts that share common properties and avoids the use of long alphabetical lists of undifferentiated terms. Guide terms are applied within the AAT in a way that obviates, or at least greatly reduces, the need for links. It would appear to a casual observer that there is an overlap between the use of certain guide terms and the use of links. Guide terms that include the phrase "by location or context" seem to duplicate links 3C (Conceptual/Locational Context or Setting), 3H (Agent/Locational Context or Setting) and 3P (Activity/Locational Context or Setting), all of which link terms in the objects hierarchies to their associated agents, activities, or broad concepts on the basis of locational context or setting. These links are defined by the rules given below:

- 3C Conceptual/Locational Context or Setting: To or from terms in the Associated Concepts facet (CP) and the locational context or setting for the concept (terms from the Built Environment hierarchies of the Objects facet).
- 3H Agent/Locational Context or Setting: To or from terms in the Agents facet (HG) and the locational context or setting for the concept (terms from the Built Environment hierarchies of the Objects facet).
- 3P Activity/Locational Context or Setting: To or from terms in the Activities facet (KD, KG, KM, KT) and locational context(s) or setting(s) for actions (terms in the Built Environment hierarchies of the Objects facet).

These links are specifically defined to prevent their use when the result would be, in fact, a "kind of x" rather than a concept linked to its associated context. Guide terms are used as a structural device to position or collocate legitimate pre-coordinated terms that happen to be a combination of objects and locations resulting in a "kind of x." For example:

*<public buildings by location or context>*
    city halls
    *hôtels de ville*
    *Rathäuses*

The issue is not a matter of post-coordinating a pair of terms into a new term by means of a link but rather a matter of positioning a term or concept in the knowledge base. For example, it is legitimate to use 3C Conceptual/Locational Context or Setting to link *rural land use* and *farmland*, or the broader term *agricultural land*. This use fits the rule, and the linked concepts do not form a "kind of x." 3H Agent/Locational Context or Setting can be used to link *agriculturists* to *agricultural land*, or *farmers* to *farmland*, and the 3P Activity/Locational Context or Setting links *farming* to *farmland*. Such links do not create a concept that is a "kind of x."

## 7.3 Another View of BT/NT

The 1A and 1B links, Alternate Broader and Alternate Narrower Term, caused the AAT editors to reconsider the placement of many terms in the Associated Concepts facet. In general, the terms found in that facet are exceptionally broad, *architecture*, for example, or *propaganda*. They may easily have multiple meanings: Is *architecture* a practice, the products of an activity, or something else entirely? Words with multiple meanings are called homographs, and lexicographers have techniques for handling them. Since homographs may represent entirely distinct physical objects as well as more intellectual variations of a concept, they often need to be placed in more than one hierarchy. The use of the parenthetical qualifier, or gloss, distinguishes the multiple meanings of terms and allows them to be placed in the appropriate location in the hierarchies. For example, the following notation would be used to indicate the first meaning of *architecture(activity)*, while *architecture(built environment)* might be used to indicate the products of the practice. In the early work on building links, it became apparent that some terms worked better if they were taken out of the Associated Concepts hierarchy and placed in a more specific hierarchy where the meaning and subsequent use of the term was made clear. One distinct advantage of the hierarchical structure is the ability to define terms more clearly.

## 7.4 Whole/Part and Non-physical Entities

Links 2A and 2B (Whole to Part and Part to Whole) contain an unresolved challenge: Can they be used with other than physical entities? Take, for example, the effort on the part of some editors at the AAT to link the concept *dating* (a homonym with no conflicting meaning in the domain of art and architecture) to the concept *archeology* or *cool colors* to *blue* and *green* and the various shades of those colors. The most logical link to use is the whole/part link, but the link application rules as interpreted by the project coordinator hold that the link can only be used with physical objects. There is an overwhelming insecurity about extending the use of the link to intellectual rather than physical entities. The basic argument revolves around the link definition and whether something other than a physical entity can meet the definition:

> Links should be made between a whole and its parts or between a part and its associated whole only:
>> When the parts are necessary and sufficient for understanding the whole,
>> OR
>> When the whole can only be understood in terms of, or is distinguished by virtue of, the parts AND the relationship would be relevant to potential users AND the parts are somehow different by their association with the whole or are somehow special by virtue of being part of the particular whole.
> This type of link may not be reciprocal; thus the need exists for two links, 2A and 2B.

One difficulty is that the parts of a nonphysical entity can seem to be arbitrary. Stated differently, can an individual be an *archeologist* if that person does not engage in the activity of *dating*? Is *dating* a required aspect of *archeology* and, along with other activities, sufficient to understand *archeology*? The debate will go on, but within the context of the AAT, 2A and 2B can only be applied to physical entities.

## 7.5 Necessary vs. Sufficient Links

This discussion begs the question of the existence of a necessary set of links versus a sufficient set. The necessary set of links seems to be that which arises from the definitions of the concepts being linked apart from the context in which the concept is used. A sufficient set would include those links that derive from the context in which the concept is used. Links that arise out of an application context may not meet the rigor of the links as defined by the AAT, but they may be important to a body of users. For example, some individuals may consider it appropriate to link the concepts of *security* with *locks*, *peepholes*, and *alarms* using link 3Q (Activity/Equipment Needed or Produced). However, nothing in the definition of the object terms suggests such a link. Nonetheless, there is a logic to it that might be important to a particular application, and in that context such links can be encouraged. There is an easy analogy in the MARC record formats that allow for local subject headings (field 659), which can contain anything useful to a particular application. There is no implication that entries in this field would be useful to anyone else, and their presence in the 659 field rather than the standards-driven 650 field makes that clear. A similar situation could exist with interconcept links developed and implemented in a local system: While there is no reason to hide their existence, there is also no reason to force their acceptance on any other application.

## 8. IMPACT ON THE USERS

Earlier it was suggested that the user operates at a significant disadvantage when the syndetic structure of a system is idiosyncratic, unlabeled, inconsistent, and/or incomplete. Users of such a system have no indication of why two concepts are linked or of the directionality of the link (although most are bidirectional), nor can they expect to find similar concepts linked throughout the system. In a system underpinned by rules which, to the best of human implementation, result in standardized, labeled, consistent, and complete linking, the user recognizes several benefits:

- Because of the hierarchical structure, and the fact that each hierarchy is identified, what is being linked is known (e.g., agent linked to activity) and users can determine if following that link might lead to information useful to their information queries.
- In the case of instantiation links, users viewing the thesaurus itself (rather than its application in a database) will be able to see the range of structurally related terms that are also conceptually related through a link to another term or set of terms. This will facilitate a productive focusing of a search strategy.
- Users can anticipate that similar pairs of terms will be linked and can anticipate framing questions that rely on being able to traverse links.
- Users will be able to differentiate among multiple links leading from a concept and to select the most productive.

## 9. CONCLUSION

Work to date in information science has treated related terms in highly individuated ways, heavily dependent on the world-view of the individual making the related-term link. In those cases where rules have been created, their application is severely hampered by two factors: the lack of a coherently structured knowledge base to which the links can be applied and the level of interpretation or judgment that must be exercised by individuals applying the rules. Establishing agreement on the definition of a link and determining the rules for its implementation are both difficult tasks. Differences in opinion actually reflect the complex interplay of multiple world views. Each person conceives of the world and its constituent parts as held together by a structure of relationships, and within bounds, there is a great deal of variety. The group process used by the AAT was one way to mitigate the differences and reach a testable compromise. The process begins by building a "world" (the hierarchically structured thesaurus), then linking its constituent parts together by a structure (interconcept links). Without first defining and agreeing on the world, the second process is doomed; conversely, attempting to build links without a structured thesaurus is an equally impossible task.

The group process undertaken by the AAT editors runs counter to historic methods of working with links in either the information or computer sciences. In the former, cross references have been developed by individuals absent rules other than the world-view of that individual. In computer science, there first exists a fundamental difference from information science in that knowledge is coded for a specific application and hence the links reflect or are driven by some particular need; second, except for graphing sentence structures, there are only loose rules regarding what should be linked and what a link means (Woods, 1985). Further differences between these two communities may be seen in the link "kind of x." The distinction between a legitimate use of a link and the perceived need to link concepts for the purpose of capturing "kind of" is a critical difference that is neither articulated or enforced in semantic nets or frames. Part of the problem arises from the difference between the basic objectives of modeling in artificial intelligence, a branch of computer science, and information science. A major focus of knowledge structuring in artificial intelligence is on modeling a specific part of the world to solve a particular problem. In contrast, information science aims to model the world for any potential problem, having no specific application in mind other than such generic ones as indexing, classification, and so forth. The result of this difference is that information scientists work at the concept level, not at the instance level. One might expect there to be considerable overlap, particularly in the frame environment, for example, where the knowledge engineer develops the canonical or generic CHAIR frame before proceeding to the subclass of *continuous bow Windsor armchairs*, and specific instances thereof. But these worlds remain separate, with the overlap there in theory ready to be tapped.

## Endnotes

1. Toni Petersen was with RILA (Répertoire international de la littérature de l'art = International Repertory of the Literature of Art) and Pat Molholt and Dora Crouch were with Rensselaer Polytechnic Institute.

2. The contributed vocabularies were: Avery Index to Architectural Periodicals, Library of Congress Subject Headings, Royal Institute of British Architecture (RIBA) Architectural Periodicals Index, and RILA.

3. The use of < > surrounding a concept indicates that the concept is used for organizational purposes only and cannot be used as an indexing term. Such terms are called guide terms.

## References

American National Standards Institute. (1980). *American National Standard Guidelines for Thesaurus Structure, Construction, and Use*. New York: ANSI. (Z39.19-1980)
*Art & Architecture Thesaurus*. (1994). (2nd ed.; T. Petersen, Dir.). New York: Oxford University Press.
British Standards Institution. (1987). *Guide to Establishment and Development of Monolingual Thesauri* (2nd ed.). London: BSI. (BS 5723:1987)

Crouch, D., Molholt, P., & Petersen, T. (1981). *Indexing in Art and Architecture: An Investigation and Analysis. Report to the Council on Library Resources.* Council on Library Resources.

International Organization for Standardization. (1986). *Documentation—Guidelines for the Establishment and Development of Monolingual Thesauri* (2nd ed.). [Geneva:] ISO. (ISO 2788-1986(E))

Molholt, P. (1990). The use of inter-concept relationships for the enhancement of semantic networks and hierarchically structured vocabularies. *Proceedings of the Electronic Text Research Conference,*Waterloo, Canada, October 30, 1990.

Molholt, P. (1996). *A Model for Standardization in the Definition and Form of Associative, Interconcept Links.* Ph.D. dissertation, Rensselaer Polytechnic Institute.

Neelameghan, A., & Rao, I. K. R. (1976). Non-hierarchical associative relationships: Their types and computer-generation of RT links. *Library Science with a Slant toward Documentation,* 13, 24-42.

Nutter, J. T. (1989). *A Lexical Relation Hierarchy.* TR-89-6 Department of Computer Science, Virginia Polytechnic Institute and State University, Blacksburg, VA

Soergel, D. (1974). *Indexing Languages and Thesauri: Construction and Maintenance.* Los Angeles: Melville Publishing.

Woods, W. A. (1985). What's in a link: Foundations for semantic networks. In R. J. Brachman & H. J. Levesque (Eds.), *Readings in Knowledge Representation,.* Los Altos, CA: Morgan Kaufmann Publishers.

# Chapter 11

# Relationships in Medical Subject Headings (MeSH)

Stuart J. Nelson, W. Douglas Johnston, and Betsy L. Humphreys
*National Library of Medicine, Bethesda, MD, USA*

**Abstract:**
Recent efforts to make some of the relationships within MeSH more explicit have led to a deeper understanding of the nature of these relationships. This chapter will explore the relationships represented in MeSH in the light of that understanding. Every term that occurs may be thought of as representing a concept. One or more terms, comprising one or more concepts, grouped together for important reasons, form a descriptor class. The descriptor class is the basic building block of the thesaurus. Relationships among concepts can be represented explicitly in the thesaurus, most notably as relationships within the descriptor class. Hierarchical relationships are at the level of the descriptor class. The hierarchies are key in allowing expanded retrievals. The hierarchical relationships, traditionally thought of as broader or narrower (parent-child) relationships, are better understood as representing broader and narrower retrieval sets. Nevertheless, these hierarchical relationships often reflect important broader-narrower relationships between preferred concepts in descriptor classes. Other types of relationships present in the thesaurus include associative relationships, such as the Pharmacologic Actions or see-related cross references, as well as forbidden combination expressions, such as the Entry Combination.

## 1. INTRODUCTION

The Medical Subject Headings (MeSH) have been produced by the National Library of Medicine (NLM) since 1960. The MeSH thesaurus is NLM's controlled vocabulary for subject indexing and searching of journal articles in MEDLINE, and books, journal titles, and non-print materials in NLM's catalog (Bachrach & Charen, 1978). Translated into many different languages, MeSH is widely used in indexing and cataloging by libraries and other institutions around the world.

Forty years of heavy use have led to a significant expansion in the content of MeSH and to considerable evolution in its structure. It is one of the most highly sophisticated thesauri in existence today. The relationships currently represented in MeSH provide good examples of the types of relationships useful in any thesaurus.

Recently, the maintenance environment for the Medical Subject Headings was redesigned. The altered data structure allows more explicit representation of the relationships, and makes clearer the roles of the relationships and the objects (term, concept, and descriptor class) involved. The new system design has made possible a deeper understanding of these thesaural relationships. It supports the development and

171

*C. A. Bean and R. Green (eds.), Relationships in the Organization of Knowledge, 171–184.*

maintenance of a rapidly expanding vocabulary. It is hoped that the new data structure will support more advanced technology in information retrieval, such as identifying the appropriate MeSH term within the Metathesaurus of the Unified Medical Language System (UMLS) for such purposes as semi-automated indexing (Schuyler et al., 1993; Nelson et al., 1999). There were other benefits obtained from the redesign process as well, including the development of a mission statement for MeSH. This statement provides a framework from which it is possible to explore the goals and requirements of MeSH. A deeper appreciation of the importance of intention or purpose to the representation of relationships has also emerged.

Understanding MeSH requires an understanding of its structure. There are three major components to the Medical Subject Headings: the Headings themselves, the Subheadings (also known as Qualifiers), and the Supplementary Concept Records. This chapter includes a discussion of the historical MeSH structures, a review of the mission statement of MeSH, and descriptions of the relationships in the MeSH thesaurus discussed in the following order: equivalence relationships, including entry terms and synonyms; hierarchical relationships; and associative relationships.

## 2.  THE HISTORICAL MESH STRUCTURE: EXPLICIT AND IMPLICIT REPRESENTATIONS

One way to understand the types of relationships within MeSH is to review some of the data elements of each MeSH component. Many of the data elements contain information about relationships, both inter- and intra-descriptor. As is evident in other chapters of this book, it is nonsensical to talk of relationships without talking of meaning; any discussion of the record elements must include how the meaning is represented. The records for the different MeSH components will be discussed in turn, though some of the elements are common to more than one type of record.

### 2.1  Main Headings

Main headings are the meat of the MeSH thesaurus. They are used to describe what an article or book is "about." That is, as index terms they provide an indication of the major topics under consideration.

Among the data elements in the record for a main heading are:

MESH HEADING (MH)

This is the term used in the MEDLINE database as the indexing term. The term reflects a meaning; its use indicates the topics discussed by the work cited.

ENTRY TERM, PRINT

These terms, which are printed in the MeSH publications, are used as pointers to the MH. The presence of an entry term in the record is an indication that this topic should be indexed by the given MH.

ENTRY TERM, NON-PRINT

These terms are the entry terms that are not printed. For a variety of reasons, trade names, lab numbers, and some permutations of other terms, either entry terms or the MH, may not be selected for printing.

RUNNING HEAD, MESH TREE STRUCTURES

While primarily an indicator of what should appear on the printed page, the running head often provides a general category of where the MH will appear in the hierarchy.

MESH TREE NUMBER

The tree numbers indicate the places within the MeSH hierarchies, also known as the Tree Structures, in which the MH appears. Thus, the numbers are the formal computable representation of the hierarchical relationships.

CAS TYPE 1 NAME

For chemical names, the structural name assigned by the Chemical Abstracts Service (CAS) in accordance with the American Chemical Society naming convention. This structural name is a synonym for the MH.

CAS REGISTRY/EC NUMBER

For chemicals, the CAS registry number assigned to this compound. For enzymes, the Enzyme Commission number provides a classification of the activity of the enzyme. In both of these cases, the number is a formal computable synonym of the Heading.

RELATED CAS REGISTRY NUMBER

For chemicals, these are the registry numbers of congeners and derivatives indexed by the same MH.

SEMANTIC TYPE

Every term is assigned one or more semantic types (general categories) from the UMLS Semantic Network (McCray & Hole, 1990). These categories help assign meaning to a term.

CONSIDER ALSO (XREF)

The notation in this field alerts the user of possible terms with different morphemes (e.g., for kidney, "consider also terms at renal"). A user is thus alerted to possible semantic relationships not represented in the usual orthographic representation as seen in a book.

ENTRY COMBINATION

This field is present as an indication that a combination of a qualifier and the MH should be indexed by a different MH. It forbids, and in some systems prevents, the establishment of a relationship between a qualifier and a MH, forbidden because the meaning can be expressed in a different manner covered by a different MH. For example, the MH/SH combination "Pregnancy/complications" is forbidden, and the user is pointed to the MH "Pregnancy Complications."

## FORWARD CROSS REFERENCE (SEE ALSO REFERENCE)
A MH that is closely associated with or should be carefully differentiated from the MH.

## ANNOTATION
The written instructions given to indexers at NLM for correct use of the MH. It often elucidates meaning as well as usage, and may indicate special relationships with other headings.

## ALLOWABLE TOPICAL QUALIFIERS
The topical subheadings or qualifiers that may be assigned to the MH by indexers. Some qualifiers which might otherwise be allowed are forbidden and given (with the MH) as Entry Combinations.

## MESH SCOPE NOTE
This short piece of free text provides a type of definition, in which the meaning of the MH is circumscribed. Other MHs frequently appear in scope notes, usually in ALL CAPS. These represent relationships, which are often very important, but which may not otherwise be represented in the MeSH structure.

## PHARMACOLOGICAL ACTION
The actions and uses of various chemicals are indicated by a different MH in this field. These relationships are descriptive, often indicating why the particular chemical may be of interest.

## PREVIOUS INDEXING
The expression here indicates how articles were indexed in MEDLINE prior to the establishment of the MH. This is a historical representation of how the meaning was expressed prior to the advent of the MH.

## 2.2 Qualifiers

Historically, subheadings or qualifiers have been of several different types. The ones of most interest are the topical qualifiers. Included in the data elements are those listed below:

## SUBHEADING
The term that is used in the MEDLINE database to qualify the MH indexing terms. Its use indicates how the meaning of the MH should be refined (i.e., which particular aspect of the topic is addressed in the work cited).

## QUALIFIER TYPE
The types into which a qualifier can be categorized include topical, form, geographic, and language. These general types determine allowable usage of the qualifier. The topical qualifiers can be thought of as modifiers of the meanings of MHs, while form, geographic, and language qualifiers are essentially descriptive of the citation.

## QUALIFIER CROSS REFERENCE
An entry term to the subheading.

MESH SCOPE NOTE

A type of definition which characterizes the modification of meanings allowed by the usage of the subheading.

TREE NODE ALLOWED

The node annotations indicate in which MeSH Tree subcategory(ies) the subheading is usually allowed. The areas or topics that generally relate to the subheading are listed here.

## 2.3  Supplementary Concepts

Supplementary Concept Records are edited and added to MeSH daily. Preferred names in these records can be assigned to a special data element (Name of Substance) within the MEDLINE record of a citation. As many of the names of the data elements imply, the bulk of these records are related to chemicals and drugs. Data elements include:

NAME OF SUBSTANCE (NM)

This name, the preferred name of the substance, is the term used in the MEDLINE database to represent a Supplementary Concept. It can be thought of as analogous to the MH.

SYNONYMS

Entry terms to the NM, indicating that the topic should be indexed under the Name of Substance. These are often not true synonyms, but names of substances that are equivalent for retrieval purposes, for example, salts, trade names, and lab numbers.

CAS TYPE 1 NAME

For chemical names, the structural name assigned in accordance with the American Chemical Society naming convention. This structural name is a synonym of the NM.

CAS REGISTRY/EC NUMBER

For chemicals, the CAS registry number assigned to this compound. For enzymes, the Enzyme Commission number provides a classification of the activity of the enzyme. These numbers are a formal computable representation of the meaning.

RELATED CAS REGISTRY NUMBER

For chemicals, these are the registry numbers of congeners and derivatives indexed by the same named substance. These are usually the numbers for the Synonyms discussed above.

HEADING MAPPED TO (HM)

When citations are assigned an NM, the one or more MHs in this field are also assigned to the MEDLINE record. There is a structural or functional relationship between the NM and the MHs in this data element.

INDEXING INFORMATION

This information consists of MHs associated with the substance that should be considered in indexing or retrieving.

NOTE

This note is a free text definition, in which the meaning of the NM is circumscribed.

PHARMACOLOGICAL ACTION
   The actions and uses of the various chemicals are indicated by the MHs in this field.
PREVIOUS INDEXING
   The HM which was used to index the citations in the MEDLINE databases before
   the Supplementary Concept was created.

## 2.4 The Historical MeSH Structure Representation: A Comment

As with many thesauri, the historical structure of MeSH emphasized the relationships of items within the thesaurus to the main terms. In the database in which the vocabulary was maintained and in databases such as MEDLINE, the Main Heading, the Qualifier, or the Name of Substance was identified as a single term. Relationships were noted and maintained at the term level. The emphasis on term-level relationships led to some imprecisions and loss of ability to represent other relationships. For example, since the late 1980s, entry vocabulary was noted as being related to the Main Heading as synonymous, broader, related, or narrower, but relationships between entry terms were not and could not be noted.

In redesigning the MeSH thesaurus to a concept-oriented structure, it became possible to represent explicitly other important relationships. It became apparent that a Main Heading did not represent a single concept; rather, a Main Heading represented one or more concepts, and constituted a descriptor class (hereinafter referred to as a descriptor.) The important distinction between the meaning of the term used to represent a Main Heading and the usage of that term (to represent the class of concepts entailed by the descriptor) is then more apparent, and the nature of a given hierarchical relationship in a thesaurus is clarified. These distinctions then make it possible to appreciate the differences between a thesaurus and a concept representation scheme.

## 3. THE GOALS OF MESH:
## LOGICAL CONSTRAINTS ON THESAURUS CONSTRUCTION

In defining the role of the Medical Subject Headings, it seemed appropriate to develop a formal statement of the goal of MeSH. It is "to provide a reproducible partition of concepts relevant to biomedicine for purposes of organization of medical knowledge and information."

This statement bears close examination, as many of the words selected for it have deep meanings. In order for MeSH to provide a *reproducible partition of concepts*, the headings must be approachable, make meaningful distinctions, be scientifically valid and current, and reflect a consistent approach. To provide a *partition* implies that the knowledge space must be covered in its entirety, without multiple ways of expressing the same ideas. That the headings partition *concepts* reflects the reality that not every concept we might wish to express is sufficiently distinct in its meaning that it would serve well as a Main Heading. That MeSH must cover all ideas *relevant* to biomedicine simply reflects the fact that many ideas not central to biomedicine might nevertheless be of interest. That MeSH's role is one of *organization* is not a surprising claim, but serves to emphasize that it is not solely for indexing or for cataloging, but also to support retrieval. The emphasis on *knowledge and information* accentuates the idea that the role is not one of characterizing data such as might be seen in a clinical or research environment, but material at a higher level of intellectual organization.

## 3.1 Meaningful Distinctions

Main Headings should be distinct in meaning (as well as spelling) from other Main Headings in the thesaurus; that is, they should not overlap in meaning. The constraint of distinctness, necessary to achieve a partition, can be easily defined in the MeSH thesaurus. Since descriptors consist of classes of concepts, distinct descriptors are just those with concepts whose meaning does not overlap that of a concept in any other descriptor, and whose application will achieve a partition of the literature.

The one acceptable exception to this rule is for descriptors in a hierarchical relationship. Broader descriptors whose meaning encompasses the meaning of their descendants are usual. If two descriptors are in a hierarchical arrangement, the common NLM indexing convention is to assign the most specific descriptor that covers the topic discussed in an article.

However, if the overlapping or duplicate descriptors are not in a hierarchical arrangement, the indexer or searcher would have no way to determine which descriptor to use. Under those circumstances, indexing would necessarily be inconsistent and searching arbitrary. For example, the component concepts of the MeSH descriptor "Exercise," "Isometric Exercise," and "Aerobic Exercise" overlap in meaning. They are not sufficiently distinct in meaning to be useful in this thesaurus.

In other cases, the descriptor itself may be clear but its application would not be. For example, we might wish to make a distinction between "DNA Fingerprints" and "DNA Fingerprinting." The meanings are distinct, but the literature is not. Discussions do not clearly distinguish between the process and the product. By way of contrast, we can note that "Radiography" and "Radiographs" are sufficiently distinct in the literature to warrant making them separate descriptors.

## 3.2 Approachability

To be approachable, the thesaurus must be organized in a clear and intuitive manner. Names of descriptors need to reflect the broad meaning of the concepts involved. The hierarchical relationships must be intellectually accessible to users of MeSH (e.g., clinician, librarian, and indexer). An indexer must be able to assign a given Main Heading to an article and a clinician must be able to find a given Main Heading in the tree hierarchy. Consistency in style, both in naming and in arranging the hierarchical relationships, are important aspects of this approachability. Which relationships are and are not represented in a hierarchy becomes a significant issue for the thesaurus developer. It is not possible to develop rules that are applicable in all cases. Nevertheless, the goal of a principled approach to developing hierarchies remains an ideal.

## 3.3  Scientific Validity and Currency

Thesaurus terminology must not only be those terms currently used in the documents indexed by the MeSH vocabulary (e.g., journal articles), it must also be consistent with currently accepted scientific theories and results in the corresponding biomedical field. There is an essential tension between the currency of a representation and its recognized validity. Today's hypothesis or theory may easily be disproven; on the other hand, it may become a valid standard. Only time and further experience, both enemies of currency, will tell.

## 4.  EQUIVALENCE AND SUBSTITUTIONARY RELATIONSHIPS ENTRY VOCABULARY AND THE DESCRIPTOR CLASS

The relationship of entry terms to main headings is one of the most essential in any thesaurus. Traditionally, entry vocabulary has been thought of as synonyms and quasi-synonyms of the main heading (quasi-synonyms are nonsynonymous terms which are otherwise indicative of the same concept, e.g., "dryness" would be a quasi-synonym of "wetness.") (National Information Standards Organization, 1994). Soergel (1985, p. 219) refers to these relationships as "equivalency," though we would prefer to reserve that term as describing, in a mathematical sense, the essential relationship of synonymy. Moreover, these equivalence relationships are not the only ones appropriate in entry vocabulary. In MeSH, the presence of an entry term can be interpreted as an indicator that the Main Heading is the appropriate method of representing that specific meaning for the purpose of organizing literature. In an environment in which MeSH is used, the Main Heading could be used as an appropriate substitute for the entry term. This type of relationship can thus be thought of as substitutionary.

As noted in 2.4, the primary entities in MeSH have been the Main Heading and the term. In the process of designing a new MeSH maintenance system, it was desirable that a third entity, the concept, should be explicitly represented. In the development of the new system, the nature of Main Headings, as a cluster of one or more concepts, became clearer. In the new maintenance system, the identification of synonymy between entry terms is made by explicit reference to concepts. The new system can store the fact that "Laser Scalpel" and "Laser Knife" are synonyms of each other and entry terms to "Laser Surgery." The new system formally represents that each term names the same concept.

The distinction between a descriptor, term, and concept in a single thesaurus is not new to the literature, but it has not been fully developed or exploited. As Soergel says, "One must carefully distinguish between the plane of concepts and the plane of terms . . ., lest confusion reign. The relationships between concepts and terms . . . are muddy at best" (1985, pp. 217-218). The three-level structure in MeSH (descriptor class, concept, and term) helps to make these relationship less "muddy."

## 4.1 What Is a Concept?

The ordinary definition of a concept is the common idea or meaning expressed by synonymous words or terms. For example, the terms "Cardiac Arrest" and "Heart Arrest" express the same concept. This notion of a concept is not one of a novel or abstruse entity; indeed, a concept may be identified by the class of synonymous terms. For computational purposes, a precise way of identifying synonyms is all terms that are members of the same concept class. Synonyms constitute a true equivalence class. They may be substituted for one another in an arbitrary expression without changing the meaning.

### 4.1.1 Relationship Between Concepts and Terms

The thesaurus literature has recognized the existence of concepts as distinct from terms in statements such as the one that the broader_than (BT) and narrower_than (NT) relationships are "really" between concepts and only between terms by derivation (Maniez, 1988, p. 220). Part of the reason for the confusion between concepts and terms is that it is necessarily difficult to talk of a concept without using at least one term. Often a concept has a preferred term, which is typically used to refer to the concept and may be viewed as the name of the concept (Soergel, 1985, p. 218; National Information Standards Organization, 1994, p. 2). However, since the identity of the preferred term may change, thesauri often use an arbitrary alphanumeric or numeric string as a Unique Identifier (UI), the persistent name of a concept. A term may change its meaning (think of how "gay" has changed in meaning over the past 50 years), but the UI should remain with the meaning to which it was originally assigned.

### 4.1.2 Relationship Between a Concept and Descriptor: The Descriptor Class

As noted earlier, the historical view of a descriptor in MeSH was as a group of terms, with the preferred term being the name of the Main Heading. Now, since a descriptor consists of one or more concepts, how is the name of the Main Heading or descriptor chosen? One term in each concept set is the preferred term for that concept. Analogously, one of the concepts in a descriptor class is the preferred concept; the name of that descriptor then is the preferred term of the preferred concept. For example:

    Descriptor = Coronary Disease
    Concept 1 = Coronary Disease
    Concept 2 = Coronary Occlusion
    Concept 3 = Coronary Stenosis

Concept 1 is the preferred concept, with the other two concepts being subordinate. Each of the terms shown is the preferred term for each concept. (Other terms are not shown.) In general, the preferred concept would be the one somehow "broadest" in meaning; however, this broader relationship is poorly defined. Recognizability by a user is important, as well as the possibility that the user might look for the less common concepts under this name.

Since this role as preferred term of preferred concept may change, MeSH uses an arbitrary alphanumeric string, the Unique Identifier (UI), as the unchanging name of each descriptor. The descriptor UI (the D number) is not the same as the Concept UI (an M number). Using the UIs permits the representation to remain clear and the attributes of various objects to be linked to the appropriate object.

The new MeSH maintenance system attaches to a descriptor only those properties or fields that are appropriate to it. The list of allowable qualifiers is an attribute of the descriptor. Importantly, as discussed in Section 5, the position in a hierarchy is an attribute of the descriptor. On the other hand, the scope note or definition is an attribute of a single concept. Multiple definitions, one for each concept, can then be represented within the descriptor record.

The question may arise if a concept could be a member of more than one descriptor class. Allowing a concept to be in more than one descriptor class would destroy any hope of achieving a partition of the information space. MeSH does not permit membership in multiple descriptors. The polyhierarchical arrangement of descriptors is sufficient to support the goals of MeSH.

## 4.2 Relationship of Substitutionary Equivalence: Descriptors and Entry Terms

The Main Heading and entry terms are the names of the concepts in a descriptor class. In most bibliographic databases, and in MEDLINE in particular, the descriptor name (the preferred term of the preferred concept) is the one assigned and attached to the citation record. An entry term may be a synonym of the descriptor name, or it may be a name of an additional concept in the descriptor. The relationship between the entry term and the descriptor name can be thought of as one of substitutionary equivalence. The terms function equivalently in retrieval systems that employ MeSH as it was designed to be used.

This relationship is not as restrictive as that of synonymy, though it may be mistaken for synonymy. While entry terms are closely related to Main Headings, they need not be synonymous to the Main Heading or to each other. This practice is justified because it is often impractical and usually undesirable to restrict the entry vocabulary to strictly synonymous terms. Most indexed domains have limited scope, which may have few or no documents about a given group of synonyms. Retrieval in the domain does not require fine granularity for every term. For example, MeSH contains a descriptor for "Whales" but the domain of MeSH is biomedicine and not zoology. In the MEDLINE citation database, there are not sufficient citations to create a separate descriptor for each specific whale species. Nevertheless, it is useful to have the species names as entry terms to the descriptor. Gains in precision of retrieval by creating more specific descriptors would be small.

The guiding principle in the development of entry vocabulary is the degree to which the distinction between the entry terms and the preferred term become important in conceptually partitioning the literature. If the body of literature is hopelessly fragmented by overly fine distinctions or if meaningful distinctions cannot be made, the utility of MeSH is reduced.

## 4.3 Relationships Between Entry Terms and the Preferred Term

Most thesauri do not make explicit the relationships between the entry term and the preferred term except to note that they are equivalent to each other (and to indicate the preferred term) for purposes of indexing and retrieval (Soergel, 1985, p. 218; National Information Standards Organization, 1994, p. 15). For some time MeSH has gone beyond this and labeled some relations within descriptors, primarily the relationship of each entry term to the preferred term. For example, "Laser Microsurgery" is an entry term to "Laser Surgery" and we have labeled this relationship as Narrower. Other entry term relationships are labeled as Broader or Synonymous.

Relationships within descriptors are not identical to the relations between descriptors, also often referred to as BT and NT, that are represented in thesaurus hierarchies such as the MeSH Tree Structures. The relationship of belonging to the same descriptor class is somehow closer. The nature of the relationship is readily apparent: The preferred term is the descriptor name used in the database to represent the meanings named by the entry term. This is a relationship of substitutionary equivalence.

## 5. HIERARCHICAL RELATIONSHIPS: TREES, SUBSUMPTION, AND MESH IN DOCUMENT RETRIEVAL

The hierarchical relationships are fundamental components in a thesaurus and can be powerful tools for retrieval. MeSH has long formalized its hierarchical structure in an extensive tree structure, currently at nine levels, representing increasing levels of specificity. This structure enables browsing for the appropriately specific descriptor, and is the basis of automatic and very powerful searching of all more specific topics.

The hierarchical relationships in the MeSH trees reflect a number of aspects of the main heading, both definitional and intentional. However, the relationships represented in the traditional hierarchies were implicit and not well defined. The relationship was termed a "broader than" relationship. Without a more formal definition of this relationship, such a statement is almost meaningless. "Broader than" relationships can be as formal as a set of meronymic and hyper/hyponymic relationships, for example, the set composed of "is_a," "part_of," "conceptual_part_of," and "process_of" (see National Information Standards Organization, 1994, pp.17-19). A thesaurus using only these relationships would approximate a concept representation scheme. While subsumption is often an important part of the arrangement of the hierarchies, other needs come into play with MeSH.

Many examples of hierarchical relations are instances of the part/whole and class/subclass relationships, which are relatively well understood, not only theoretically but also in their application. However, these relationships do not capture all hierarchical relationships and may not well explain any of them. A classic example is the case of "Accidents," which has as a narrower term, "Accident Prevention." Clearly, "Accident Prevention" is not part of "Accidents" nor is it included in the class of "Accidents." Soergel gives the following "hierarchy test" for retrieval of documents: "Should a search for documents dealing with A find all (or most) documents dealing with B? If yes, A is broader than B (and conversely, B is narrower than A)" (1985, p. 252). Given this test, it is easy to see that the BT/NT relationships thus represented are at the level of the descriptor.  The Soergel definition defines the nature of this relationship.

Moreover, a search for documents about accidents in MEDLINE should find documents about accident prevention.  It is the relationship of "aboutness" that is fundamental to a hierarchy in a thesaurus used for document retrieval.  The relationships of part/whole and class/subclass have a role in subject retrieval because if a subject is about a subclass, then it is also likely about the class.  Further analysis of this notion of subject or aboutness might provide us with rules for assigning if not using a hierarchy in document retrieval (Maron, 1977; Harper, 1989).

Arranging material hierarchically with these criteria should result in the placement of a descriptor in more than one hierarchy.  This is a perfectly reasonable thing to do.  What is less obvious is that the narrower descriptors ("children") of a given descriptor do not need to be identical in different trees.  For example, consider the descriptor "Nose."  As a child of "Sense Organs," "Nose" should appropriately have the children "Vomeronasal Organ" and "Olfactory Bulb."  However, as a child of "Face," its children should include "Nasal Bones."  A search based on the descriptor "Nose" in the context of the "Sense Organs" hierarchy should retrieve citations about the olfactory bulb, but not those about nasal bones.

Many individuals have tried to use MeSH as a concept representation language with only modest success.  That the relationships in the MeSH tree structures were designed with a different view, and with a different (and not formal) meaning of "broader_than," has frustrated their efforts.  The MeSH hierarchical structure was designed to reflect a view of the literature for a user.  Articles are indexed with the most specific headings available.  The use by a searcher of a parent heading would allow a broader search.  In the ELHILL system, this was known as an "explode," and required the searcher to indicate that they wished to include all the more specific terms.  The trees thus indicate what appears to be a useful set of relationships, based on the perceived needs of searchers.

Since its hierarchical relationships are between descriptors,  there are practical reasons for a MeSH descriptor to have different children in different trees.  The MeSH hierarchy differs substantially from a concept representation language.  Hierarchical relationships in concept representation are at the level of the concept; in the MeSH thesaurus, these relationships are at the level of the descriptor.

## 6.  ASSOCIATIVE RELATIONSHIPS:
### THE "SEE RELATED" CROSS-REFERENCE AND OTHER ATTRIBUTES

Associative relationships have often been thought to be similar to hierarchical relationships, but somehow looser and less clearly defined.  These are often relationships for which inclusion in an "explode" type of search is not mandatory, but should be considered under certain circumstances.  Another use for the associative relationship is to point out in the thesaurus, the existence of other descriptors, which may be more appropriate for a particular purpose.  They may point out distinctions made in the thesaurus or in the way the thesaurus has arranged descriptors hierarchically.

Many associative relationships are represented by the "see related" cross reference.  The categories of relationships seem to be greater in number and are certainly more varied than hierarchical relationships. (See Harper's 1989 analysis of the associative relationships in MeSH.) While some of these relationships may have definitional value, the most that can be said of them for certain is that they serve as important reminders of the impossibility of representing all the important relationships between ideas in a set of hierarchies.

One attribute which can be thought of as an associative relationship within the MeSH thesaurus is the Pharmacologic Action. Limited to chemicals (which comprise approximately half of the Main Headings in MeSH), this relationship allows the aggregation of chemicals by actions or uses. Two chemicals with the same Pharmacologic Action thus share an association by virtue of sharing the same property.

An Entry Combination, which points or maps users to a different descriptor rather than allowing them to use a combination of a descriptor with a specific qualifier, is a different type of associative relationship. These relationships attempt to maintain the distinctions between usages of descriptors where a meaning represented by the descriptor/qualifier combination may overlap the meaning of a different descriptor.

## 7. SUMMARY

The transition of MeSH from a term-based structure into a concept-oriented structure has shed some light on important relationships within a thesaurus. A descriptor represents one or more concepts. The role of entry vocabulary is to provide a guide for the proper choice of a descriptor. Avoiding overlap in meaning between descriptors emerges as another motivation for the use of entry vocabulary, as well as the associative relationships provided by the Entry Combination. The hierarchical relationships are of primary importance as keys to literature organization of a body of literature. The "broader than/narrower than" relationship in thesaurus hierarchies is one of representing a broader or narrower retrieval. The differences between a document-retrieval thesaurus and a concept-representation language become apparent.

## References

Bachrach, C. A. & Charen, T. (1978). Selection of MEDLINE contents, the development of its thesaurus, and the indexing process. *Medical Informatics*, 3, 237-254.

Harper, C. R. (1989). Associative relationships in the MeSH thesaurus. *Associate Project Report*. National Library of Medicine.

Maniez J. (1988). Relationships in thesauri: Some critical remarks. *International Classification*, 15, 133-138.

Maron, M. E. (1977). On indexing, retrieval, and the meaning of about. *Journal of the American Society for Information Science*, 28, 38-43.

McCray, A. T. & Hole, W. T. (1990). The scope and structure of the UMLS semantic network. In Miller, R. A. (Ed.), *Proceedings of the Fourteenth Annual Symposium on Computer Applications to Medical Care*, pp. 126-130. New York: IEEE Computer Society.

National Information Standards Organization. (1994). *Guidelines for the Construction, Format, and Management of Monolingual Thesauri*. Bethesda, MD: NISO Press. (ANSI/NISO Z39.19-1993).

Nelson, S. J., Aronson, A. R., Doszkocs, T. E., Wilbur, W. J., Bodenreider, O., Chang, H. F., Mork, J., & McCray, A. T. (1999). Automated assignment of Medical Subject Headings. *Journal of the American Medical Informatics Association, Symposium Supplement*, 1127.

Schuyler, P. L., Hole, W. T., Tuttle, M. S., & Sherertz, D. D. (1993). The UMLS metathesaurus: Representing different views of biomedical concepts. *Bulletin of the Medical Library Association*, 81, 217-222.

Soergel, D. (1985). *Organizing Information*. Orlando, FL: Academic Press.

# Chapter 12

# Lateral Relationships in Multicultural, Multilingual Databases in the Spiritual and Religious Domains: The OM Information Service

A. Neelameghan

*Documentation Research and Training Centre, Indian Statistical Institute, Bangalore, India*

**Abstract:**

Mapping a multidimensional universe of subjects for linear representation, such as in class number, subject heading, and facet structure is problematic. Into this context is recalled the near-seminal and postulational approach suggested by S. R. Ranganathan. The non-hierarchical associative relationship or lateral relationship (LR) is distinguished at different levels—among information sources, databases, records of databases, and among concepts (LR-0). Over thirty lateral relationships at the concept level (LR-0) are identified and enumerated with examples from spiritual and religious texts. Special issues relating to LR-0 in multicultural, multilingual databases intended to be used globally by peoples of different cultures and faith are discussed, using as example the multimedia OM Information Service. Vocabulary assistance for users is described.

## 1. INTRODUCTION

### 1.1 Structure and Relationships

Conceptualizing and communicating ideas about an entity, whether concrete or abstract, presupposes cognition of that entity. It implies demarcating and discriminating that entity from other entities, or recognizing a boundary about that entity. In the physical world, the sensory experiences (i.e., seeing, hearing, touching, tasting, and smelling) provide for such discrimination. In intellection, such discrimination may be achieved by recognizing the dissimilarities in attributes; that is, by using differentiating attributes (characteristics) of the entity—the basic principle of classification. This gives rise to the idea of structure within a class of entities and among different classes of entities. A complex class or system may be constructed by an assembly of simpler elements or subsystems. For example, in a faceted classification model, compound subjects and complex subjects can be constructed by a combination of facets. Simon (1962) noted that the relationship among the components of a subsystem is stronger than the relationship among the subsystems. S. R. Ranganathan (1967, ch. O) named the strength of relationship among the components of a subject as Bond Strength. The relationship among the subsystems (e.g., facets) may be hierarchical or non-hierarchical as would be the case among the elements within a subsystem. Different structures, such as a combination or assembly of entities, give rise to different kinds of

*C. A. Bean and R. Green (eds.), Relationships in the Organization of Knowledge, 185–198.*

relationships and the same elements assembled in different ways give rise to different relationships among the elements and different properties of the assembled entity; chemical structures are examples. The papers of the symposium *Hierarchical structures* (Whyte, Wilson, & Wilson, 1969) deal extensively with the concept of hierarchy. In contrast, this chapter deals essentially with non-hierarchic associative relationships or lateral relationships (LRs) in parallel with 'lateral thinking' elaborated by De Bono (1970).

## 1.2 Multidimensional Universe of Subjects

The universe of subjects is multidimensional in the sense that to identify any one entity in that universe, several coordinates (characteristics) may be required. In transforming or mapping that universe for unidimensional representation as in a class number, a subject heading, a faceted structure, etc., the principal and difficult task is that of retaining the original immediate-neighborhood relationships perceived among the components in the linear structure (Neelameghan, 1971; Ranganathan, 1967, pt. Q). If that is not possible, the issue is which component is to be chosen as the reference point, which one is to placed closest to it, which one in the second remove, and so on according to their respective bond strength (or strength of relationship) so as to facilitate recognizing the subject presented in a linear format. Ranganathan (1967, pt. R) suggested that since the variety and number of ideas are too numerous at the phenomenal level, diving deeper to the near-seminal level may permit the variety and number to coalesce into fewer types or categories. He further postulated the existence of five Fundamental Categories of ideas: Personality (core entity of study), Matter (material, property), Energy (action), Space, and Time, and their organization into this linear sequence reflecting the strength of bond between the core entity category and each of the other categories. This sequence of facets, called the Absolute Syntax, elaborated by Ranganathan (1967, ch. XJ) and Neelameghan (1975a), is also claimed to parallel best the way in which a majority of normal persons organize components of a subject when thinking or communicating about the subject. In a recent paper, Neelameghan (1998) discussed how the lateral relationships are represented in the facet structure model based on Ranganathan's General Theory of Knowledge Classification.

LRs are discussed in this chapter using as a case study the databases of the OM Information Service (OMIS).

## 2. OM INFORMATION SERVICE

### 2.1 Features and Databases

OMIS (1998) is a multicultural, multilingual information service in the spiritual and religious domains. The objective of OMIS is to provide a preliminary source of information for comparative and analytical studies, to prepare discourses and lectures, and to support and supplement attempts to understand the spiritual concepts and precepts of different faiths and cultures.

The technical details of OMIS are described by Rajashekar, Ravi Srinivas, &

Neelameghan (1998). OMIS consists of three hypertext-linked multimedia (text, sound, and images) databases:

- OM is a database of extracts (currently about 18,000) from the sayings, discourses, sermons, dialogues, poems, and writings of religious leaders, mystics, saints, prophets, and scholars and from religious texts, scriptures, and epics, together called Sources (about 900). Ranging from 3000 BCE to the present, and spanning across many faiths, cultures, and religions of the world, these extracts comprise the principal database.
- OMBIO is a database of life sketches/descriptions of the Sources with pictures in some cases (about 125 at present).
- OMBIB is a bibliography of source books (about 475 at present).

Searching the OM database is essentially concept-based and can be qualified by one or more concept terms or name(s) of Source(s) using Boolean operators. Hypertext links and user interfaces to navigate among the records of the different databases have been provided.

## 2.2 Vocabulary Control: Usual Requirements

Vocabulary control is necessary both within and across databases to facilitate searching across databases using one and the same search expression. AACR2 rules have generally been followed in rendering names of Sources in all the three databases. The common problems of alternative names, pseudonyms, popular names, etc., are also found in the spiritual texts. Consistency is required in rendering Name of Subject/Concept not only in all the indexed fields within a database but also across databases to facilitate hypertext linking. The usual problems of spelling variation, hyphenation, abbreviations, compounding of terms, etc., are all encountered, but are not considered in this chapter. Only certain additional issues relating to culture-sensitive terminology and LRs in developing the thesaurus and glossary to assist online searching in the databases of OMIS are addressed.

## 3. LANGUAGE OF EXTRACTS AND QUERIES

### 3.1 Language of Extract

The extracts in the OM database are all in English. They have been extracted from English language materials, or from those in other languages (e.g., Sanskrit, Pali, Arabic, Persian, Yiddish, Hebrew, Tamil, and others) translated into English. The dialogue language of the system is also English.

In many of the original texts, especially those translated into English, special terms of the original language transliterated into the English alphabet are provided in parentheses along with the English translation or vice versa. Alternatively, the transliterated term from the original text is given in the text with its meaning in English either as a footnote or in a glossary in the book.

## 3.2 Use of Terms of the Original Language

The reasons for using terms of the original language (transliterated into English) in the text by the translating and/or commenting author include:

- There is no exact equivalent term to the original in the English language (e.g., *Atman, Brahman, Nibbana, Sefirot, Einsof*).
- The English term used is only a near-equivalent to the term in the original language.
- The term in the original language requires several words or a whole sentence in English for its correct interpretation or understanding (e.g., *Anaagaami* (Pali): The third stage of sainthood before attaining Arahantahood).
- Giving the original term along with its interpretation helps comparative study of two or more of such interpretations by different scholars.

In some translated texts, the same English term may be used to denote slightly different concepts for which there may be different terms in the original work. For example, the English term 'Mind' is used for both the Sanskrit terms *Manas* and *Chitta*, which terms are given in parentheses in the text or in a footnote. The reverse case also occurs: The same term in the original language (transliterated into English alphabet) may denote slightly different concepts for which different English terms are given in the text. For example, in Sanskrit the terms *Buddhi* is used for 'Reason,' 'Intellect,' and 'Intelligence,' and *Prajna* is used for 'Mind,' 'Awareness,' and 'Understanding.' On the other hand 'Intelligence' may also be an interpretation for *Chetana*.

For similar reasons, a user, whose first language is English but who is knowledgeable about works in other languages, tends to use terms of the original language (transliterated into English alphabet) in the OMIS search session. Likewise, a user, not proficient in English or in the special terminology of the spiritual field, may not know the English-language equivalent for a term in the original language.

Might such uses of terms of different languages represent also differences in the nature of relationships among the terms within a language and across the languages?

## 4.  LATERAL RELATIONSHIPS (LR)

The following distinct types of LRs arise at different levels among multiple (and multilingual) databases in an information system (Neelameghan, 1998):

## 4.1  LR Type 0 (LR-0)

Consider the concepts represented by the terms to be used in a search expression. At least two different user needs may be represented by different relationships among the concepts, for example, a combination of the terms "Value of repentance, Sins, Destruction" can give rise to two different interpretations, namely, "Value of repentance is in the destruction of sins" and "Destruction of the value of repentance by sins." Use of appropriate search expressions representing the two different user interests could retrieve different sets of records. The relationship among the concepts in each set of retrieved records is **Inter-concepts relationship** or **LR-0**. This type of relationship will be discussed in more detail in section 5.

## 4.2 LR Type 1 (LR-1)

The search expression "Mysticism. Christianity. Middle Ages" applied to the OM database may retrieve one or more texts/records. This represents a relationship among the records retrieved in relationship to a particular query, **Inter-records relationship** or **LR-1**.

## 4.3 LR Type 2 (LR-2)

When several databases are accessible, identifying those to be searched in relation to a specific information need depends on a knowledge of the contents of each of the databases. A user selecting two or more of the databases for further search perceives a relationship among them, **Inter-databases relationship** or **LR-2**. Knowledge of the contents of the databases and the search experience can be helpful in subsequent searches in those databases.

## 4.4 LR Type 3 (LR-3)

When a user identifies several sources (e.g., websites) as possible sources likely to provide information to a specific query, those sources are related to each other with respect to the specific information need. This is **Inter-sources relationship** or **LR-3**, which can be useful in further searches in those sources.

## 5.  INTER-CONCEPT RELATIONSHIP (LR-0)

Neelameghan (1975b, 1998) identified several specific types of non-hierarchical associative relationships among concepts, essentially LR-0, as mentioned above. Indicating the specific type of relationship by using a role indicator or other devices in the search expression, plus vocabulary tools, such as thesauri, subject headings lists, classification schemes, and class numbers, will help in retrieving more relevant records and minimizing the chances of retrieval of nonrelevant ones, especially those arising from certain combinations of the search terms and indicative of different relationships among them (see 4.1). In examining the extracts in the OM database for developing vocabulary tools, several of the LRs noted in the earlier work have been found to occur in the spiritual and religious domain as well. Table 1 is a brief enumeration of specific types of LRs among concepts.

(a)  =  TERMS DENOTING
(b)  =  EXAMPLE
(c)  =  THESAURUS ENTRY

SERIAL NO.:    01
(a)  Process and Device or Medium or Method
     used  in the Process
(b)  Nirvana through Renunciation
(c)  NIRVANA
        (Through)
        RT RENUNCIATION
     RENUNCIATION
        (For Attainment of)
        RT NIRVANA

SERIAL NO.:    02
(a)  Process and resulting Product
(b)  Liberation is a result of Self-sacrifice
(c)  SELF-SACRIFICE
        (Leads to)
        RT LIBERATION
     LIBERATION
        (Result of)
        RT SELF-SACRIFICE

SERIAL NO.:    03
(a)  Processes occurring in Sequence
(b)  The successive Stages of Nibbana
(c)  NIBBANA
        (Stages of)
        RT MAGGA
            PHALA
            SATAPANNA
            SAKADAAGAAMI
            ANAAGAAMI
            ARAHANTA
        MAGGA
        (Stage to)
        RT NIBBANA
     [similarly for other RT terms]

SERIAL NO.:    04
(a)  Process and its Property (Attribute)
(b)  Benefits of Praying
(c)  PRAYING
        (Attribute)
        RT BENEFITS
     BENEFITS
        (Attribute of)
        RT PRAYING

SERIAL NO.:    05
(a)  Process and Property of Object associated
     with the Process
(b)  Human Transformation and Purity of Heart
     of aspirant
(c)  TRANSFORMATION
        (Depends on)
        RT PURITY OF HEART
     PURITY OF HEART
        (Necessary for)
        RT TRANSFORMATION

SERIAL NO.:    06
(a)  Process and Person usually associated with
     the Process
(b)  Confession of Sinner
(c)  CONFESSION
        (Done by)
        RT SINNER
     SINNER
        (Doer of)
        RT CONFESSION

SERIAL NO.:    07
(a)  Property and Action performed on it
(b)  Absolution of Sin
(c)  SIN
        (Action by)
        RT ABSOLUTION
     ABSOLUTION
        (Action on)
        RT SIN

SERIAL NO.:    08
(a)  Entity and Device used in Producing it
(b)  Bhakti is a means to Liberation
(c)  BHAKTI
        (Means of)
        RT LIBERATION
     LIBERATION
        (Attained by)
        RT BHAKTI

Table 1.  Summary Enumeration of Specific Types of  LR-0

SERIAL NO.: 09
(a) Entity considered as attribute of another Entity
(b) Renunciation is characteristic of Monastic life
(c) RENUNCIATION
    (Characteristic of)
    RT MONASTIC LIFE
MONASTIC LIFE
    (Characterized by)
    RT RENUNCIATION

SERIAL NO.: 10
(a) Entity and its Application capability
(b) Prophets can Forecast future events
(c) PROPHET
    (Ability for)
    RT FORECASTING
FORECASTING
    (Ability of)
    RT PROPHET

SERIAL NO.: 11
(a) Thing as material and the Thing made out of it
(b) Cross made of Wood
(c) CROSS
    (Made of)
    RT WOOD
WOOD
    (Material for)
    RT CROSS

SERIAL NO.: 12
(a) Thing and parts associated with it
(b) Angel with Halo
(c) ANGEL
    (Associated with)
    RT HALO
HALO
    (Associated with)
    RT ANGEL

SERIAL NO.: 13
(a) Entity and its Characteristic Property
(b) Boundless, changeless, essence of existents, eternal, incomprehensible, inexpressible, non-duality, omnipresence, without beginning are all attributes of the Supreme Being

(Cont.—Top of next column)

(c) SUPREME BEING
    (Attribute)
    RT BOUNDLESS
       CHANGELESS
       ESSENCE OF EXISTENTS
       ETERNAL
       INCOMPREHENSIBLE
       INEXPRESSIBLE
       NON-DUALITY
       OMNIPRESENCE
       WITHOUT BEGINNING
BOUNDLESS
    (Attribute of)
    RT SUPREME BEING
[similarly for other RT terms]

SERIAL NO.: 14
(a) Entity and its Measure or Device for measuring
(b) Acuteness of Pain
(c) PAIN
    (Measure)
    RT ACUTENESS
ACUTENESS
    (Measure of)
    RT PAIN

SERIAL NO.: 15
(a) Entity and its usual Place of occurrence or manipulation
(b) Priest in the Temple
(c) PRIEST
    (Location)
    RT TEMPLE
TEMPLE
    (Location of)
    RT PRIEST

SERIAL NO.: 16
(a) Entity and its Predecessor or Precursor
(b) Relationship between Salvation and Renunciation
(c) RENUNCIATION
    (Precursor to)
    RT SALVATION
SALVATION
    (Preceded by)
    RT RENUNCIATION

Table 1. Summary Enumeration of Specific Types of LR-0—Cont.

SERIAL NO.:    17
(a)  Situation or condition and What may occur
     in that situation or condition
(b)  Enlightenment and Peace of Mind
(c)  ENLIGHTENMENT
        (Conducive to)
        RT  PEACE OF MIND
     PEACE OF MIND
        (Occurs with)
        RT  ENLIGHTENMENT

SERIAL NO.:    18
(a)  Near Synonymous or Near Equivalent
     concepts (see also 31)
(b)  Liberation and Salvation
(c)  LIBERATION
        (Near equivalent)
        RT  SALVATION
     SALVATION
        (Near equivalent)
        RT  LIBERATION

SERIAL NO.:    19
(a)  Two concepts usually used or occurring
     concurrently
(b)  Repentance and Forgiveness
(c)  REPENTANCE
        (Precedes)
        RT  FORGIVENESS
     FORGIVENESS
        (Follows)
        RT  REPENTANCE

SERIAL NO.:    20
(a)  Contiguous concepts based on definition
(b)  Buddhism—four types of doubts: Doubt
     about the Teacher Buddha; Doubt about
     the Teaching, Dhamma; Doubt about the
     Order, Sangha; Doubt about the Training,
     Sikkha.  These hinder Spiritual Progress
(c)  SPIRITUAL PROGRESS
        (Obstacles)
        RT  DOUBT ABOUT BUDDHA
            DOUBT ABOUT DHAMMA
            DOUBT ABOUT SANGHA
            DOUBT ABOUT SIKKHA
     DOUBT ABOUT BUDDHA
        (Obstacle to)
        RT  SPIRITUAL PROGRESS
     DOUBT ABOUT DHAMMA
        (Obstacle to)
        RT  SPIRITUAL PROGRESS
     [similarly for other RT terms]

SERIAL NO.:    21
(a)  Concepts having common elements in their
     definitions
(b)  Revelation and Enlightenment
(c)  REVELATION
        RT  ENLIGHTENMENT
     ENLIGHTENMENT
        RT  REVELATION

SERIAL NO.:    22
(a)  Two persons interacting in a special
     context
(b)  Guru and Disciple
(c)  GURU
        RT  DISCIPLE
     DISCIPLE
        RT  GURU

SERIAL NO.:    23
(a)  Apparent Opposite concepts which
     however may also be construed as
     interacting factors
(b)  Impact of Failure on Success
(c)  SUCCESS
        (Impact by)
        RT  FAILURE
     FAILURE
        (Impact on)
        RT  SUCCESS

SERIAL NO.:    24
(a)  Antonymous concepts
(b)  Modesty and Arrogance
(c)  MODESTY
        RT  ARROGANCE
     ARROGANCE
        RT  MODESTY

SERIAL NO.:    25
(a)  Coordinate concepts—concepts in one and
     the same array derived by division of
     superordinate concept using a single
     characteristic
(b)  Religions - Buddhism, Judaism,
        Christianity, Islam
(c)  BUDDHISM
        RT  CHRISTIANITY
            ISLAM
            JUDAISM
     CHRISTIANITY
        RT  BUDDHISM
            ISLAM
            JUDAISM
     [similarly for other RT terms]

Table 1.  Summary Enumeration of Specific Types of  LR-0—Cont.

SERIAL NO.: 26
(a) Comparison relationship among concepts
(b) Comparison of Unselfish Action with Renunciation
(c) RENUNCIATION
    (Compared with)
    RT UNSELFISH ACTION
    UNSELFISH ACTION
    (Compared with)
    RT RENUNCIATION

SERIAL NO.: 27
(a) Differentiation relationship among concepts
(b) Difference between Renunciation and Relinquishment
(c) RENUNCIATION
    (Differentiated from)
    RT RELINQUISHMENT
    RELINQUISHMENT
    (Differentiated from)
    RT RENUNCIATION

SERIAL NO.: 28
(a) Mutual influence among entities
(b) Influence of Meditation on Mental Stress
(c) MEDITATION
    (Influence on)
    RT MENTAL STRESS
    MENTAL STRESS
    (Influenced by)
    RT MEDITATION

SERIAL NO.: 29
(a) Model or Case study relationship
(b) Ramakrishna Paramahamsa is a model of Renunciation
(c) RENUNCIATION
    (Model)
    RT Ramakrishna Paramahamsa
    RAMAKRISHNA PARAMAHAMSA
    (Model of)
    RT RENUNCIATION

SERIAL NO.: 30
(a) Causal Relationship
(b) Einsof generates or causes Sefirot
(c) EINSOF
    SN Infinite in Kabbalah, Jewish Mysticism
    (Causes)
    RT SEFIROT
    SEFIROT
    (Caused by)
    RT EINSOF

SERIAL NO.: 31
(a) Equivalence relationship (see also 18)
(b) God, Allah, Bhagawan, the Infinite, Einsof, Iswara, Providence, Supreme Being, the Creator, are different Names for the same Entity
(c) GOD
    (Equivalent to)
    RT ABSOLUTE SPIRIT
    ALLAH
    BHAGAWAN
    EINSOF
    ETERNAL BEING
    INFINITE BEING
    ISWARA
    ABSOLUTE SPIRIT
    (Equivalent to)
    RT ALLAH
    BHAGAWAN
    EINSOF
    ETERNAL BEING
    GOD
    INFINITE BEING
    ISWARA
    [similarly for other RT terms]

Table 1. Summary Enumeration of Specific Types of LR-0—Cont.

In Table 1, the relationships at serial numbers 26 to 31 are additions. The *Near Equivalence* and *Equivalence* relationship can be used within and also among terms from different faiths, cultures, and languages. For example:

LIBERATION
   (*Near equivalent*)
   RT MOKSHA (Hinduism, Sanskrit)
      NIBBANA (Buddhism, Pali)
      NIRVANA (Hinduism, Sanskrit)
      SALVATION

HOLY WORD (Christianity, The Bible)
   (*Equivalent to*)
   RT KALMA (Islam)
      SABD (Indian scriptures)
      SAUT-E-SARMADI (Sufism)
      TAO (Taoism)
      UDGIT (Hinduism, Upanishads)

UDGIT (Hinduism, Upanishads)
   (*Equivalent to*)
   RT HOLY WORD (The Bible)
      KALMA (Islam)
      SABD (Indian scriptures)
      SAUT-E-SARMADI (Sufism)
      TAO (Taoism)

MONASTIC LIFE
   (*Equivalent to*)
   RT SANNYASA (Hinduism)

SANNYASA (Hinduism)
   (*Equivalent to*)
   RT MONASTIC LIFE

ATMAN
   (*Near equivalent*)
   RT BRAHMAN
      SELF
      SOUL

BRAHMAN
   (*Near equivalent*)
   RT ATMAN

## 6.  INTERCULTURAL COMMUNICATION

### 6.1  Global Perspective

International intercultural information exchange and intercultural studies have taken place since the discovery of international trade routes in the mid-15th century.  But they have become much more frequent and wider in scope and depth in recent decades, thanks to the rapid expansion of international and intranational travel, communications, publications, and now Internet websites (Vrajaprana, 1998).  Such exchanges have also become institutionalized through university study and research centers and programs, as well as through the work of societies, such as Christian missions, Buddhist societies, Vedanta societies, Zen groups, and so on.

### 6.2  Concept Acquisition

Concept acquisition by a person is influenced, among other factors, by the needs of daily life, and the cultural and societal environment to which the person is attuned (see, for example, Beghtol, this volume).  The concepts are usually expressed and communicated through a natural language native to or acquired by the person, giving rise to differences in the concepts used by persons belonging to different cultural groups.  For example, certain South Pacific Islanders are reported to have the concept of two primary colors only, those that they need in daily life.  On the other hand, the same group not only recognizes but also has distinct names for over thirty varieties of a single species of fish, because they need such elaborate classification for use in their daily life in the environment they live. Peter Farb (1973) discusses many such differences in conceptualization and related terminology among different cultural groups. Such differences in concepts and related terms are common in the discourses, writings, and other communications in the spiritual and religious domains. For instance, some faiths do not use concepts related to 'after-life,' 'reincarnation,' etc., while others do.

## 6.3 Issues

In this context, an information system intended for use by the global community will have to deal with issues such as the following:

- There will be concepts originating in one cultural group that are not found in other groups; however, the latter group would also be interested to learn about and research such concepts.
- An entity may be viewed from different perspectives by different cultural groups; hence differences may arise in the perceived relationships among the concepts.
- Arising from the foregoing are problems in the terminology used by the different groups.
- How may a global multicultural, multilingual information system accommodate and reflect in its vocabulary tools, user interfaces, and other user aids, these differences in concepts and the relationships among them, to support correct interpretation of texts, comparative studies, etc., by scholars with differing cultural orientations?

An information service such as OMIS, is intended to be used globally, that is, by persons belonging to different faiths, cultures, and linguistic groups, with a view to promoting intercultural and interfaith understanding and comparative studies. Therefore, it is necessary to facilitate searching the databases by assisting users to use the terms of the natural language to which he/she is attuned; and to recognize appropriate relationships among the concept terms that are pertinent to his/her culture, faith, or language background. Two specific types of assistance are offered.

### 6.3.1 Thesaurus

Two types of thesaurus are being developed. In one, all terms irrespective of their cultural and linguistic origin are included in a single listing. This assumes that the nature of relationships among concepts perceived by different cultural groups does not differ. For example:

RENUNCIATION
*(Attribute of)*
RT MONASTIC LIFE
   SANNYASA
   SELF-LESS ACTION
   SPIRITUAL LIFE
   YOGI
*(Attainment through)*
RT BHAKTI
   DEVOTION
   JNANA
   SACRIFICE
   SELF-LESS ACTION
   YOGA

SANNYASA
*(Equivalent to)*
RT MONASTIC LIFE
*(Attribute)*
RT RENUNCIATION
*(Follower)*
RT SANNYASIN
   SANNYASINI
   YOGI

BHAKTI
*(Leads to)*
RT RENUNCIATION
   LIBERATION
   MOKSHA
   VIMOCHAN

The terms in bold are transliterations of the corresponding Sanskrit terms. More examples can be found in earlier sections.

TASAWWUF
*(Equivalent to)*
RT MYSTICISM (Sufism)
*(Basis)*
RT DIVINE PATH
   HAQIQA
   RELIGIOUS LAW
   SHARI'A
   TARIQA
   TRUTH

AQIQA
*(Equivalent to)*
RT TRUTH
*(Basis of)*
RT TASAWWUF

Here the terms in bold are transliterations of corresponding Arabic/Persian words occurring in Islamic Sufi literature.

In the OM database, every substantive term (i.e., excluding terms included in the stopword list) occurring in the Extract (including terms transliterated into English), is indexed. In the PC version of the database, a Pascal program VOCON, described by Chowdhury, Neelameghan, & Chowdhury (1996), helps in generating a thesaurus and also in selecting terms from it to formulate search expressions. Thus, the user can also select terms from other languages transliterated into English for search formulation.

In an alternative approach, the MTM program developed by Davies (1997) may be used to generate separate-but-linked thesaurus lists for terms selected from the different language groups. The program can handle as many as nine languages that use English/Roman scripts. Concepts may be represented by codes, class numbers, etc., and the program treats these as though they were natural language terms. Here, the differences in the perceived relationships among the concepts of a particular linguistic or cultural group can be reflected in the thesaurus. A user may select term(s) from any of the languages represented in the thesaurus list to formulate search expressions, and the program will link the corresponding terms in the other languages represented and search the database using all of the selected terms. The multilingual thesaurus can be called online in the PC version of the OM database using the VOCON program.

### 6.3.2 Glossary

Another help feature provided to the user is an online glossary of the terms from other languages transliterated into English. This facility is now available for the PC version of the OM database. It uses a Pascal program called SELN. The program permits the selection of term(s) from the text of a record retrieved in response to a query (from one or more databases) and displaying online the corresponding record(s) from the GLOSS database, currently containing about 5000 terms, resident in the system. The details are given in Neelameghan (1999).

## 7. CONCLUDING REMARKS

Differences in concepts and relationships among concepts do occur in the spiritual and religious domains across different cultural and linguistic groups. In databases for these culture-sensitive domains intended for use by the global community, online assistance should be provided to users to assist them, among other things, to recognize the differences in concepts and the relationships among them in the different cultures and faiths. Tools and devices should also be provided to enable users with different cultural orientations and language backgrounds to formulate search expressions by selecting words in the language to which each may be attuned, and by correctly interpreting the relationship among concepts in the context of the cultural or religious group from which certain special terms may have originated. Some preliminary solutions, in the form of a thesaurus and a glossary and user interfaces are discussed in this chapter. Further work in this regard with terms from Sanskrit is being carried out by Dr. Padma Upadhyay at the Manipal Institute of Technology, Udupi, India.

### References

Chowdhury, G. G., Neelameghan, A., & Chowdhury, S. (1996). VOCON: Vocabulary control online in MicroIsis databases. *Knowledge Organization*, 22, 18-22.

Davies, R. (1997). *Multilingual Thesaurus Management* (MTM) (Version 3.1) [Computer software]. Ottawa: Bibliomatics.

De Bono, E. (1970). *Lateral Thinking: A Textbook of Creativity*. London: Ward Lock Educational.

Farb, P. (1973). *Word Play: What Happens When People Talk*. New York: Alfred A. Knopf.

Neelameghan, A. (1971). Classification, Theory of. In A. Kent & H. Lancour (Eds.), *Encyclopedia of Library and Information Science*, 5:147-174. New York: Marcel Dekker.

Neelameghan, A. (1975a). Absolute syntax and structure of an indexing and switching language. In A. Neelameghan (Ed.) *Ordering Systems for Global Information Networks: Proceedings of the Third International Study Conference on Classification Research*, 165-176. Bangalore: Sarada Ranganathan Endowment for Library Science.

Neelameghan, A. (1975b). Non-hierarchical associative relationships: Their types and computer generation of RT links. In *Seminar on Thesaurus in Information Systems, Bangalore, 1975 December 1-5*, AA:A1-A8. Bangalore: Documentation Research and Training Centre.

Neelameghan, A. (1998). Lateral relations and links in multi-cultural, multimedia databases in the spiritual and religious domains: Some observations. *Information Studies*, 4, 221-246.

Neelameghan, A. (1999). An online glossary for a multilingual database. *Information Studies*, 5, 83-94.

*OM Information Service* (OMIS) [Online]. (1998). Available: <http://144.16.72.175/~om> (full version) or <http://ukko.grainger.uiuc.edu/omasp> (some pictorial and audio data may be missing) [2000, February 15].

Rajashekar, T. B., Ravi Srinivas, R., & Neelameghan, A. (1988). Designing a multimedia information service for the Internet and CD-ROM. *Information Studies*, 4, 125-142.

Ranganathan, S. R. (1967). *Prolegomena to Library Classification* (3rd ed., assisted by M. A. Gopinath). Bombay: Asia.

Simon, H. (1962). The architecture of complexity. *Proceedings of the American Philosophical Society*, 106, 467-482.

Vrajaprana, P. (1998). Vedanta in cyberspace, the vedanta movement and the electronic frontier. *Prabuddha Bharata*, 103, 91-103

Whyte, L. L., Wilson, A., & Wilson, D. (1969) *Hierarchical Structures*. New York: American Elsevier.

Chapter 13

# Relationships in Ranganathan's Colon Classification

M. P. Satija
*Library Science Department, G N D University, Amritsar, India*

**Abstract:**
Ranganathan's Colon Classification (CC) treats knowledge as a multidimensional structure, enshrining a multiplicity of complex relations. This complexity is manipulated within the CC on the basis of numerous of Ranganathan's contributions to subject analysis, including the modes of formation of subjects; an objective rationale for the arrangement of main classes; the PMEST facet formula, extended by the postulate of rounds and levels; a general dependency principle for collocation of related components in a facet formula; phase relationships between the components of complex interdisciplinary subjects; the recurrence of an APUPA arrangement throughout the linear ordering of materials; and an absolute syntax of ideas.

## 1. INTRODUCTION

Classification is a tool to map the universe of knowledge and represents its structure at some given time. S. R. Ranganathan's Colon Classification (CC) excels in this endeavor. As Fran Miksa has pointed out, "There is virtually no area of Ranganathan's work and personal life in which [the] quest for discovering the inner or essential order behind the visible world is absent" (1998, p. 67).

Until the Industrial Revolution in the mid-1800s, the growth of knowledge was slow, and boundaries between subjects were clear. Main classes consisted of broad areas (e.g., the three categories of Francis Bacon, the ten main classes of the Dewey Decimal Classification [DDC]), and the structure of knowledge was simple. With the coming of industrialization, democracy, and the universalization of education, the growth of knowledge increased at a brisk pace. The end of World War I further accelerated its rate of growth. Knowledge inevitably became more specialized. Presently, the information revolution threatens to engulf us.

Ranganathan perceived this acute proliferation of knowledge while designing his system of classification and later continued his studies of knowledge growth to mold and rejuvenate his system accordingly. He conceived of CC as a way to develop a composite classification to move beyond the monolithic hierarchical structure of the DDC, which Ranganathan perceived as inadequate for coping with the twentieth century's multidimensional knowledge.

199

*C. A. Bean and R. Green (eds.), Relationships in the Organization of Knowledge, 199–210.*

## 2. SUBJECTS AND THEIR KINDS

Ranganathan (1967, sect. CR3) defined a subject as an organized, systematized, and coherent body of ideas whose length and breadth fall within the comprehension of a typical scholar. A subject is independent of its length of treatment in a document. It could fill a multivolume encyclopedia or could be confined to a small journal article or less.

Ranganathan recognized three kinds of subjects, namely, basic subjects, compound subjects, and complex subjects.

### 2.1 Basic Subjects

**Basic subjects** are coherent chunks of knowledge without any ramification or focus. These are elemental and form the basic or core facet of both compound and complex subjects. As they are postulated by the classificationist in keeping with socio-academic conditions, their number and boundaries change over time. In the current (7th) edition of the Colon Classification there are broadly two types of basic subjects (Ranganathan, 1987, pp. 66-68), main basic subjects and non-main basic subjects.

**Main basic subjects** are divided into the following five kinds, based on their mode of formation:

| Kind | Examples |
|---|---|
| Traditional main classes | Physics, law, literature |
| Fused basic subjects | Biochemistry, medical jurisprudence, geopolitics |
| Distilled basic subjects | Research methodology, management science, careerology |
| Agglomerate basic subjects | Social sciences, behavioral sciences, biological sciences |
| Subject bundles | Deep sea sciences, space missions, polar expeditions |

**Non-main basic subjects** are also known as compound basic subjects (Ranganathan, 1987, sect. DE71, p. 67). These apply to restricted areas of studies within a main class. These are of four types:

| Kind | Examples |
|---|---|
| Systems basic subjects | Allopathy system of medicine, homeopathy system, Marxist economy |
| Special basic subjects | Child medicine, sports medicine, small-scale industry |
| Environment basic subjects | Tropical medicine, space medicine, high altitude engineering, low temperature physics |
| Canonical basic subjects | Arithmetic, algebra, geometry in mathematics Heat, light, electricity in physics |

## 2.2 Compound Subjects

Compound subjects are formed by adding one or more isolate facets to a basic subject (Ranganathan, 1965, sect. K01, p. 96). For example, Agriculture of wheat, Agriculture in India, and Agriculture of wheat in India are all compound subjects. The number of such subjects in the universe of knowledge is virtually infinite and keeps growing.

## 2.3 Complex Subjects

Complex subjects are formed by the interaction of two or more different basic or compound subjects, usually taken from different disciplines. Hence, a complex subject is commonly interdisciplinary.

## 3. MODES OF FORMATION OF SUBJECTS

D. W. Langridge (1969, p. 2) aptly says that the modes of forming subjects represent a topology of relationships and act as guiding ideas in recognizing and formulating relationships among concepts constituting a subject. In order to study the nature and structure of knowledge, Ranganathan investigated how subjects were formed. These modes of formation have a natural, innate effect on the structure of the subject. "Obviously the mode of formation of subjects leaves its impress on the structure of the subject" (Ranganathan, 1967, sect. PA3). These modes are of three kinds, depending on the kind of subjects produced, and are subject to further division (Satija, 1992):

**Modes of formation of subjects**
Specialization subjects
  Fission
    Dissection
    Denudation
  Lamination
Interdisciplinary subjects
  Loose-assemblage
  Fusion
Multidisciplinary subjects
  Distillation
  Agglomeration
  Subject bundles

## 3.1 Specialization Subjects

Fissioned subjects are cohesive and have unitary structures formed by fragmentation of relatively bigger chunks of knowledge. Dissection is the process of slicing a subject into equally ranked subdivisions, thus forming an array of coordinate classes. Dividing the earth into continents is the process of dissection, as is the division of continents into countries and countries into states and so on. When dissection is applied repeatedly to a single entity, the process becomes **denudation**. The chain Earth—Europe—Western Europe—France reflects the process of denudation, which can be compared to peeling off the successive layers of an onion. The result is a chain of classes. Dissection and denudation are relative processes.

**Lamination** is the process of producing compound subjects by layering isolates onto a basic subject. For example, Agriculture of wheat, Agriculture in India, and Agriculture of wheat in India are all compound subjects formed by lamination. An early mode used in forming subjects, lamination remains the predominant mode. Subjects formed by lamination are specializations, subjects of greater intension than basic subjects. Their specialization increases by ongoing layering of laminae, which can be added to any practical limit.

## 3.2 Interdisciplinary Subjects

Since World War II, interdisciplinary subjects have emerged as an antidote to the increasing specialization of subjects. **Loose assemblage** and **Fusion** are the first and last stages, respectively, of the formation of interdisciplinary subjects. Loosely assembled interdisciplinary subjects are complex subjects such as Psychology for nurses, Law for social workers, and Statistics for librarians. Two subjects from different disciplines are brought together on ad hoc basis. When this ad hoc relationship solidifies irreversibly into a new subject, the result is fusion. Biochemistry, Geophysics, Nuclear medicine, Medical jurisprudence are basic subjects formed by fusion.

## 3.3 Multidisciplinary Subjects

During the last year of his life, in association with his colleagues at the Documentation Research and Training Centre, Bangalore, Ranganathan isolated three more modes of formation of subjects. All are multidisciplinary modes. **Agglomeration** is a cluster of neighboring subjects having a generic name, for example, Natural science, Physical science, Bioscience, Medical sciences. These are formed either by the affinity of their subject contents or by a common research methodology. Their dissection leads to main classes. **Distilled subjects** are seemingly unitary subjects formed through the distillation of mature feedback and experience across many subjects. Examples include Research methodology, Management science, and Careerology. **Subject bundles** are ad hoc, loosely assembled, multidisciplinary, mission-oriented, and highly practical. Some examples are Ocean sciences, Space science, Antarctica expedition, Sinology, and West Asia studies. International agency projects also commonly fall into this category.

A modification of Iyer's scale of the integration of subjects illustrates the progressive order of internal cohesiveness (1995, p. 20). Note that lamination is half unitary and half federated.

```
↑   Fission
    Fusion                          Unitary
    Distillation                    subjects
    Lamination
    Agglomeration
    Loose-assemblage                Federated
    Subject bundles                 subjects
```

## 4. SEQUENCE OF BASIC SUBJECTS

Ranganathan laid great emphasis on the arrangement of basic subjects in his CC. For him the essence of library classification lay in a helpful sequence of documents and subjects. The CC provides objective solutions to unraveling the intricate web of relationships in knowledge and represents them in a linear form.

Ranganathan's first division of knowledge is into traditional disciplines, which he arranges in the order of their evolution as academic studies, namely:

Science and Technology
Humanities
Social Sciences

The social sciences are the most recent academic disciplines to emerge; science and technology, however, were studies (of curiosity) of even primitive humans.

Within each discipline the CC has an order of main classes based on objectively stated principles. Sciences (including technology), in classes A to M, have been arranged in order of increasing concreteness: B, Mathematics, is the most abstract of the sciences, while M, Useful arts (which includes crafts and applied technologies), is the most concrete in the group. Within this arrangement, theory and practice alternate, theory always preceding practice or its applications. For example, B, Mathematics, precedes C, Physics, which in turn precedes D, Engineering. E, Chemistry, precedes F, Chemical technology. Similarly I, Botany, is followed by J, Agriculture. This internal arrangement is based on the principle of dependency, first promulgated by Auguste Comte. Unlike Dewey, Ranganathan preferred to collocate the theory and practice of a subject. Indeed the Library of Congress Classification earlier followed this principle.

In the humanities, which are spread over main classes N to S, the arrangement is in order of increasing richness of subject content. Thus:

| | | | |
|---|---|---|---|
| N | Fine arts | Q | Religion |
| O | Literature | R | Philosophy |
| P | Linguistics | S | Psychology |

The order in the social sciences, in main classes T to Z, is of increasing artificiality of subject content:

| | | | |
|---|---|---|---|
| T | Education | X | Economics |
| U | Geography | Y | Sociology |
| V | History | Z | Laws |
| W | Political Science | | |

One may fault this arrangement. For example, economic and social laws are not artificial, but are based on human nature and thus should not come so far down in the order of classes.

In an article published prior to the release of CC, R. S. Parkhi (1933) commended its arrangement of main classes as logical and evolutionary. Elucidating his viewpoint, he described the Generalia class as the complete microscopic view of knowledge that precedes the entire universe of knowledge. Physical sciences, C-F, study the matter and forces which constitute this universe. B, Mathematics, pervades every science. G, Biology, is vital science. Classes H-K are in evolutionary order of life on the earth. Classes L-P classes are application subjects for the well being and prosperity of humankind. From Q, Religion, to T, Education, are the moral and mental development of individuals, which in fact depend upon the correct application of classes L-P, which in turn depend on classes A-K. Classes U-Z study the geographical and social sciences, the latest areas of knowledge to engage the human mind. Here W, Politics (and Government), precedes the creation and distribution of wealth in X, Economics, while Y, Sociology, and Z, Law, keep society intact and going.

Ranganathan subsequently added as a main class $\Delta$, Spiritual experience and mysticism, positioned between the sciences on the one hand and the humanities and social sciences on the other. (See fig. 1 for a diagrammatic representation of the overall arrangement of main classes.) $\Delta$ is at the confluence of two different streams of knowledge, the sciences and the humanities, the two different cultures of C. P. Snow. Ranganathan treats spiritual experience as the fountain head of all knowledge, thus refuting Snow's theory. At the base are the generalia subjects. As we move from the end of each half to the middle the subjects on each side culminate in the central subject $\Delta$, Spiritual experience and Mysticism (Parkhi, 1933, sect. DB2, p. 52).

The philosopher and classificationist H. E. Bliss endeavored to discover a permanent main class order based upon scientific and educational consensus. Such consensus can never be permanent. Ranganathan based his order instead on concrete and objectively stated principles. These principles are helpful in placing newly emerging main classes at their logical places in the array of main classes. The number of basic subjects has increased to about eight hundred in CC-7 without any problem of assigning subjects their rightful place in the lengthy array of basic subjects.

## 5. FACET ANALYSIS

### 5.1 Facet Formula

To mechanize the arrangement of categories and facets within categories, Ranganathan,

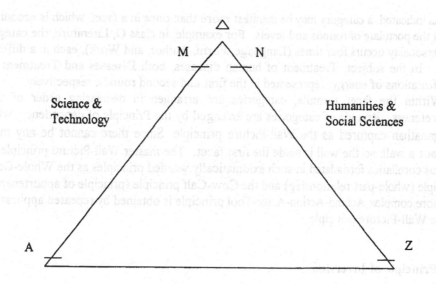

Generalia classes a/z, 1/9

Figure 1. Arrangement of main classes in CC

after a long trial, finally settled on a general and all encompassing facet formula popularly known as PMEST (Personality/Matter/Energy/Space/Time). In the sequence, the basic facet—usually represented by main class—or its amplification by system (Sm), environment (Env), or specialization (Sp), precedes other facets. The phenomenon of the recurrence of categories is tackled by the **postulate of rounds and levels**. Ranganathan postulated that space and time occur in the last round of the facet formula. [P], [M], and [E] can occur in various rounds and in various levels within a round—except [E] which has only rounds and no level; energy always completes a round. The grand general facet formula may be represented as follows (numbers preceding a category indicate its round, while subscripted numbers following a category indicate its level):

(Sm F), (Env F), (Sp F), $[1P_1]...[1P_m]$; $[1M_1]...[1M_m]$: [1E], $[n\text{-}1P_1],...[n\text{-}1P_m]$; $[n\text{-}1M_1]...[n\text{-}1M_m]$: [n-1E], $[nP_1]...[nP_m]$; $[nM_1]...[nM_m]$: $[S_1]$. $[S_2]$ '$[T_1]$ '$[T_2]$

In the current edition of the CC, the total number of facets and their general sequence is as follows (Ranganathan, 1987, ch. DD, pp. 49-50):

Field of study → System → Environment → Specials → Object of study → Kinds/Parts of objects → Properties of the object → Action on the object → Kind of action → Method of action → Agent of action → Instrument of action → Space → Space qualifier → Time → Time qualifier.

## 5.2 Syntax of Facets

As indicated, a category may be manifest more than once in a facet, which is accounted for by the postulate of rounds and levels. For example, in class O, Literature, the category [P] personality occurs four times (Language, Form, Author, and Work), each in a different level. In the subject, Treatment of human diseases, both Diseases and Treatment are manifestations of energy, represented in the first and second rounds, respectively.

Within the facet formula, categories are arranged in decreasing order of their concreteness. Rounds of categories are arranged by the Principle of dependency, which Ranganathan captured as the Wall-Picture principle: Since there cannot be any mural without a wall, so the wall is made the first facet. The master Wall-Picture principle has various corollaries formulated in such axiomatically worded principles as the Whole-Organ principle (whole-part relationship) and the Cow-Calf principle (principle of appurtenance); the more complex Actand-Action-Actor-Tool principle is obtained by repeated applications of the Wall-Picture principle.

## 5.3 Principle of Inversion

The CC follows the Principle of Inversion first used by the Universal Decimal Classification [UDC]. In the citation order represented by Ranganathan's PMEST formula, categories are arranged in order of decreasing concreteness. [P] Personality is the most concrete and [T] Time the most abstract; [E] Energy lies midway being as concrete as it is abstract. On the shelves or in a classified database, however, the order of subjects is from general to specific, that is, from abstract to concrete. Overall order within a class comes out to be:

General treated generally
General treated specially
Special treated generally
Special treated specially

This order is achieved by ingeniously fixing the value of indicator digits.

## 5.4 Absolute Syntax

In his spirited quest for discovering a natural order of facets, Ranganathan proposed the idea of an "absolute syntax of facets," by which he meant a sequence in which component facets of a subject "arrange themselves in the minds of the majority of persons" (Ranganathan, 1967, sect. XJ3). Indeed, he conjectured that absolute syntax may be the "same for a large majority of persons irrespective of their mothertongue [sic]," so that absolute syntax and linguistic syntax do not necessarily coincide. He further believed that absolute syntax was close to his own PMEST citation order, arrived at by rigorous postulates and principles.

The basic question is whether there exists such an absolute syntax of ideas in the minds of the majority of adults, free from the incessant impact of the mother tongue and its grammar as impressed on human minds since infancy. There is no empirical evidence that it exists at all. Nevertheless, as Iyer asserts, "If a particular way of structuring a subject can be easily understood in translation to another language, regardless of the linguistic variations of individual tongues, then an absolute syntax may exist at some level" (Iyer, 1995, p. 184). Arthur Maltby (Sayers, 1975, p. 223) points out that Ranganathan believed in knowledge synthesis rather than in its mere division for mapping and information retrieval; this makes the search for the absolute syntax of ideas worth pursuing.

## 5.5 Phase Relations

Another important category of relationships utilized by the CC are phase relations. When isolates interact and they belong to two different main classes or they belong to the same category within a given main class or they are related in a non-hierarchical way, a complex subject is formed, comprised of two or more phases. Six types of relationships between these phases—which have been subject to various enumerations and designations across time—are recognized in the 7th edition of the CC (1987, ch. DP, p. 106; Satija, 1989, pp. 84-85):

| Kind | Example |
|---|---|
| General phase relation | Relations of Political Science with History |
| Bias phase relation | Mathematics for Biologists, Psychology for Doctors |
| Comparison phase relation | Physics compared with Chemistry |
| Difference phase relation | Difference between Mysticism and Metaphysics |
| Tool phase relation | Mathematical Physics |
| Influencing phase relation | Influence of the British constitution on the Indian constitution |

The number of relations is quite small, but it should be noted that phase relations supplement other relationships depicted through PMEST.

These relationships are intended to be self evident. The general phase relation comprehends any relationship not expressed through the other five, while the difference phase relation is simply a specific case of the comparison phase relation. These relations can occur at three levels, namely, between two main classes for interdisciplinary subjects, between two facets of the same category (intrafacet relationships), and between two isolates belonging to the same array within a facet (intra-array relationships). Therefore, there are 6 x 3 = 18 phase relations in all. Definitive rules for primary and secondary phases and for notation ensure the expression of the relationships in a precise and consistent way.

## 6.  APUPA PATTERN

Ranganathan was not content with his broad, though thoroughly formalized order. Within a given specific class he arranged documents on the shelves in what is referred to an APUPA pattern, as demonstrated in figure 2. The letters of the acronym stand for different pockets of subjects in a given class: A is an Alien (or related) subject zone; P is a Penumbral region; U is the Umbral region, having core documents on the subjects. The general APUPA pattern is achieved by postulating two kinds of common auxiliaries ("common isolates"): Anteriorizing Common Isolates (ACIs) and Posteriorizing Common Isolates (PCIs). Common isolates are like the standard subdivisions of DDC and are attachable to any class, irrespective of its specificity. ACIs are not the subject proper, but approaches to a subject. They include, for example, bibliographies, synopsis, histories, and statistics. ACIs are filed anterior to the subject proper. This forms a penumbral region, having less of the subject proper. Then follows the pure subject proper, with all its subdivisions. For example, basic and compound subjects could constitute the umbral region in the pattern. This is followed by another penumbral region, formed by fitting documents of the umbral region with PCIs. These are documents about the subject that are best read after the mastery of the core subject by advanced students or researchers. These include educational and research institutes on the subject, critical reviews, and recent advances in the subject. Thus the umbral region is surrounded on both sides by penumbral regions of differing natures, which in turn are sandwiched between two different alien regions.

Going beyond this Ranganathan (1951/1981, p. 228) asserts that arrangement is "everywhere APUPA." Core documents of immediate interest to a reader form that reader's Umbral region. It is invariably surrounded on either side by documents of lesser interest, which form penumbral regions. On the left of the left penumbral region and on the right of the right penumbral region are Alien areas. This arrangement automatically sets forth the general to specific order of subjects. So in the CC, APUPA prevails at every point.

The APUPA pattern is one of the logical and pedagogically useful arrangements of documents on the shelves of an open access library (Satija, 1989, p. 228). It uniformly weaves a useful pattern of documents on the shelves or of their surrogates in a bibliography. The arrangement is so impeccable that it is appropriate to say that to browse a CC classified library is itself an education. This has been achieved by investigating deeply the structure of knowledge and arranging its components in a way most useful to the most users. For this Ranganathan evolved apt principles and tools. It is fit to conclude with Fran Miksa (1998, p. 67) that Ranganathan "treated library classification as a single unified structure of ideas which followed from a cohesive set of basic principles."

## 7.  CONCLUSION

Today, as Alvin Toffler foresees, relationships in knowledge are changing as we reorganize its production and dissemination. We are linking concepts to one another in startling ways. Data are being interrelated in new ways by giving context, which allows data

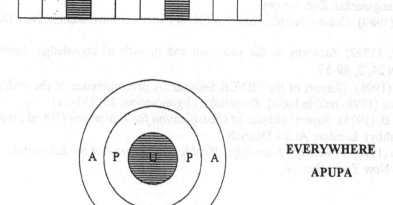

Figure 2.  APUPA pattern

to be converted into knowledge (Toffler, 1991, p. 82).  There is an urgent need to discover new modes of formation of subjects and identify new relationships among subjects and concepts, as recommended in the 1998 FID conference (Satija, 1998).  The Colon Classification is currently under revision (Neelameghan, 1999).  It is expected that the revised edition will assimilate changing relationships in knowledge.

## References

Iyer, H. (1995). *Classificatory Structures: Concepts, Relations and Representations*. Frankfurt am Main: INDEKS Verlag.

Langridge, D. W. (Ed.). (1969). *The Universe of Knowledge*. College Park, MD: School of Library and Information Services, University of Maryland.

Miksa, F. (1998). *The DDC, the Universe of Knowledge and the Post Modern Library*. Albany, NY: Forest Press/OCLC.

Neelameghan, A. (26 March 1999). Circular letter to prospective members of the CC revision committee.

Parkhi, R. S. (1933). Colon scheme of library classification. *Modern Librarian*, 3, 2, 87.

Ranganathan S. R (1951/1981). *Classification and Communication*. Bangalore: Sarada Ranganathan Endowment.

Ranganathan, S. R. (1965). *A Descriptive Account of the Colon Classification.* Bombay: Asia.

Ranganathan, S. R. (1967). *Prolegomena to Library Classification* (3rd ed., assisted by M. A. Gopinath). Bombay: Asia.

Ranganathan, S. R. (1987). *Colon Classification* (7th ed.; M. A. Gopinath, Ed.). Bangalore: Sarada Ranganathan Endowment.

Satija, M. P. (1989). *Colon Classification, 7th Ed.: A Practical Introduction.* New Delhi: Ess Ess.

Satija, M. P. (1992) Anatomy of the evolution and growth of knowledge. *Lucknow Librarian* 24, 2, 49-57.

Satija, M.P. (1998). [Report of the FID/CR Seminar: A preconference of the 49th FID conference (1998) held in India]. *Knowledge Organization,* 25, 211-213.

Sayers, W C. B. (1975). *Sayers' Manual of Classification for Librarians* (5th ed., revised by A. Maltby). London: Andre Deutsch.

Toffler, Alvin (1990). *Powershift: Knowledge, Wealth, and Violence at the Edge of the 21st Century.* New York: Bantam.

# Chapter 14

# Relationships in the
# Dewey Decimal Classification System[1]

Joan S. Mitchell
*OCLC Forest Press, Dublin, OH, USA*

**Abstract:**
The Dewey Decimal Classification (DDC) system is a general knowledge organization tool used worldwide. The system features well-defined categories, well-developed hierarchies, meaningful notation, and a rich network of relationships. The nature of relationships in the DDC is richer than is apparent from a linear view of the system. The DDC accommodates the three basic thesaural relationships in the notational and structural hierarchy; through notes in the schedules, tables, and Manual; and in entries in the Relative Index. Derived relationships are shown through the synthesized notation, or through abridgment leading to broader classification. Options and translations provide alternative relationships. Additional relationships may be displayed through mapping of other thesauri.

## 1. BRIEF INTRODUCTION TO THE DDC

The Dewey Decimal Classification (DDC, Dewey) system is a general knowledge organization tool used worldwide in 135 countries. The DDC is owned by OCLC Forest Press, and is published in both full (Dewey, 1996) and abridged (Dewey, 1997) print editions, as well as an electronic (Dewey for Windows, 1996–) version; a Web version is under development. The DDC has also been translated into over thirty languages.

The DDC is developed and updated continuously in the Dewey editorial office at the Library of Congress under an agreement between OCLC Forest Press and the Library of Congress. The system features well-defined categories, well-developed hierarchies, meaningful notation, and a rich network of relationships. This chapter will focus on the relationships found or derived from the DDC and the relationships that may be mapped to the DDC. The DDC accommodates the three basic thesaural relationships: hierarchical, equivalence, and associative relationships. The various relationships are displayed in the notational and structural hierarchy; through notes in the schedules, tables, and Manual; and in entries in the Relative Index. Those that can be derived are shown through the synthesized notation or through abridgment leading to broader classification. Options and translations provide alternative relationships. Additional relationships may be displayed through mappings of other thesauri.

In order to understand the relationships within, derived from, or mapped to the DDC, it is important to have a basic understanding of the design of the system. The DDC is

*C. A. Bean and R. Green (eds.), Relationships in the Organization of Knowledge, 211–226.*

divided into ten main classes, which together cover the entire world of knowledge. Each main class is further divided into ten divisions and each division into ten sections. (Not all the numbers for the divisions and sections have been used.) Arabic numerals are used to represent each class in the DDC. A decimal point follows the third digit, after which division by ten continues to the specific degree of classification needed.

Below are the ten main DDC classes with their popular descriptions. The first digit in each three-digit number represents the main class. For example, 500 represents science.

| | |
|---|---|
| 000 | Computers, Information & General Reference |
| 100 | Philosophy & Psychology |
| 200 | Religion |
| 300 | Social Sciences |
| 400 | Language |
| 500 | Science |
| 600 | Technology |
| 700 | Arts & Recreation |
| 800 | Literature |
| 900 | History & Geography |

The second digit indicates the division. For example, 500 is used for general works on the sciences, 510 for mathematics, 520 for astronomy, 530 for physics, and so forth.

| | |
|---|---|
| 500 | Science |
| 510 | Mathematics |
| 520 | Astronomy |
| 530 | Physics |
| 540 | Chemistry |
| 550 | Earth Sciences & Geology |
| 560 | Fossils & Prehistoric Life |
| 570 | Biology & Life Sciences |
| 580 | Plants (Botany) |
| 590 | Animals (Zoology) |

The third digit in each three-digit number indicates the section. For example, 510 is used for general works on mathematics; the specific branches of the discipline are divided among 511-519.

| | |
|---|---|
| 510 | Mathematics |
| 511 | General principles of mathematics |
| 512 | Algebra, number theory |
| 513 | Arithmetic |
| 514 | Topology |
| 515 | Analysis |
| 516 | Geometry |
| 517 | (Unassigned) |
| 518 | (Unassigned) |
| 519 | Probabilities and applied mathematics |

The DDC is developed on the basis of literary warrant; that is, a threshold of published literature determines the need for category creation. The system includes over 25,000 entries in the core disciplinary outline of knowledge in 000-999. These are called the schedules. Supplementing the schedules are seven auxiliary tables of notation that may be added to numbers in the schedules to show form, place, time, people, language, genre, and other aspects. The schedules also are extended by internal tables, and by using add instructions from other parts of the schedules.

Each entry in the schedules and tables consists of a class number and caption. Some entries have special labels or captions that indicate a structural hierarchy different from the notational hierarchy. Many entries have one or more notes that explain the hierarchical, equivalence, and associative relationships between that class and other classes in the DDC. The entries may also contain instructions for extending the notation to include additional aspects through the use of internal tables, notation from elsewhere in the schedules, or the auxiliary tables.

## 2. RELATIONSHIPS IN THE SCHEDULES AND TABLES

### 2.1 The Hierarchical Relationship

The hierarchical relationship in the DDC is expressed through notation and structure. In the DDC, all topics (aside from the ten main classes) are part of the broader topics above them. Certain notes (i.e., definition, scope, relocation, class-here, class-elsewhere, see-reference, preference, and option notes) have hierarchical force for a class and all its subordinate classes. There is a strong inheritance principle at work in the hierarchical relationship, whether that relationship is described through the notation or through other devices in the DDC.

### 2.1.1 Notational Hierarchy

In many places throughout the DDC, the hierarchy is expressed by length of notation. Numbers at any given level are usually subordinate to a class whose notation is one digit shorter, coordinate with a class whose notation has the same number of significant digits, and superordinate to a class with numbers one or more digits longer. The following example shows the notational hierarchy for several kinds of racket games.

| | | |
|---|---|---|
| 796 | Athletic and outdoor sports and games | |
| 796.3 | Ball games | |
| 796.34 | Racket games | |
| 796.342 | | Tennis (Lawn tennis) |
| 796.343 | | Squash |
| 796.345 | | Badminton |
| 796.346 | | Table tennis |
| 796.347 | | Lacrosse |

## 2.1.2 Structural Hierarchy

Sometimes other devices must be used to express the hierarchy when it is not possible or desirable to do so through the notation. Special types of headings, notes, and entries indicate relationships among topics that violate notational hierarchy.

Dual and multiple headings are used to indicate when a topic and the main subconcept share the same number and hierarchical structure:

| | | |
|---|---|---|
| 972 | Middle America　Mexico | |
| 636.2 | Ruminants and Camelidae　Bovidae　Cattle | |

Several types of notes are used to indicate the hierarchical relationship. When part of a topic is not included in the direct subdivisions of the number, a see reference leads one to its location:

> 512.02　　　Abstract algebra
> *For subdivisions of abstract algebra, see 512.2-512.5*

A centered entry indicates and relates structurally a span of numbers that represents a single concept for which there is no specific hierarchical notation available. A symbol ">" in the number column identifies a centered entry, and it is so called because the span appears in the print edition of the DDC in the center of the page rather than in the number column. For example, the subdivisions of 512.02 Abstract algebra are not notational subdivisions of 512.02, but are located elsewhere under a centered entry:

> \>　　512.2-512.5　　Subdivisions of abstract algebra
> 　　　　　　　Class comprehensive works in 512.02

## 2.1.3 Generic, Whole-Part, and Instance Relationships

The DDC supports generic, whole-part, and instance relationships through the notational and structural hierarchy. A simple example of the generic relationship expressed through the notational hierarchy is the development for the plant subclass 583.3 Ranunculidae:

| | |
|---|---|
| 583.3 | Ranunculidae |
| 583.34 | Ranunculales (Ranales) |
| 583.35 | Papaverales (Rhoeadales) |
| 583.36 | Sarraceniales |

Ranunculidae are part of 583 Magnoliopsida (Dicotyledons), which in turn are a kind of Angiospermae (Flowering plants). The generic relationship between Magnoliopsida and Angiospermae is expressed through the structural hierarchy instead of the notational hierarchy:

> \>　　　　583-584　Angiospermae (Flowering plants)
> 　　　　　　Class comprehensive works in 580

The whole-part relationship is expressed through the notation and structure. Categories of wholes and their parts are found throughout the DDC. For example, here is the discipline of mathematics and its major parts:

| | |
|---|---|
| 510 | Mathematics |
| 511 | General principles |
| 512 | Algebra, number theory |
| 513 | Arithmetic |
| 514 | Topology |
| 515 | Analysis |
| 516 | Geometry |
| 519 | Probabilities and applied mathematics |

In the following example from medicine, the mouth and its parts are displayed in the notational hierarchy:

| | |
|---|---|
| 611.31 | Mouth |
| 611.313 | Tongue |
| 611.314 | Teeth |
| 611.315 | Palate |
| 611.316 | Salivary glands |
| 611.317 | Lips |
| 611.318 | Cheeks |

In Table 2, the parts of Norway are developed on coordinate notation; the whole-part relationship is revealed through the structural hierarchy:

| | |
|---|---|
| —481 | Norway |
| > | —482-484 Divisions of Norway |
| —482 | Southeastern Norway (Østlandet) |
| —483 | Southwestern Norway (Sørlandet and Vestlandet) |
| —484 | Central and northern Norway (Trøndelag and Nord-Norge) |

The instance relationship is sometimes displayed explicitly in the notational and structural hierarchy, and sometimes accommodated through optional arrangements. For example, specific oceans and seas are listed on coordinate notation under the Table 2 notation for oceans and seas:

—162 Oceans and seas
*For Atlantic Ocean, see T2—163;*
*for Pacific Ocean, see T2—164;*
*for Indian Ocean, see T2—165;*
*for Antarctic waters, see T2—167…*

At 005.133 Specific programming languages, the addition of an optional arrangement is suggested to identify specific programming languages by name:

005.133 Specific programming languages
Arrange alphabetically by name of programming language, e.g., C++

## 2.1.4 Polyhierarchical Relationships

Sometimes, the same concept can be considered as a member of more than one category.  The structural hierarchy also addresses polyhierarchical relationships.  For example, the comprehensive number for craters is 551.21, the number for volcanoes.  A note leads one to 551.21 for craters from another possible category, 551.44 Depressions and openings.  Craters formed by meteorites are potentially members of the general category for craters or the category for meteorites as agents of geological change.  The latter has been chosen, and a see reference leads from 551.21 to 551.397 for meteorite craters:

> 551.21  Volcanoes
>       Class here comprehensive works on craters
>       *For meteorite craters, see 551.397*
>
> 551.397  Meteorites
>       Class here meteorite craters
>
> 551.44  Depressions and openings
>       *For craters, see 551.21*

## 2.2 The Equivalence Relationship

One of the basic rules in number building in the DDC is that one cannot add subdivisions for a topic unless the concept approximates the whole of the concept represented by the number.  Therefore, the equivalence relationship is important in the DDC, and is supported by a number of different types of headings and notes that identify synonyms, variant and former names, and variant spellings.  Antonyms are treated in the same manner as synonyms.  Several devices are available to denote an equivalence relationship for narrower or broader concepts.

In headings, the equivalence relationship is indicated by parentheses.  The term or phrase in parentheses may be a synonym; an equivalent proper adjective for a people, language, or area; an acronym or the spelled-out version of an acronym (depending on which form is the better known); the vernacular form of a geographic name; or the popular version of a scientific name:

> 153.8   Will (Volition)
> —9635  Gur (Voltaic) languages [Table 6]
> 538.364  Electron paramagnetic resonance (EPR)
> 572.86   DNA (Deoxyribonucleic acid)
> —49453  Fribourg (Freiburg) [Table 2]
> 595.799  Apoidea (Bees)

When it is not practical to specify the equivalence relationship within the heading, a variant or former name note is included as shown:

> 530.475  Diffusion and mass transfer
>       Variant name for mass transfer: mass transport

641.8654    Cookies
            Variant name: biscuits (United Kingdom)

—6751       Democratic Republic of the Congo  [Table 2]
            Former names: Belgian Congo, Zaire

Several notes are used to define the equivalence relationship. Topics in the note may be equivalent, narrower, or broader in scope, but have been deemed to have the same importance as the concept defined in the heading. In some cases, this results in what Aitchison, Gilchrist, and Bawden (1997) call "upward posting," for example, the equivalence between the city of Bologna and the province of Bologna in Table 2.

746.7       Rugs
            Class here carpets

—4541       Bologna province  [Table 2]
            Class here Bologna

—0832       Infants  [Table 1]
            Children from birth through age two

## 2.3 The Associative Relationship

Two kinds of notes indicate the associative relationship in the DDC schedules and tables: the class-elsewhere note and the see-also reference note.

552         Petrology
            Class structural geology in 551.8

004.7       Peripherals
            *See also 004.64 for communication devices*

Since the DDC is developed on the basis of literary warrant, associative relationships are often treated as equivalence or hierarchical relationships because that is how they are treated in the published literature.

Sometimes the equivalence relationship is used instead of the associative relationship to incorporate topics in a hierarchy that are related, but are not equivalent or subordinate concepts. For example, the equivalence relationship is used in sociology to equate the sociology of religious institutions with the sociology of religion; these are actually related concepts.

306.6       Religious institutions
            Class here sociology of religion

Polyhierarchical relationships often include associative and hierarchical elements, as seen in the earlier example of meteorite craters. Because craters have been made equivalent to volcanoes at 551.21 through the device of the class-here note, a see reference is used to reflect the resulting structural hierarchical relationship between 551.21 Volcanoes and

551.397 Meteorites for meteorite craters.  The relationship between the two categories at
the caption level is at best associative.

Conversely, the associative class-elsewhere note is sometimes used to draw attention to
subordinate topics in the same hierarchy:

> 512          Algebra, number theory
>                    Class foundations of algebra in 512.9

## 3.  RELATIONSHIPS IN THE RELATIVE INDEX

A key feature of the DDC is the Relative Index.  The Relative Index is an alphabetical
list of subjects with the disciplines in which they are treated subarranged alphabetically under
each entry.  Because disciplines provide the context for topics in the DDC, the Relative
Index provides a useful reverse display of topics and the disciplines in which they appear.
The see-also reference in the index serves three functions in showing relationships among
topics in the index: equivalence (Use), hierarchical (BT), and associative (RT).

The see-also reference leads from the nonpreferred form of the index entry to the
preferred form (the equivalence function) on the premise that it is useful to give at least one
number with the nonpreferred form:

> Elderly persons              305.26
>                              T1—084 6
>     see also Older persons

In the example above, Elderly persons is the nonpreferred term; Older persons is the term
with full indexing.

The see-also reference is used to link index entries to broader concepts under which
additional subentries may be found (the hierarchical function):

> Player pianos          786.66
>     see also Mechanical musical instruments

Sometimes, the reference leads to the broader term for a category that may not be the
first one considered in a general knowledge organization tool:

> Earthquakes              551.22
>     disaster services    363.3495
>     social effects       303.485
>       see also Disasters

Earthquakes are most commonly thought of as part of 551 Geology, but are also a type of
disaster.

The see-also reference is additionally used to provide links between associated concepts
in the Relative Index:

> Job hunting              650.14
>     see also Résumé writing

Résumé writing          808.06665
    *see also* Job hunting

In the schedules and tables, homographs are handled through the hierarchical structure, for example, "Mercury" appears as the caption at 669.71 (referring to the element) and at 523.41 (referring to the planet). In the Relative Index, these entries are disambiguated by the addition of a qualifier:

Mercury (Element)     669.71
Mercury (Planet)      523.41

If one meaning of the term is the most common one, that meaning is not required to be qualified. For example, cold in the sense of temperature appears without a qualifier in the Relative Index:

Cold              536.56
Cold (Disease)
  medicine       616.205

## 4. RELATIONSHIPS IN THE MANUAL

The schedules, tables, and Relative Index all contain references to the Manual. One of the key functions of the Manual is to provide advice on the choice of a number for a topic. This advice often includes discussions on polyhierarchical and associative relationships.

### 170 vs. 303.372
**Ethics (Moral philosophy) vs. Belief systems and customs**

Social ethics may be a subject either in moral philosophy or in methods of social control. Social ethics in 170 refers to the rightness or wrongness of conduct as it affects individuals or society. Social ethics in 303.372 refers to beliefs and systems of beliefs influencing the way society and its institutions operate. . .

### 355 vs. 623
**Military science vs. Military and nautical engineering**

Use 623 for physical description, design, manufacture, operation, and repair of ordnance; use 355-359 for procurement and deployment, and also for the units and services that use the ordnance. . .

## 5. RELATIONSHIPS IN SYNTHESIZED NOTATION

Only a fraction of potential DDC numbers are explicitly listed in the DDC. It is often necessary to synthesize (build) a number in order to represent a concept. Each synthesized number brings together elements from multiple hierarchies in a syntactic relationship. There are four sources of notation from which to build numbers: Table 1 Standard Subdivisions; Tables 2-7; other parts of the schedules; and add tables in the schedules. Standard subdivisions may be added for any concept that is equivalent to the category. Other numbers may be synthesized upon instruction.

Table 1 is used to add aspects such as form and time and to introduce aspects from other tables such as place (Table 2) or ethnic group (Table 5):

A medical journal                                      610.5
  61              Medicine (from 610)                   [topic]
  05              Journals (Table 1)                    [form]

Computer science in the 1970s                          004.09047
  004             Computer science                      [topic]
  09047           1970-1979 (Table 1)                   [time]

The Internet in Scandinavian countries                 004.6780948
  004.678         Internet                              [topic]
  09              Geographic treatment (Table 1)
  48              Scandinavia (Table 2)                 [place]

Jewish ceramic arts                                    738.089924
  738             Ceramic arts                          [topic]
  089             Racial, ethnic, national groups (Table 1)
  924             Jews (Table 5)                        [group]

In the examples above, the Table 1 notation serves as a type of relational operator. In many places in the DDC, the operator or facet indicator is eliminated to shorten the notation, and the aspect is added directly to the base number through an instruction in the schedule:

Higher education in France                             378.44
  378             Higher education                      [topic]
  44              France (Table 2)                      [place]

As already illustrated, Table 2 provides geographic notation. Table 3 is used to introduce forms and genres in literature and (to a limited extent) in the arts. Table 4 is used to extend aspects of languages. Table 5 provides notation for racial, ethnic, and national groups. Table 6 provides notation for specific languages. Table 7 provides notation for groups of persons. (Note: Table 7 will be eliminated in the next edition of the DDC because notation for the same concepts is already available in Table 1 or in the schedules.)

Numbers are also synthesized from internal tables and instructions for direct addition from the schedules:

Vertebrate mechanics                                   571.316
  571.3           Morphology
  1               Facet indicator for animals (from 571.1 Animals)
  6               Vertebrates, from 596

In this example, two hierarchies are linked together: the hierarchy for morphology/physiology/biology (570) and the hierarchy for vertebrates/animals (590).

Another example is the nocturnal behavior of bats, in which two hierarchies in the same division of the DDC (590) are linked together:

| | |
|---|---|
| Nocturnal behavior of bats | 599.41518 |

| | |
|---|---|
| 599.4 | Bats |
| 1 | Facet indicator for general topics (from table under 592-599) |
| 518 | Nocturnal behavior, from 591.518 |

The bats example also can be used to illustrate another useful feature of the DDC: meaningful notation. Across the DDC, the notation 94 (derived from 599.94) is used to represent "bats" the mammal; other notation is used to represent "bats" the sports equipment.

| | |
|---|---|
| Bats | 599.4 |
| conservation technology | 639.9794 |
| physiology | 571.194 |
| Bats (Sports equipment) | |
| baseball | 796.35726 |
| manufacturing technology | 688.76357 |
| cricket | 796.35826 |
| manufacturing technology | 688.76358 |

## 6. INTRADISCIPLINARY AND INTERDISCIPLINARY RELATIONSHIPS

The earlier example of craters illustrated how intradisciplinary relationships among aspects of a topic are handled. What about topics that cross disciplines? Relationships among disciplines are often addressed directly in the schedules:

305.231 Child development

Class here interdisciplinary works on child development

*For psychological development of children, see 155.4; for physical development of children, see 612.65*

The same set of relationships is displayed in the Relative Index; the interdisciplinary number appears opposite the main index entry:

| | |
|---|---|
| Child development | 305.231 |
| physiology | 612.65 |
| psychology | 155.4 |
| sociology | 305.231 |

The Manual also contains advice on the relationships among disciplines for certain topics. For example, the following discussion of cognitive science, a topic important in psychology and artificial intelligence, appears at 153 vs. 006.3 in the Manual:

> Class cognitive science . . . in 153 if the goal is to understand better how the human mind works. Class cognitive science in 006.3 if the goal is to produce computer systems with better artificial intelligence. If in doubt, prefer 153.

Of course, the final advice could be ignored in nonlinear application of the DDC, that is, both numbers could be assigned.

## 7. FLEXIBLE STRUCTURES

One method of extending the relationships in the DDC is through the introduction of flexible structures. A flexible structure is an alternative view that is derived from or linked to a general organization scheme to address an information need that is not easily accommodated through the existing structure (Mitchell, 1998).

### 7.1 Derived Relationships

The abridged edition of the DDC is the simplest flexible structure that may be derived from the DDC. It is a logical abridgment of the full edition of the DDC based on the literary warrant of small library collections. Abridged numbers provide an alternative for smaller collections to use logically broader notation in a less complex structure. One unfortunate side effect of departures from notational hierarchy in the full edition is that the same structure must be accommodated in the abridged edition. For example, since Norway and its parts are on coordinate notation in the full edition, the abridged edition must also include the coordinate notation for Norway and its parts in order to avoid false abridgment.

Flexible structures may also be introduced through options and translations. Throughout the DDC, alternative relationships are provided through options. Options provide alternatives to the standard structure in terms of jurisdictional emphasis; racial, ethnic, national group emphasis; language emphasis; topical emphasis; or emphasis by some other special characteristic (Mitchell, 1995). A simple option is to give prominence to a literature other than American literature in English by moving both literatures to different positions in the hierarchical structure. One option is to vacate 810 and merge American literature in English with 820 English literature, thus freeing 810 for a literature of local importance regularly at a deeper level in the hierarchy. For example, the Vietnamese translation of the DDC could merge the standard meaning of 810 with 820, and use 810 for Vietnamese literature (895.922 in the English-language standard edition).

Translations of the latest editions of the DDC are currently underway in Arabic, Chinese, Greek, Hebrew, Icelandic, Italian, Korean, Norwegian, Russian, and Spanish. The French translation of Edition 21 was published in 1998 (Dewey, 1998). German and Vietnamese translations are under discussion. In a translation, expansions or use of options may alter some of the existing relationships in the English-language standard edition. For example, in Table 2 in the Italian translation (Dewey, 1993), the equivalence relationship between the province and city of Bologna has been replaced by a hierarchical relationship through expansion:

    —4541        Provincia di Bologna
    —45411       Comune di Bologna

Several researchers are exploring derived views of the DDC. Cochrane and Johnson (1996) have proposed use of the thesaural relationships in the DDC as an aid to bibliographic searching. Pollitt (1998) is testing the derivation and presentation of facets from the DDC as an aid to online searching. Vizine-Goetz (in press) is experimenting with the development of pathfinders accessible from a restructured set of DDC classes.

## 7.2 Mapped Relationships

Relationships within the DDC can be dynamically altered through the linking of thesauri and subject heading lists to the system. The linking of other thesauri enriches the vocabulary in the DDC and provides an alternative view within the general organizational framework of the DDC. A mapped thesaurus enables the DDC to offer domain-specific vocabulary and relationships to the specialist. The specialist can simultaneously use the DDC's general knowledge framework for the exploration of interdisciplinary or tangential topics. Olson and Ward (1998) are experimenting with mapping *A Women's Thesaurus* to the DDC to overlay the relationships found in women's studies on the existing DDC structure. Iyer and Giguere (1995) have proposed seven relationships for the linking of the American Mathematics Society Mathematics Subject Classification to the DDC:

- Exact matches,
- Specific to general,
- General to specific,
- Many to one,
- Cyclic mapping strategies,
- No matches, and
- Specific and broad class mapping.

In conjunction with OCLC's CORC[2] (Cooperative Online Resource Catalog) project, Vizine-Goetz (1999) has developed various mapping strategies for Library of Congress Subject Headings (LCSH), along with assessments of the strength of the association between source and target terms. The strength of the association varies depending upon the method used to link class numbers with headings.

| CORC Abbreviation | Source of Term | Association Method | Strength of Relationship |
|---|---|---|---|
| IM | Editorially mapped LCSH | Intellectual | Strong |
| SHC | Subject Headings for Children | Intellectual | Strong |
| NF | LCSH assigned in NetFirst records | Intellectual | Moderate to Strong |
| SM | OCLC WorldCat | Statistical | Moderate |
| FM | Dewey for Windows (from WorldCat) | Statistical | Weak to Moderate |

Terms with the IM designation have the strongest association—Dewey editorial staff members have intellectually linked them to the DDC. Terms with an SHC designation are also strongly associated with the DDC, but often at a broader number that represents the concept in the abridged edition of the DDC. These LC subject headings were extracted from the WorldCat database by processing LC MARC records with headings used in the LC Annotated Card Program (AC)/Subject Headings for Children's Literature, then the candidate mappings were reviewed by the Dewey editors to match numbers in Abridged Edition 13. OCLC NetFirst editors have linked the LC subject headings with the NF designation to DDC numbers in records for Internet-accessible resources. The two remaining sets of terms have been automatically linked to the DDC using statistical techniques. The abbreviation SM is used to identify terms associated with the DDC using a term co-occurrence measure. This measure was applied to over 710,000 WorldCat records that contain MARC 082 (DDC number) and a subject heading field, MARC tag 600-651. The terms labeled FM consist of LC subject headings that are included in the Dewey for Windows database through straight frequency mapping from WorldCat.

There is still much work to be done on coding the nature of mapped relationships, and how the relationship is to be used will affect the definition of the link (Mitchell, 1998).

## 8. ASSESSMENT OF RELATIONSHIPS IN THE DDC

The nature of relationships in the DDC is richer than is apparent from a linear view of the system. As discussed in this chapter, the hierarchical relationship goes beyond that of the notation itself and is embedded in the structure of headings, notes, and entries in the DDC. No special labeling exists for the different kinds of hierarchical relationships, but the type can often be determined from the context in which it appears (e.g., a taxonomic schedule, parts of a discipline, a listing of geographic features). The DDC stretches the equivalence relationship to accommodate literary warrant and practical classification concerns. The associative relationship is employed liberally throughout the DDC to connect related topics distributed within and among disciplines.

Each synthesized number brings together elements from multiple hierarchies in a syntactic relationship. Additional aspects are often introduced by special notation, as in the addition of geographic area through 09. In some instances, the facet indicator is eliminated to shorten the notation, thus resulting in a loss of explicit relational information.

Direct revision is not the only answer to improving relationships in the DDC. Flexible structures that are derived from or linked to the DDC show great promise in modifying and expanding the network of relationships in the system.

## Endnotes

1. DDC, Dewey, Dewey Decimal Classification, Forest Press, NetFirst, and WorldCat are registered trademarks of OCLC Online Computer Library Center, Inc. CORC is a trademark of OCLC Online Computer Library Center, Inc.

2. CORC (Cooperative Online Resource Catalog) is a Web-based service being developed by OCLC in partnership with several hundred volunteer libraries, with the goal of assisting libraries in providing their users with well-guided access to Web resources. CORC provides tools for the cooperative creation, maintenance, and use of metadata for Web resources.

The CORC toolkit includes facilities for automatic classification of Web resources using the DDC, and for the development of pathfinders based on the DDC. For more information, see http://purl.oclc.org/corc.

**References**

Aitchison, J., Gilchrist, A., & Bawden, D. (1997). *Thesaurus Construction and Use: A Practical Manual* (3rd ed.). London: Aslib.

Cochrane, P., & Johnson, E. (1996). Visual Dewey: DDC in a hypertextual browser for the library user. In R. Green (Ed.), *Knowledge Organization and Change: Proceedings of the Fourth International ISKO Conference*, 95-106. Frankfurt am Main: INDEKS Verlag.

Dewey, M. (1993). *Classificazione Décimale Dewey* (Ed. 20, edizione italiana diretta da L. Crocetti con la collaborazione di D. Danesi; 4 vols.). Rome: Associazione Italiana Biblioteche.

Dewey, M. (1996). *Dewey Decimal Classification and Relative Index* (21st ed.; J. S. Mitchell, J. Beall, W. E. Matthews, Jr., & G. R. New, Eds.; 4 vols.). Albany, NY: OCLC Forest Press.

Dewey, M. (1997). *Abridged Dewey Decimal Classification and Relative Index* (13th ed.; J. S. Mitchell, J. Beall, W. E. Matthews, Jr., & G. R. New , Eds.). Albany, NY: OCLC Forest Press.

Dewey, M. (1998). *Classification Décimale Dewey et Index* (Ed. 21, version française sous la coordination de R. Couture-Lafleur et L. Cabral; 4 vols.). Montreal: ASTED.

*Dewey for Windows* [Computer software]. (1996- ). Dublin, OH: OCLC Forest Press.

Iyer, H. & Giguere, M. (1995). Towards designing an expert system to map mathematics classificatory structures. *Knowledge Organization*, 22, 141-147.

Mitchell, J. S. (1995). Options in the Dewey Decimal Classification system: The current perspective. *Cataloging & Classification Quarterly*, 19(3/4), 89-103. Also published in A. R. Thomas (Ed.), *Classification: Options and Opportunities*, 89-103. New York: Haworth.

Mitchell, J. S. (1998). Flexible structures in the Dewey Decimal Classification. *Knowledge Organization*, 25, 156-158.

Olson, H. A. & Ward, D. B. (1998). Charting a journey across knowledge domains: Feminism in the Dewey Decimal Classification. In W. Mustafa el-Hadi, J. Maniez, & A.S. Pollitt (Eds.), *Structure and Relations in Knowledge Organization: Proceedings of the Fifth International ISKO Conference*, 238-244. Würzburg: ERGON Verlag.

Pollitt, A. S. (1998). The application of Dewey Decimal Classification in a view-based searching OPAC. In W. Mustafa el-Hadi, J. Maniez, & A.S. Pollitt (Eds.), *Structure and Relations in Knowledge Organization: Proceedings of the Fifth International ISKO Conference*, 176-183. Würzburg: Ergon Verlag.

Vizine-Goetz, D. (1999). *Term Associations in the Enhanced DDC Database* [Online]. Available: <http://www.oclc.org/~vizine/DDC_CORC/DDC_TermAssociations.htm> [2000, February 9].

Vizine-Goetz, D. (In press). Dewey in CORC: Classification in metadata and pathfinders. *Journal of Internet Cataloging.*

# Index

# Information Knowledge and Science Management

1. C. W. Choo, B. Detlor and D. Turnbull: *Web Work*. Information Seeking and Knowledge Work on the World Wide Web. 2000                           ISBN 0-7923-6460-0
2. C. A. Bean and R. Green (eds.): *Relationships in the Organization of Knowledge.* 2001                           ISBN 0-7923-6813-4

Kluwer Academic Publishers – Dordrecht / Boston / London